W9-AFC-477

◇

The French New Autobiographies

◇

Crosscurrents

Crosscurrents: Comparative Studies in European Literature and Philosophy
Edited by S. E. Gontarski

Improvisations on Butor: Transformation of Writing, by Michel Butor; edited, annotated, and with an introduction by Lois Oppenheim; translated by Elinor S. Miller (1996)

The Ghosts of Modernity, by Jean-Michel Rabaté (1996)

The French New Autobiographies: Sarraute, Duras, and Robbe-Grillet, by Raylene L. Ramsay (1996)

◆

THE FRENCH NEW AUTOBIOGRAPHIES

Sarraute, Duras, and Robbe-Grillet

◆

Raylene L. Ramsay

University Press of Florida

GAINESVILLE TALLAHASSEE TAMPA BOCA RATON

PENSACOLA ORLANDO MIAMI JACKSONVILLE

01 00 99 98 97 96 6 5 4 3 2 1

Library of Congress Cataloging-in-Publication Data

Ramsay, Raylene L.
The French new autobiographies: Sarraute, Duras, and Robbe Grillet/Raylene L. Ramsay.
p.   cm. — (Crosscurrents)
Includes bibliographic references and index.
ISBN 0–8130–1397–6 (cloth: alk. paper)
1. French prose literature — 20th century — History and criticism. 2. Autobiography. 3. Self in
literature. 4. Sarraute, Nathalie — Criticism and interpretation. 5. Duras, Marguerite — Criticism
and interpretation. 6. Robbe-Grillet, Alain, 1922– — Criticism and interpretation. I. Title.
II. Series: Crosscurrents (Gainesville, Fla.)
PQ629.R36   1996
843'.91409 — dc20   95–49495

The University Press of Florida is the scholarly publishing agency for the State University
System of Florida, comprised of Florida A & M University, Florida Atlantic University, Florida
International University, Florida State University, University of Central Florida, University of
Florida, University of North Florida, University of South Florida, and University of West Florida.

University Press of Florida
15 Northwest 15th Street
Gainesville, FL 32611

For Gail, Janice, Karen, and Malcolm

◇

Contents

◇

◆

Foreword

◆

The Crosscurrents Series is designed to foreground comparative studies in European art and thought, particularly the intersections of literature and philosophy, aesthetics and culture. Without abandoning traditional comparative methodology, the series is receptive to the latest currents in critical, comparative, and performative theory, especially that generated by the renewed intellectual energy in post-Marxist Europe. It will as well take full cognizance of the cultural and political realignments of what for the better part of the twentieth century have been two separated and isolated Europes. While Western Europe is now moving aggressively toward unification in the European Community, with the breakup of the twentieth century's last colonial empire, the former Soviet Union, Eastern Europe is subdividing into nationalistic and religious enclaves with the collapse of the Communist hegemony. The intellectual, cultural, and literary significance of such profound restructuring, how history will finally rewrite itself, is difficult to anticipate. Having had a fertile period of modernism snuffed out in an ideological coup not long after the 1917 revolution, the nations of the former Soviet Union have, for instance, been denied (or spared) the age of Freud, most modernist experiments, and postmodern fragmentation. While Western Europe continues reaching beyond Modernism, Eastern Europe may be struggling to reclaim it. Whether a new art can emerge in the absence — or from the absence — of such forces as shaped Modernism is one of the intriguing questions of post–Cold War aesthetics.

The series follows Michel Butor's intellectual biography, *Transformation in Writing*, with another examination of writing (and so genre) in transformation, writing reaching beyond the teleology of Modernism, Raylene Ramsay's *The French New Autobiographies: Sarraute, Duras, and Robbe-Grillet*. Ramsay focuses on six "intergeneric rewritings": Nathalie Sarraute's *Enfance* (Childhood) and *Tu ne t'aimes pas* (You Lack Self-Love), Marguerite Duras' *Emily L.* and *L'Amant de la Chine du nord*, and Alain Robbe-Grillet's *Le Miroir qui revient* (The Returning Mirror) and *Angélique ou l'enchantement*. These postmodern writers, for whom the Second World War is "the central historical event in [their] lives," have developed a species of generically indeterminate text, "sliding between fact and fiction, between true and false memories, between the disguised and revealed unconscious and between genders." Analyzing these "impossible texts," Ramsay positions herself in "the reader's situation as she/he struggles to decipher texts that are neither autobiography nor fiction and both autobiography and fiction at once." These "new autobiographies," an "autofictional genre," are not so much a realignment of genres as a folding of the self as self into the textual narrative, a reinscription of the body as the body of the text.

The series henceforth will continue to critique the developing, often conflicting currents of European thought through the prism of literature.

S. E. Gontarski
Series Editor

◇

Acknowledgments

◇

I am grateful for permission to reproduce all or part of the following studies:

"The Art of the (Im)possible: The Autobiography of the French New Novelists," *Australian Journal of French Studies* 25, no. 1 (1988): 71–91. This article was an early formulation of some of the ideas developed in chapters 1 and 2.

"Autobiographical Fictions: Duras, Sarraute, Simon, Robbe-Grillet Rewriting History, Story, Self," *The International Fiction Review* 18, no. 1 (1993): 25–33. This article was reworked and reprinted as "Autobiographical Fictions," in *The Contemporary Novel in France*, ed. William Thompson (Gainesville: University Press of Florida, 1995); it inspired major sections of chapter 3, "Rewriting History, Story, Self."

"The Second World War as History and Story, Text and Pre-text, Order and Chaos in Robbe-Grillet's Autobiography, *Le Miroir qui revient*," *Literature and History* 2, no. 2 (1991): 54–69. This article is reprinted here, with minor modifications, as chapter 4.

A revised version of "The Angel in the Mirror in Robbe-Grillet's New Autobiographies" (forthcoming in the proceedings of the colloquium "Robbe-Grillet à 70 ans," edited by Michel Rybalka) constitutes chapter 5.

The following earlier publications helped shape chapters 6 and 7: "The Unselfloving Woman in Sarraute's *Tu ne t'aimes pas*," *French Review* 67, no. 5 (April 1994): 793–802; "La Nouvelle Autobiographie de Nathalie Sarraute et la question du sexe du texte," *Degré second* 13 (December 1992): 51–58; "Reading Sarraute's *Enfance*: Reflections on Critical Validity," *Romanic Review* 80, no. 3 (May 1989): 445–61; "Voice(s) in Nathalie Sarraute's *Enfance*," *New Zealand Journal of French Studies* 9 (1988): 83–94.

Chapter 8 developed out of the article "Through a Textual Glass, Darkly: Masochism in the Feminine Self and Duras' *Emily L.*," *Atlantis: A Women's Studies Journal/Revue d'Etudes sur la Femme* 17, no. 1 (Fall-Winter 1991): 91–104.

Chapter 9 is a modified version of "Writing Power in Duras' *L'Amant de la Chine du nord*," *College Literature* 21, no. 1 (February 1994): 45–62.

INTRODUCTION

This study of the French "new autobiographies" grew out of my earlier interest in the innovative novels and film scenarios published in the sixties and seventies by Alain Robbe-Grillet, Marguerite Duras, and Nathalie Sarraute, writers often grouped as French "new novelists"—although Sarraute's first experimental text, *Tropismes*, appeared as early as 1939. More particularly, the curious character of the conceptions of the self in the work of these writers in the eighties constituted the compelling origin of my project. Drawn by pure reading pleasure and by intellectual challenge into the planetarium of this new boundary-crossing genre, I encountered self-conscious, experimental texts in the present tense, not dissimilar to the thought-provoking "practice of writing" that had been seen to characterize the so-called *nouveau roman*.[1] At the same time, this textual world had become explicitly personal, the product of a writing from a particular body, an intimation of sexual fantasies (Robbe-Grillet), of emotional inner trembling (Sarraute), or intense, desiring, unconscious life (Duras). The challenge was to take account of the distinctive character of these three powerfully original fictional universes while analyzing the nature of their common transformations of traditional narrative and generic structures.

The first two chapters of my study investigate the alleged return from new novel to traditional autobiography in the most widely read and popular new autobiographies—in *Enfance* (Sarraute), *L'Amant* (Duras), and *Le Miroir qui revient* (Robbe-Grillet). All three texts offer a colorful and individuated evocation of the geographical and historical contexts of the author's childhood during the first half of this century. Sarraute plays out scenes from her infancy in Switzerland and in Russia and her early years as an émigré in Paris, Duras' adolescence is set in colonial French Indochina, and the backgrounds of Robbe-Grillet's coming to maturity as a writer are Brittany and Paris, particularly prior to and including the period of the Second World War. Childhood places—Ivanovo, Sadec, Brest—genealogies, ancestral stories, and, above all, the powerful family romance, the relations between child, siblings, and parental figures provide an evident autobiographical and psychological coherence in all three works. My first chapter is a descriptive study of these traditional autobiographical figures; the second develops the analysis of the ways in which these narratives draw on and make visible the conventions of autobiography and yet undermine and rewrite these from within.

For, despite their historically and geographically bounded settings, the traditional familial stories are fragmented, uncertain about their origins, and often contradictory. The constructed nature of these representations of the past is raised to subject position by the perverse and subversive character of their functioning, by curious inversions, or by self-conscious dialogues within the text. In all of these narratives, the illusion of the real and of truth created by the mimetic autobiographical representations and pacts of tradition is rendered suspect. Metaleptic slidings (that is, unjustified movements from one level of narrative to another) between fiction and autobiographical truth, the conflating of history and story that makes the boundaries of the two uncertain, and the movement between story and metatextual comment on the uncertain, or textual, or otherwise invented, nature of the story are writing practices common to all three works. Self-conscious examination of the arbitrary nature of the conventions of the only apparently natural traditional autobiographical genre, *mise en scène* of the problems of the representation of memory (the past) in the present, and display of the intertextual mechanisms function to generate the text in a pirouette before the reader, seeking her or his critical attention. At the same time as the self-portrait moves us to emotional identification with the child on one level, and with the searching after the origins and truths of a writer's personality and vocation on another, we are caught up in a critical and unsettling deconstruction of both the childhood and the writers' selves as products of language. I argue that the complexity of this experience initiates the reader into an "art of the impossible." This is the attempt to uncover, necessarily through language and narrative conventions, the truths of a childhood or a self concealed by this very ready-made language.

The third chapter goes beyond the detecting of the double nature, at once traditional and deconstructionist, emotional and critical, of the memories explored in a number of representative texts. Its goal is to investigate the "rewriting" of "History, Story, Self, and Gender" as this rewriting configures a new autofictional genre. Setting out in pursuit of the commonalities in the experimental forms of all these works, it finds itself on the track of the origins and meanings of strangely circular and reversible movements between fiction and autobiography, self and other, story and history. What is found to characterize and connect all the new autobiographies is just this telescoping movement of apparently incompatible opposites, collective stereotype (*lieux communs*), and individuated experience, for example, into new "complementary" forms—contradictory but not mutually exclusive.

The subsequent readings of individual works tease out possible senses of the "complementary" and often "chaotic" mobile constructions of the new genre, considered in the context of what has been called the "postmodern debate." The central question here is whether the challenging inversions that these structures effect constitute a liberating rewriting of traditional story, history, and gendered self with ethical and political implications, or whether this subversion is merely a demonstration or skeptical deconstruction of imprisonment within linguistic systems and ready-made discourses. Language and the law are presented as ready-mades (Robbe-Grillet), as impediments to desire (Duras), as instruments too grossly and imperfectly fashioned to translate microscopic psychological movements (Sarraute). And yet, as signs of the underlying structures that created them, as indices of the repression of the violence of desire, as the surface trembling of yet intact regions of affect, or as generators of the autofictional writing that reshapes them, they hold subversive potential.

The chapter analyzing the account of the Second World War, the central historical event in the lives of all these writers, particularly as it appears in Robbe-Grillet's *Le Miroir qui revient* [*The Re-turning Mirror*], narrows the focus of the same question. Are Robbe-Grillet's memories of the war subversive? Is his recalling of a possibly "collaborationist" experience through intertext, memory, and fantasy a liberation? For whom? What is seen in Robbe-Grillet's "returning" but distorted and non-referential water "mirror" in *Le Miroir qui revient* is history redefined by its relation to story, myth, and fantasy, and to the body as the latter re-creates history in the present of the writing. In this first work of an autobiographical trilogy, presented on the front cover not as a novel ("roman") but nonetheless as a form of romance ("romanesque"), the narrator's recollections of events, stories, heroic representations or myths of the war are indirectly related to the war's shadow side. The skeptical searchlight that, by intermittent bursts, sweeps public representations of History and Holocaust, also fleetingly illuminates a coextensive private concern with the writer's own implication in disorder (collaboration with Nazi ideology and sadistic sexual fantasy).

The relation between external History and the lived personal experience of history—and, specifically, the question of whether shadows are cast by Robbe-Grillet's apparently shadowless ludic play with his own experience of war or his own violent sexual fantasies—take center stage in the next chapter. This essay looks at the use and abuse of the "angel in the mirror," the textual/sexual figure of the feminine, Angélique, particularly as she is represented in the second, more daringly intimate work of the trilogy, *Angélique ou l'enchantement*. Angélique then recurs in *Les Derniers Jours de Corinthe* as Marianic, Salomé, or Angélique, as you like it. I argue that the sado-erotic thematics dominating the representations of sexuality in Robbe-Grillet's *Angélique* derive not only from a ludic play with words reflecting words or from the collective underground representations of our culture but also from Robbe-Grillet's own sexual preferences and his staging of a sadomasochistic structure of the psyche.

The similar but reversed masochistic-sadistic frames that organize Marguerite Duras' new autobiographies, examined subsequently, more clearly play the role of an individuated psychoanalysis. This is what Doubrovsky labels "autocritique" or what that critic has also described as Duras' writing for the unconscious.

For Doubrovsky, given the evident referential dimension of these texts he describes as "autofictions," the equivalence possible in fiction between the remembered, the imagined, and the perceived cannot be sustained in the new genre. The new autobiographies turn out to participate in the dubious domain of an *entre-deux*, to be monsters of mixed genre and gender. Such an indeterminacy (neither one but both) could also be seen to be a property of the sadistic and masochistic themes and impulses staged self-consciously in all of Duras' and Robbe-Grillet's new autobiographies. The narrator, looking at himself in the central episode of the sea-changed mirror in *Le Miroir qui revient* and, again, in the mirror of the writer's study-bedroom in *Angélique ou l'enchantement*, cannot anchor himself in the mirror's floating image or see himself directly. To know himself, he must move between this "real" image and the "imaginary" figures of Angélique or the "monstre marin" [marine monster/monstrous sailor]. The dual marine monster who devours little girls or is devoured by the mother ("péri en mer" [devoured by the sea/the mother]), like the beautiful siren and captive victim, Angélique, has origins both in experience and in texts, in the personal and the collective imagination, in the inside and the outside. The conceptions of the self in the new autobiographies can be read as decentered or postmodern in their showcasing of their foundation by language or intertext. Yet, all these works also foreground the insistence that self-knowledge passes inevitably through the dual vehicle of the knowledge of the other and the other's knowledge of oneself.

The question of who "ravishes" whom, or who seeks self-affirmation and who self-dissolution in this relation with the other, is examined in greater detail in a later chapter on Duras and autobiographical mirror-gazing. The thematics of domination and submission, which are so central in the new autobiographies, inevitably put into play the issue of gender differences or, indeed, of similarities, between "masculine" and "feminine" writers. This question of the gender of the text is pursued in relation to the voices that recount Nathalie Sarraute's childhood in *Enfance*, partly in response to that writer's own vehement insistence that her text has no sex. Two voices, marked grammatically masculine and feminine, most often engage in an oppositional dialogue between what appear to be traditional "masculine" critically distanced and "feminine" intuitive and emotional ways of remembering and knowing. What generates this dialogic debate are the remembered or imagined words of the mother, father, stepmother, and of the child Sarraute once was. Both voices participate in the attempt to open the smooth, intact surfaces of these phrases that call "memories of childhood" to mind. They seek to reveal the complex, contradictory, and evanescent sensations that lie behind the unity and stability implied by their fixing in such speech acts as "A child who loves her mother thinks that no-one is more beautiful than she," or "Husband and wife are on the same side," or the child's defiant "I will tear it." Common places (places common to all), these words are also selected for their personal emotional power and impact.

In Sarraute's most recent work, *Tu ne t'aimes pas*, a text I situate between autofiction and novel, the voices that operate a *mise en scène* of these hidden tropistic movements welling up around the ready-made judgment, "Tu ne t'aimes pas" [You do not love yourself], are no longer dialogic but polyphonic and, if gendered, are generally undifferentiated. A voice embodying the lack of self-confidence, the anxiety, the sense of guilt and imposture, and the "masochism" that characterized many of the hypersensitive characters of Sarraute's earlier fictions distinguishes itself at moments. Other audible voices quibble with, contradict, or nuance this first, seeking, uncertain voice. But even as it confesses its self-doubt and lack of knowledge, the docility and self-humbling of the uncertain, unselfloving voice is incorporated in the authorial voice and countered by the author(ity) of the text. As solid, everyday surfaces are fissured by Sarraute's subversive use of language seeking to probe the composition and movements of the amorphous, swarming substances beneath, a controlling voice also emerges.

Sarraute's 1989 autofiction is once again an art of the impossible as it explores the evanescent sensations and infrapsychological responses at once concealed and evoked by the grossly fashioned judgment, "Tu ne t'aimes pas" (You lack self-love) and attempts to catch the multiplicity and elusiveness of the "enormous moving mass" of the unspoken intrasubjective world in its own more finely wrought linguistic web. Even as it deconstructs the doll-like facades of self-satisfaction, self-love, and authority and intimates the fear and fascination of vulnerability, the complexity of the self's relations with humiliation and, as in Duras' thematics, the power of self-loss, her text, both deconstructionist and authoritative, takes the reader beyond the binary divisions of (positive) self-love or (negative) self-abnegation. And, once again, from the obscure and contradictory sensations, the imperceptible squirming movements, the forays to win or protect territory, and the retreats that constitute the polyphonic, collective affective life re-created by Sarraute in *Tu ne t'aimes pas*, a recognizable self-portrait of the artist can be constituted. Behind the formula "a complex personality," the reader glimpses a "person" whose jagged edges may not quite meet but who can be grossly characterized as an ironic, distanced, even secretive but incisive observer who, at the same time, experiences contradictory desires for acceptance by the group, warmth, commonality, and love. It may be that such a swarming mass of contradictory feelings and impulses is the material of all personalities, but the choices made and the textual organization of this material are peculiarly characteristic of the writer, Sarraute.

The next chapter approaches the issue of the gender of a text and the nature of the self this text evokes from another angle as it focuses on the curious inversions operated by the proliferating specular images in Duras' *Emily L.* and seeks the meanings of Emily L.'s masochistic sacrifice of her poetry to her love for "the Captain." The Durassian subject takes form in the movement between looking and being looked at. The character Emily L. watched empathetically in her indecency, in her closeness to death, embodies the disturbing strangeness of the perverse desire of the watching narrator to be "ravished." The telescoping of the dichotomies of the fearful and opposite states at the origins of writing (self-loss in the other, and separation from the other) involves a similar movement between a "masculine" position of desire that seeks to "kill" and a "feminine" position excited by self-dispossession. Curiously, and perhaps problematically, this "feminine" impulse to self-dissolution is valorized in *Emily L.* much as the lack of self-love is preferred to self-satisfaction in Sarraute's *Tu ne t'aimes pas*.

Duras speaks from what she has called a "wild country" of buried desire in which the contours of self and the distance or disconnection between self and other disappear in a distinctively Durassian "ravishing." Sarraute claims to be working in the domain of the universal, the tiny psychological movements or "tropisms" common in substance to everyone, a domain in which the "I" for her is no one, or a "puff of air." These two writers appear to have no need to conceal the personal fascination exerted by such interpersonal domains. Robbe-Grillet also claims that the generators of his texts, and even his own fantasies, are ready-made, what is displayed for all on "the walls of the city." But he also pretends to establish a conscious, scientific distance between his own emotions and his use of this material. Only his characters or alter egos are victims of a fascination and of vertigo.

The "common places" privileged in the work of the three writers are also very different. In the final instance, far from being collective or impersonal in character, the creative works and indeed the paratexts (photographs, interviews, television appearances) of all three writers reveal very different styles and personalities and gender mix, much as the areas the three explore are quite distinctive. All work self-consciously through and on the language "in power" but Sarraute's distinctive rhythm of dialogue and narrative and use of metaphors, Duras' poetic repetitions and cinematic images in slow motion, and Robbe-Grillet's assemblage techniques create recognizable signatures. Style itself is a choice among competing possibilities; a function of an individuated history and set of preoccupations, conveying emotional tonality and psychological impulses that lean toward domination or toward self-loss, toward paranoia or hysteria.

My reading of *L'Amant, Emily L.*, and *L'Amant de la Chine du nord* against the backdrop of the vast corpus of Duras' intergeneric rewritings (novels rewritten as film scenarios, as plays, or as autobiography, plays that become novels or films), my sense of the aesthetic play of white page against black type, silence against sound, and sound against image is, for example, a sense of an eminently sensual if also artful (linguistic) world. In this self-centered *and* self-forgetting discourse, words may function as an analytic tool for the probing (and re-creating) of sensations or of knowledge of the emotional relation to the mother or unexplored (unselfloving) regions of the self, as in Sarraute. They are also a nonrational means of discovering, through the personal relation to father/brother(s) and lover, the depths of universal *ennui*, humiliation, desire, fear, and domination close to disorganization and madness and an intense life of desire. Kristeva has seen this, in her study of Duras, as the sounding, through the body, of "the pain and suffering in the modern world."

All of the new autobiographies are texts that live dramatically in the present of their textual unfolding. They all predicate an absent or lost origin, an exile in language at the same time as they seek the impossible recovery (re-membering) of the past and its meanings through language. In this respect, Duras' work is similar to the work of Sarraute. Both writers seek to explore or touch a prelinguistic, perhaps preconscious "real" behind appearances but, paradoxically, through consciousness and language; through art and the inversions art alone can operate. Robbe-Grillet's assemblages of memories, fantasies, and literary theory maintain an apparently more controlled distance from the vertigo of ravishing than Duras' scenarios and dialogues, despite the reiterative violence against the bodies of young girls and the fear of death by drowning in the feminine that intrude increasingly into his stories. The elements of pastiche in his work seem closer to the intellectual distances and critical irony in Sarraute. Yet, the multiple present spaces, traversed by fleeting shapes from the past forming and re-forming, and indeed, the sense of art at work, on the track of its own "criminal" origins, recall those of Duras. If there is a major difference between these writers, it is that Robbe-Grillet chooses to situate his imaginary alter egos at the sadistic pole in aggression against the "feminine," Duras and Sarraute prefer, rather, a thematics of self-loss and a "feminine" masochism.

Such individuation of both writing and reading self, I argue, may nuance the ethically fraught question of whether reference, in these autofictions, is to personal history or to text—that is, whether this writing escapes the postmodern double bind, the "prison house of language" (the language of the tribe from which none escape), without falling back into a retrograde realism or essentialism. My final chapter takes the example of *L'Amant de la Chine du nord*, a textual "rewriting" of *L'Amant* to argue for the liberating implications of the specificity of the contexts that generate the new autobiofictional texts and their conceptions of self. This rewriting produces a new version of Duras' life and of her relations with the mother, the brother, and the lover and, more generally, with sexual power. Remembering the past comes to transform the present much as recollection in the present alters (betrays, loses) the past. In the final instance, such reversals in the new autobiographies, their complementarity and chaotic forms, are to varying degrees both a staging and a subversion— that is, both an analytical demonstration and an alteration of the textual/sexual forms of power in place.

The blurring of reality and unreality in the writer's memory, staged self-consciously within the text by the author as I have argued in another book, reflect ideas that are in the contemporary cultural air, ideas of the indeterminacy of the world (wave *and* particle, continuity and discontinuity) or of the "chaotic" nature (new statistical orders that emerge from disorder) of complex structures, for example.² These autofictional texts rephrase central contemporary intellectual debates often in the form of metafictional reflection (reflection on the text incorporated in the text).

Both autobiographical fiction and metatextual reflection must, of course, pass through a further filter, that of the reader's response. The sliding between fact and fiction, between "true" and "false" memories, between the disguised and the revealed unconscious, and between genders in the new autobiographies is presented not only in terms of the principle of "complementarity" (contradictory but not mutually exclusive opposites)—which, I argue, inheres in and characterizes the structure of all these works—but also in terms of the reader's situation. She or he struggles to decipher texts that are neither autobiography nor fiction and both autobiography and fiction at once, texts where fiction can indeed be truer than "truth." Reading (understanding) these rewritings of history, story, and gendered self involves hidden movements between the specific and individuated gendered bodies (the desires, fantasies, and disavowals) of these authors in text and the gendered reader's (my) own body and text.

◇

one

◇

NEW AUTOBIOGRAPHIES FOR OLD?

Nathalie Sarraute's widely read *Enfance* (Gallimard, 1983), now in paperback edition, was adapted for a successful theatrical season at the Barrault Théâtre du Rond-Point on the Champs-Elysées and has appeared as a talking book in many Parisian bookstores. *L'Amant* (Editions de Minuit, 1984) carried off the rich Ritz Hemingway literary prize of 1986 for Marguerite Duras, along with a Prix Goncourt, figured on the New York Times list of best-sellers over a considerable period, and has sold more than two million copies. The film adaptation by Jacques Annaud in 1992 was a major commercial success. *Le Miroir qui revient* (Editions de Minuit, 1984), perhaps the most accessible of Alain Robbe-Grillet's works, is also available as a talking book, read aloud by its author.

At first sight, the readable and dramatic works of the eighties seemed to be evidence of a movement away from the earlier "new novels" of these writers, widely perceived as experimental and difficult, if not unreadable. Although autobiography draws upon techniques perfected for the novel (first person narrative, dialogue, (chrono)logical development),[1] nonetheless, at least in the general understanding, it is the genre par excellence that imposes truth conditions; what Paul Eakin calls the "referential aesthetic of autobiography."[2] Autobiography appears to be related to nonfictional genres (biography, diary, memoirs, chronicle) rather than to fiction; to memory rather than to the imagination. Eakin argues that it is the reader's recognition of a referential intention that accounts for the felt difference in the experience of reading an autobiography and that of reading a work taken to be a fiction. Postmodern adepts might respond with echoes of Barthes' provocative formulation that, in the field of the subject, there is no referent.[3] Yet, many of Barthes' autobiographical writings are themselves, as Eakin states, profoundly ambivalent about the self and the possibilities for its expression in language. For Eakin, if autobiography is always a kind of fiction, it is also "nothing if not a referential art"[4] at least in the sense that the text creates the self understood as author of the text. The writer is also a reader, a reader of his own self-writing.

A number of critical reviews assumed that the popular success and apparent accessibility of this first wave of autobiographies by writers associated with the dissident French *nouveau roman* grouping of the 1950s stemmed from the return to the orthodoxy of a realist, humanist tradition.[5] My first three chapters investigate whether these autobiographical texts are indeed traditional autobiographical expression of a preexisting self by means of a referential language. How persuasive is the evidence that the opaque pages of the French *nouveau roman*, seeking new structures within its own linguistic relationships, have been turned again? Have they returned to their transparency as mimesis, mirror of a real world outside language, in this case, mirror of the memory? From the *nouveau roman*, and from metafiction in general, readers have learned to be suspicious of referentiality, to collaborate with the indeterminacy and discontinuity of the text, and to negotiate the uncertain boundaries between fact and fiction with language—as both fiction and reality—as the mediator. Could the reader's function have returned simply to the traditional one of distinguishing between the author's fantasy and experience? Might the theoretical underpinnings of a self-referential text, that is, the recognition that no sign-system is the reality that it purports to represent and the suspicion of the ideological meanings constructed and imposed by our language or carried by the conventions of the novel (plot, character, chronology, coherence, and so forth), now be losing their initial force, becoming dogma, to constitute an object of suspicion in their turn?

The collective linguistic representations borrowed from the "walls of the city" (Robbe-Grillet), the linguistic clichés that represented universal psychosocial interaction (Sarraute), or even anonymous unconscious prelinguistic interpersonal desire and flow (Duras) for which the characters had become the interchangeable vehicles appeared to be giving way to individuation and a concern with the personal. Far from being killed off by any theoretical "death of the author," these writers have become recognizable public figures lecturing in academic institutions around the world (Robbe-Grillet and Sarraute), writing theoretical paratexts, figuring in the literary media (in the case of Robbe-Grillet and Duras appearing with Bernard Pivot on the celebrated literary television show "Apostrophes"). They can be seen to be inscribing aspects of their own distinctive literary identity and itinerary into the stories of their lives— how I became a writer—as autobiographical conventions would require.

On my first fascinated reading, all three autobiographies did appear, if in an original and modern way and with some explicitly expressed metatextual reticence, to conform to many of the contours and conventions of the auto-biographical genre despite the absence of any clearly recognizable chrono-logical thread. Georges May discusses these contours under the headings of "Where and When?" "Who"? "Why"? "How"? and "The Point of View of the Reader" in the first part of his definition and classification of autobiography.[6] For this well-known theorist, autobiography corresponds to the human need (and to the writer's need) to understand one's life, to reveal its hidden mean-ings, and to discover a certain order. In *Enfance*, in spite of the fragmented, elliptical nature of the minidramas of childhood memory and the uncertain meanings of the phrases or gestures of mother(s) and father whose significance and relationship are open to a number of interpretations, a time line can be recovered from the events. According to Philippe Lejeune, these events begin with two undated memories from early childhood in Switzerland on vacation with the father, then cover the years from age two to six, 1902–1906 (chapters 3–15) when Natacha lives in Paris with her mother, rue Flatters. The years in Petersburg with the mother and Kolia from the age of six to the age of eight and a half follow (chapters 16–26), covering the period from 1906 to February 1909. Chapters 27–70 concentrate on the years in Paris, rue Marguerin, from eight and a half to twelve years of age, with father remarried to Véra, and can be dated from February 1909 to October 1912.[7] It might also be argued that a chronological account of the significant emotional events of Marguerite Donnadieu's childhood and adolescence is recoverable from the cinematic replays in *L'Amant* even though, in this work, these events have their origin in an ideal or absolute "absent" image–the photo that was never taken of the meeting with the Chinese lover on a ferry crossing the Mekong River. A num-ber of accounts—hunting the black panthers with the brother in the forest or at the river mouth, house-cleaning day, the mother's catastrophic investment in a land grant, her preference for the brother, the daughter's precocious at-tracting of men, the wealthy admirer, the mother's ambivalent relation to her daughter's suitor/lover, the gift of a diamond—appear not only in *L'Amant* but also in the earlier autobiographical novel *Un Barrage contre le Pacifique* (1950) and the later rewriting of *L'Amant* in *L'Amant de la Chine du nord* (1991). The repeated incidents constitute a core of apparent lived event that is reasonably consistent and does not noticeably contradict the few precise dates that Duras herself gives in the texts. These include the voyage of the family to France a year and a half after the encounter with the lover, the death of the second brother under the Japanese occupation in 1942 (although the age given for

Paulo at death seems inconsistent with other details), and the return of the mother from France to Indochina, where she remained from 1932 to 1949. Even if it is the case that the reader's only access to the authorial experience is through the materiality of the text and its analogical signs and images, that is, to an altered memory or history, there is no immediate textual evidence that the narrator's story is perversely or grossly unreliable.

As Georges May's study of autobiography predicts for the genre, the three writers are well-known figures who have already achieved success in the public sphere (literary prizes, *légions d'honneur*) and are in their "mature years" at the time of writing their first autobiography (81, 70, and 62 years old). A sense of time running out shapes a desire to save what is still accessible in the early periods of their lives from oblivion before it is too late. This autobiographical preoccupation becomes an explicit aspect of the thematics. In spite of the discomfort the words "Evoquer tes souvenirs d'enfance" (p. 9) [Evoke your childhood memories] cause her, Nathalie Sarraute's emotional voice is tempted, insists against her critical voice, "c'est encore tout vacillant, aucun mot écrit, aucune parole ne l'ont encore touché, il me semble que ça palpite faiblement . . . hors des mots . . . comme toujours . . . des petits bouts de quelque chose d'encore vivant . . . je voudrais, avant qu'ils disparaissent . . . laisse-moi . . ." (p. 11) [it's still vacillating, no written word, no word of any sort has yet touched it, I think it is still faintly quivering . . . outside words . . . as usual . . . little bits of something still alive . . . I would like, before they disappear . . . let me . . .]. (Note that Sarraute frequently uses the trailing ellipsis for effect; throughout this book, all ellipses that I have inserted editorially to indicate a break in the text are enclosed in brackets, as in the quotations from Marguerite Duras immediately below.) Duras begins her text with a reference to her age. "Un jour, j'étais âgée déjà" (p. 9) and continues: "Très vite dans ma vie il a été très tard. A dix-huit ans il était déjà trop tard. [. . .] A dix-huit ans j'ai vieilli" (pp. 9–10) [Very early in my life it was too late. It was already too late when I was eighteen. {. . .} I grew old at eighteen]. The work ends with a reference to death in the reported words of the lover. "Et puis il le lui avait dit [. . .] qu'il l'aimerait jusqu'à sa mort" (p. 142) [And then he told her {. . .} that he'd love her unto death]. "*L'Amant* reste l'éblouissement d'aimer, sans doute" [*The Lover* is doubtless the bedazzlement of love], suggests the writer at the conclusion of her conversation with Pivot recorded in 1984 for the TV program "Apostrophes." If declared authorial intention is taken to be sufficient evidence, it could be argued that Duras seeks to hold on to the wondrous state of love and to hold the aging of the body at bay, by recalling past desire. These writers all admit to the use of the autobiographical text to wrestle with oblivion, to arrest, at least momentarily, the movement toward death, a use sometimes hidden but implicit in traditional autobiography. Alain Robbe-Grillet, too, states this openly: "Construire un récit, ce serait alors—de façon plus ou moins consciente—prétendre lutter contre elle [la mort]" (p. 27) [So to construct a narrative would be a more or less conscious bid to outwit death]. Robbe-Grillet's text claims to seek to erase the "inscription," that is, the writing on the tomb. *Emily L.* presents a vision of the future in which "the book" will lie "outside the casket."

The exploration of the self, of one's life (and of one's death), repeated so tirelessly in the earlier novels, is presented as incomplete and incompetent: "les mêmes questions se posent toujours, vivaces, lancinantes, peut-être inutiles" (*Le Miroir qui revient*, p. 7) [the same questions still come up, perennial, haunting, maybe pointless]. For, as the following chapter will discuss at length, literature is the pursuit of the impossible, "la poursuite d'une représentation impossible" (p. 18) [the pursuit of an impossible representation]. Nonetheless, however reticently the autobiographical project is approached, however great the suspicion of the fixed, the ready made, and the inauthentic, the project offers at least the mirage of a second chance, a new approach or a deeper descent. "Mais à présent que je me résous, pour l'espace d'un petit livre, à me regarder de côté, ce point de vue inattendu me libère soudain de mes anciennes protections et réticences" (*Le Miroir qui revient*, p. 12) [But now that I've decided to take a sidelong look at myself in the space of a small book, the new perspective has suddenly freed me from my old defenses and reticence]. Marguerite Duras claims to be investigating the deeply concealed, what has remained unsaid. "Avant, j'ai parlé des périodes claires, de celles qui étaient éclairées. Ici je parle des périodes cachées de cette même jeunesse, de certains enfouissements que j'aurais opérés sur certains faits, sur certains sentiments, sur certains événements" (p. 14) [Before, I spoke of clear periods, those on which the light fell. Now I'm talking about the hidden stretches of that same youth, of certain facts, feelings, events that I buried]. Nathalie Sarraute's professed aim is also to uncover what has remained buried. "J'essaie de m'enfoncer, d'atteindre, d'accrocher, de dégager ce qui est resté là, enfoui" (p. 84) [I am trying to dig down to the bottom, to reach, to grasp, to release what has remained there, buried].

These explicit projects of self-knowledge bear a clear relationship to the confessional tradition that has always been central to the genre. As the extensive recent work on autobiography has pointed out, the Christian project of St. Augustine, the humanist aims of Montaigne, Rousseau's goals of moral self-improvement, the attempt by the Romantics to express the emotional depths of the individual, Gide's (Protestant) examination of conscience, and the mythologies of Leiris are based on similar quests to uncover man's true nature by introspection. It has also been suggested that the "true" nature that will be discovered is a function of the frame applied and of the particular questions selected. The Christian quest will lead inevitably to the workings of God, Montaigne finds the human reason and Rousseau moral innocence, while the Protestant self-examination reveals the subtle demons of self-deception. In their quest for self-knowledge, might the new autobiographers, then, encounter only language?

Intellectually rooted in what Sarraute in her early collection of theoretical essays had called "the age of suspicion," beyond traditional psychological analysis, influenced by structuralism and post-structuralism and by the new science of linguistics, the new autobiographers are evidently at some distance from the introspective search, in the absolute, for "un homme dans toute la vérité de sa nature" [a man in all the truth of his nature] of Rousseau's *Confessions*. They claim to be seeking new ways of seeing and being in a fragmented, multiple, aleatory, world. Some aspects of their autobiographical projects do appear to have a relation to the Surrealists' twentieth-century explorations of the secret and obscure forces that inhabit us, as Cocteau puts it. Or, rather, to derive from a more psychoanalytical (Lacanian) awareness of the (linguistic) disguises of the unconscious. In any case, they bear the clear trace of the development and popularizing of contemporary psychoanalytic theory that considers the desires of early childhood and of familial relationships to be those most likely to be fixed in the unconscious.

Nathalie Sarraute, for example, claims to lose interest in her project when it emerges from what she describes as the formless, hazy, protected spaces of childhood into the enormous, encumbered, and well-lit spaces of her experience after primary school. *L'Amant* (and more evidently again its 1991 rewriting, *L'Amant de la Chine du nord*) focuses mainly on the childhood and the early adolescent passions in French Indochina of Marguerite Duras/Marguerite Donnadieu. A series of photographs published in *Les Lieux de Marguerite Duras*, many of which were reproduced in the Thames Television documentary "Vive la France: Marguerite Duras, Portrait of an Author," focus on the mother, the young brothers, childhood poverty, the Indochinese setting and the smoldering young adolescent girl.

In Robbe-Grillet's *Le Miroir qui revient*, the adult writer, critic, and theoretician figures more frequently but ancestors, parents, and siblings still play a dominant role. These parents who are, as Robbe-Grillet puts it, already me taking shape ("déjà moi en train de prendre forme," p. 58) become the central organizing principle of formative early childhood. We catch glimpses of Robbe-

Grillet's seafaring Breton ancestors; of the great-grandfather, coast-guard on the lonely cliff paths among the flickering lights of shipwreck; of Ulysse Robbe-Grillet and his voyages under sail around the world with the Navy, his tin treasure trunk in the attic; of the father and his "legendary" heroic and fearful exploits as a sapper in the trenches of the Great War. At the Editions de Minuit, Mademoiselle Lindon showed me a number of now well-known photographs used to promote *Le Miroir qui revient*—of grandfather Paul Canu, of a very feminine-looking Alain at school age with his sister Anne-Lise, of the Robbe-Grillet clan helping with the wine-harvest (Mother, Father, Anne-Lise, and Alain), of Alain as a young man with his wife, Catherine, with schoolgirl-like braids and pleated skirt against the backdrop of the Breton sea, of the "clan" with Catherine Robbe-Grillet and Roland Barthes around the dinner table. In *Camera Lucida*, the later Barthes describes such photographs as "certificates" of presence.

The reflections in *Le Miroir qui revient* return repeatedly to the parents "to place flowers on their tomb"[8] and to attempt to grasp their influence. "Maman," protective against his childhood fears and nightmares, ever-present, intelligent, independent and assertive of mind and action, intuitive, sometimes incomprehensible, attuned to her son, loving living things, but keenly felt as censorious of his awakening and difficult male sexuality, is evoked at length with passion but also noticeable ambivalence. "Papa" with his tireless efforts for the family in his small cardboard-box making factory, absurd evening translations of Schiller, Sunday mending of the family's shoes and excursions with his two children skating on the grand canal at Versailles, his eccentricity provoked perhaps by a war wound, is evoked with great affection but less tension. The description of this close and exclusive family group contains within it, however, claims Robbe-Grillet, the seeds of the break with childhood in the form of the difficulties posed by the right-wing, anti-Semitic, monarchist parental ideology after the revelation of Nazi holocaust. I would argue that this break, although perceived as necessary, was never in fact completely effected. Robbe-Grillet's autobiographical texts continue to work out major tensions within his confrontation with his right-wing family origins and his mother's lifelong refusal to believe that the Holocaust had existed. But the desire to explain and even to vindicate these positions appears to grow stronger rather than to be exorcised.

Nathalie Sarraute's heroic soldier grandfather sent to Russia by Napoleon (the Third and not the First, to her adolescent disappointment), her Russian uncle's association with the revolutionary movement against the Czar and his mysterious death, her chemist-industrialist father's subsequent association with fellow revolutionaries in exile in France, provide a familial and historical back-drop to her story. At the heart of her theoretically cautious evocation of the "memories of childhood" ("souvenirs d'enfance," p. 9) is the early absolute attachment to the lively and beautiful mother, the anguish of her absence, the suspicion of her lack of understanding of her daughter, and the fear of rejec-tion or "abandonment" by either of her estranged parents. The nature of the increasing bond with the emotionally undemonstrative and morally austere father and the complex relationship with an unloving stepmother or the feel-ings toward the absent mother and response to her occasional visits from Rus-sia, feelings that motivate the child's decision to remain in France with the father and stepmother, are her very subject matter. The cover of the later pa-perback edition of the work contains a photograph of little Natacha around the age of four or five.

Ancestral and parental time is no less central in Marguerite Duras' autobi-ography than in Sarraute's or Robbe-Grillet's. The mythological strength of the mother's brothers of sturdy Northern French farming stock according to the mother's stories, the absence of the school superintendent father who dies when his three children are small, the mother's heroic battle in Indochina to maintain, against the encroaching sea, the worthless land grant acquired with her life savings from a corrupt colonial administration, her difficulties raising her three children alone, and her moments of great discouragement with liv-ing itself are Duras and her writing taking shape. Against the background of the story of the lover, a means of discovery of the power and the pain and pleasure of the body and of the interpersonal force of sexuality and desire, it is the complex and intense mix of love and hate, embarrassment and pride, need for money and sense of the irrelevance of material things inspired by the pow-erful/powerless figure of the mother that is at the center of the work. In the interview with Pivot, Duras discusses the difficulty of separation from the mother on her own definitive return to France. "J'ai cru mourir d'ennui d'elle. A 18 ans, c'est étrange, s'ennuyer de sa mère à ce point-là" [I thought I would die from missing her. At eighteen, it's strange to miss one's mother that much].

The unhappiness of the mother that occupies the "place of dream" accord-ing to the daughter is linked for Duras with the elder brother, addicted to opium, exploiter of the mother, "criminal" and "delinquent." Memory is colored, lu-ridly, by the relationship with this brother, his animal will to domination and devouring of the "little brother" and his possession of the mother. "Autour du souvenir la clarté livide de la nuit du chasseur" (p. 67) [And surrounding the memory is the ghastly glow of the night of the hunter]. Yet the brother exerts a strong attraction on the sister even in the presence of the lover. "Mon désir obéit à mon frère ainé, il rejette mon amant" (p. 66) [My desire obeys my elder brother, rejects the lover]. He is an object of unconscious desire, the shadow of the "assassin" that crosses the bedroom the "little white girl" shares with the Chinese lover. The "weak" lover is identified with the slightly re-tarded and defenseless "little brother,"[9] the "hunter" who roams the child-hood forests of Siam with his sister in *Un Barrage contre le Pacifique*, where there is only one brother, and whose incestuous shadow also appears recogniz-ably in the bedroom of *L'Amant*. It will take the unacceptable death under the Japanese occupation of this "little brother" who is apparently two years his sister's senior but barely able to read and write in 1942 (one of the precise indi-cations of time in the text), eleven years after his sister has left Saigon at age eighteen, to finally break the intense family bonds of desire, love, and hate. The affair with the lover is, in fact, the beginning of this lifetime process of separation.

For the sister, the body of her little brother was felt as her own body and linked with her own recent loss of a child at birth; his death (from infection but experienced imaginatively as if from oppression) becomes the huge scan-dal and injustice of death itself, "the death of immortality." The mother, "left" by the daughter is thus punished for her complicity with the elder brother, seen as responsible for the "ultimate subjection" of the beloved little brother. She will die, quite mad,[10] the narrator tells us, perhaps again in some imagina-tive exaggeration, in her imitation Louis XIV castle in the Loir et Cher be-tween her faithful servant Dô and the elder son—the one she "calls her child." Thief and vagabond, this son wastes the inheritance (the forests of the mother gambled in a single night); indigent, steals from his sister; and dies, solitary, to be buried in the mother's grave as she had requested, in what Duras terms "splendid symbolism." Readers of the novels, *Un Barrage contre le Pacifique* and *Des Journées entières dans les arbres* will recognize the passionate familial drama of the mother and her children, the absent father, the strength of the mother's passion for the profligate son, and the rage and jealousy this unjust preference causes in the daughter as a continuously powerful generative source of Duras' fiction along with the passionate love for the weaker brother. The same story (or almost), but this time focusing more explicitly on the sexual nature of the young girl's relationships with the threatened "little" brother (Paulo) whom she sees as her "child" or with the threatening and feared big-ger brother (Pierre) who has the mother beat his sister's precocious sexuality out of her while he looks on, is rewritten in *L'Amant de la Chine du nord*. Here again, it is only in the focus on the lover, identified in his powerlessness with the little brother, that some degree of distance and liberation can be established from the simultaneously attracting and repulsing figures of the mother and the powerful older brother, Pierre.

Accompanying the evocation of intense family bonds and the events that lead to the modification of these formative primary relationships, in all three writers there are descriptions of a succession of geographically situated homes. The three granite steps and front door with ornamental iron grille of the family house overlooking the treacherous sea in Brittany, near Brest, have already appeared in the New York of Robbe-Grillet's novel *Projet pour une révolution à New York*. They may, of course, recur here in ironic response to the claims by the critic Jean Ricardou that *Projet* is a self-generating text proceeding from just this initial description of a "linguistic" rather than a "real" door. The alert reader might also note the heavy red curtains separating the child's bedroom from the watching mother in the small family apartment in the Rue Gassendi of the writer's secondary studies in Paris and subsequent entry into the Ecole Nationale Supérieure d'Agronomie. These "real" red curtains bear a striking likeness to the "fictional" red curtains that separate the outside from the inside of the writer's room in the novel *Dans le labyrinthe*.

Most of these homes seem to foreground the psychological and geographical realism of the narratives of childhood memories and to respect autobiographical tradition. "As if in a break in a silvery mist" ("Comme dans une éclaircie émerge d'une brume d'argent," p. 41), in *Enfance*, the long, wooden, Christmas story house at Ivanovo emerges, with its stalactites of ice, Russian birthplace of Natacha Tcherniak (later Nathalie Sarraute). Glimpses of the father's Moscow flat (decorating the Christmas tree with a pretty blond woman after shopping in a sleigh with father) and of the storybook stately home at Kamenetz-Podolsk of lawyer uncle and beautiful aunt Aniouta (on holiday with mother) are flashed by theatrical dramatizations onto a mind-screen that does appear to reveal the memories and emotional investments of a specific author, Sarraute. In Paris, there is the small but bright and happy house in the rue Flatters with writer mother and her second husband Kolia, a Russian writer, and the grayer more forbidding house of Papa, Véra, and stepsister that becomes her permanent home while never quite feeling hers.

In *L'Amant*, again apparently providing "authentic" and "formative" background and serving as an emotional material metaphor, there is the land-grant house in disrepair that looks toward the mountain in Siam and from where the three children hunted the black panther in the swamps at the river mouth or explored the enchanted forest while the mother fought her desperate losing battle with the sea. Like the Pension Lyautet and the Lycée Français, the *garçonnière* used by the lover in Cholon, the Chinese quarter of Saigon, with the smells and constant hubbub of the crowds outside penetrating to the inside through the bamboo curtain, the homes of the Donnadieu family, however reconstructed by affective memory, appear more realistic than imagined. Their authenticity is borne out by a book that Duras has not spoken of.

Published by Gallimard in 1940 under the joint names of Marguerite Donnadieu and Philippe Rocques, *L'Empire français*, a treatise on the grandeur of France's empire, contains sections of apparently objective geographical, historical, and social description of French Indochina that could well constitute the background for "The Lover" cycle. The Mekong River, which sets the scene for the self-assertive image of defiant passage to sexual adulthood at the "absent" center of *L'Amant*, is much in evidence. "C'est à cet endroit, où le soi-disant Mékong est d'une opulence grandiose, que les Kmers bâtirent la ville de Pnom-Penh" [It is in this place, where the so-called Mekong is of a grandiose opulence that the Khmers built the city of Phnom-Penh]. In the vast gulf, "le fleuve charrie de la terre et des matériaux en suspens dans ses eaux" (p. 107) [the river carries along earth and material suspended in its waters]. In the description of Saigon "bâtie sur une vaste échelle, composée de villas et jardins que coupent de larges avenues rectilignes" [built on a vast scale, composed of villas and gardens intersected by wide straight avenues], Cholon has a dominant place. "Saigon comprend également de populeux faubourgs indigènes et en particulier Cholen, véritable cité dans la cité que peuplent 150,000 Chinois. [. . .] C'est là que se concentre la haute finance et le grand commerce chinois, qui détient toutes les minoteries et entrepôts de la Cochinchine" (pp. 113–14) [Saigon also contains densely populated native suburbs and in particular Cholon, veritable city within a city populated by 150,000 Chinese. {. . .} That's where Chinese high finance and the business interests that own all of the flour milling and warehouses of Cochin China are concentrated]. Again, "Cholen est célèbre par ses 'immeubles-restaurants,' création de la Chine moderne, ses magasins de soie et de jade, le tintamarre de ses rues et de ses fêtes nocturnes. Il est curieux de remarquer que Saigon et Cholen, séparées par une courte avenue, coexistent sans s'influencer en rien, dans leur urbanisme et dans le mode de vie de leurs habitants" (pp. 116–17) [Cholon is famous for its restaurant complexes, a creation of modern China, its silk and jade shops, the hubbub of its streets and its night festivals. One observes with surprise that Saigon and Cholon, separated by a short avenue, coexist without influencing one another in any way, in their urban organization or in the lifestyle of their inhabitants].

Descriptions like these appear to be from the rhythmically flowing pen of Donnadieu/Duras rather than in the more didactic style that seems to mark the writing of Rocques. Expressions such as "en effet," "sans doute," "en vérité" [in fact, doubtless, in truth] characterize what I assume to be the texts of this coauthor, concerned, in the political context of 1940, to establish the now politically and ideologically contested thesis of the civilizing mission and colonizing aptitudes of France. The book celebrates the organic unity, grandeur, and military strength of the French Empire and argues that France will be able to count on these many loyal sons in her current time of need. While the existence of such a text may require some rethinking of Duras' ideological positions in the war period,[11] its traditional and detailed descriptions that complement the more fragmented, subjective details of the autofictional cycle give weight to the autobiographical thesis.

It is the repeated evocation of the frail ferry crossing the powerful Mekong, the portrait of the elegant administrative villa of the scandalous "Anne-Marie Stretter," the account of the affair in the garçonnière in Cholon where the little white girl scandalously breaks down the separation between racial and social worlds—between Asian and French, White and non-White, rich and poor—that give L'Amant much of its exotic popular appeal. The details of the sticky rice from which choum-choum, an Annamite liqueur is made, of Chinese wealth and tradition, or of the restaurants in Cholon, present in L'Empire français as factual, historical description of a French colony, will recur in L'Amant de la Chine du nord to give traditional verisimilitude to this text's new (and topical) focus on the Chinese story.[12] Yet this retold story of the lover is also a strangely fictional tale. As the following chapters will argue, the real— like the conventions of autobiography—does not disappear. It is telescoped with the imaginary.

In all the "new autobiographical" evocations and imaginary transformations of personal childhood surroundings, "real" political and social contexts and comment are, then, at least indirectly present (at second hand and in the form of stories). We catch glimpses of the refined court of the Czar, the privileged world of the upper classes and intelligentsia, and of the repressive Czarist police state through the memories of the stories of Grandmother and Uncle in Enfance. Racism, capitalist exploitation, and colonialism (there has been a major ideological shift from L'Empire français) are themes that appear to emerge from personal lived experience in the autobiographical Duras, although these are problematically influenced both by the political contexts of the time of the experience and the changed contexts of the time of writing.

The underlying and complex thematics of woman's powerlessness/sexual power, the sensuality of wealth (the black Morris Léon Bollée), the freedoms and the humiliations of poverty, and the apparently natural rhythm or calamity of the annual "harvest" of children playing joyously in the Mekong River or riding the buffalo, born to die, experienced in the colonial Indochina of childhood raise different political questions in 1991 from those posed in the collective consciousness of the 1930s and 1940s or in Duras' adolescent consciousness. The "little white girl" who takes a Chinese lover is not frequentable or marriageable in the prejudiced white Saigon community; the poor, nonvirgin European girl is not a possible wife for the heir of a wealthy and traditional Chinese businessman. Yet the adolescent with whom Duras identifies in 1991 in her text rises above such ethnic and class prejudice by defiantly and transgressively asserting her freedom and assuming her sexuality. The (re)writing of her story inverts power relations, while other colonial women live their empty lives absently, waiting for Europe and for romance. Occasionally, a model of difference does emerge from this flatness and boredom like "la Dame de Vinhlong," wife of an important colonial administrator, who becomes the character of the fatally attractive Anne-Marie Stretter. A "real" referent can be demonstrated for this scandalously seductive "Lady" whose story so fascinated the young Marguerite. Letters written by her daughters and sent to Duras have appeared in print.[13]

Robbe-Grillet's autobiography too, exhumes and rewrites the skeletons in the cupboard not only of a personal past but also of a French history in a return of the repressed that is influenced by both present and past historical contexts. This past is predominantly collaborationist in sentiment if not in direct action. *Le Miroir qui revient* examines the right-wing, monarchist, antiSemitic and anglophobic sentiments of his parents and his own experience of "voluntary labor" as a turner and fitter in a German tank factory near Nuremberg during the war. This remembering of the unacceptable—the sign in the factory, "Du bist eine Nummer und diese Nummer ist nul" ("You are a number and that number is zero"), the classifications of persons (as foreign workers, Jews, and Poles) and of the gap between the sign and the reality (National Socialism with its images of blond healthy children, the helpful, smiling, young blond soldier, and the reality of the Holocaust revealed after the war)—signifies both the questioning of the bond with his family and the beginning of unceasing interrogation of the monsters of disorder concealed in the constituted forms of order, language, and self. Such a deconstructive staging takes place in the light of the attraction of "une certaine idée de l'ordre qui avait pu nous paraître grandiose" (p. 46) [a particular idea of order that had appeared awe-inspiring to us].[14]

Le Miroir qui revient can be seen as deriving from the "apologie-confession" tradition, the confession (and justification) of a right-wing past and of sexual "difference," and an attempted understanding and exorcism of these personal ghosts in the mirror. *Enfance* would not be dissimilar to the search of the Proustian "I" for past time through voluntary and involuntary memory, the emergence or evocation of a series of images or feelings from the past that take form in a sentient present marked by "now." Much as Proust's tea and madeleine evoke the emotions of forgotten experience, a spoonful of straw-berry jam "even today" brings back the feelings of deception and disquiet of the childhood experience of unwittingly taking medicine concealed in deli-cious jam. A similar formative memory of "joy" called up from the past memory of a park bench on a sunny afternoon in the Luxembourg Gardens with father closing a book of fairy tales, the joy of the natural world assimilated to self and the self dissipated in oneness with the world—"je suis dans cela, dans le petit mur rose, les fleurs des espaliers, des arbres, la pelouse, l'air qui vibre . . . je suis en eux sans rien de plus, rien qui ne soit à eux, rien à moi" (p. 65) [I am inside it, inside the little pink wall, the flowers on the espaliers, on the trees, the lawn, the vibrating air . . . I am inside them with nothing else, nothing that does not belong to them, nothing that belongs to me]—although re-created and experienced in the present of the writing, is surprisingly similar in content to Rousseau's literary past-tense description of harmony in self-loss in the fifth "Rêverie" of the classic *Les Rêveries du promeneur solitaire.* A not dissimilar experience closes the holidays in the Alps that precede high school and mark the end of childhood and of the book. The child, preparing herself for her new adventure, presses herself to the moss-covered earth for its sap to pen-etrate and spread through her body. Looking at the sky as never before, she again becomes one with the universe: "Je me fonds en lui, je n'ai pas de limites, pas de fin" (p. 255) [I melt into it, I have no limits, no end]. It is evident that the conformity to literary autobiographical models, in this case to Proust, to Rousseau, or to George Sand's biographical and literary invocations to nature is not merely a coincidence.

L'*Amant*, too, which insists on the slow filmic present/presence of the im-age—"L'image dure pendant toute la traversée du fleuve" (p. 11) [The image lasts all the way across the river]—on seeing as a Lacanian "appetite of the eye" or desire, "C'est là, dans la dernière maison, celle de la Loire, c'est là que je *vois* clairement la folie pour la première fois" (p. 40, my italics) [It's there, in that last house, the one on the Loire that I *see* her madness clearly for the first time] can be read as a kind of voluptuousness of reminiscence. It is the attempt to relive the past experience (the intensity of physical love or of a star-lit night drive with the mother), although the only means to this end is a tex-tual re-creation in a sentient present. It too contains echoes of Proust's search for lost time or of Rousseau's *Rêveries* while clearly recasting the conditions of possibility of Rousseau's (self-deceiving) autobiographical project of truth, nature, and self-knowledge.

In partial answer to our initial questions, then, these chronologies of a life, descriptions of the places of childhood, retrospective analyses of family relations, and recapture of moments of formative childhood experience, epiphany, or bliss are recognizable functions of the autobiographical genre. At the same time, past experience is shown to be filtered through memory and the imaginary and constructed in language in the present. The attitudes of the past are influenced by the present political moment; even the sentient present is a function of past text and the materiality of present language.

The following chapter will develop the argument that although the new autobiographical enterprise involves a staging of autobiographical conventions and traditional theories of the self that sometimes takes on a very narcissistic flavor, it is nonetheless clearly a child of its postmodern time (defined as what comes after and out of modernism)—that is, of what Sarraute called the "age of suspicion" or what Robbe-Grillet prefers to call "modernité." The new autobiographies will place the territories of old autobiographies, to use a Derridean term, "under erasure" ("sous râture"), that is, they will not be fully erased but simply struck out and still perceptible. Conventional autobiographical theories of self will be put under a skeptical microscope, examined for self-indulgence.

What the demonstration of the continued presence of preoccupation with theories of the self suggests is the resistance of something concealed in the traditional material placed in parentheses. This resistance or resilience of what might be designated by the very Derridean (anti)concepts of "crypt" or "remainder" or by what Umberto Eco suggests is a kind of ideal or original language[15] appears to defy those Derridean pen-strokes that put metaphysics or origins, that is, any kind of transcendental meanings, in parentheses ("sous râture"). It is significant that Eco's semiosis derives from the work of the North American linguist Pierce rather than from De Saussure. It proposes that although there is indeed no absolute identification between word and thing as De Saussure claims, some form of link between word and world exists. In a recent article entitled "Picketing the Zeitgeist: In Search of the Perfect Language," Dawn Michelle Baude discusses a similar difference between Derrida and Eco. "While both men extol the signifying chain—which runs parallel to the world but does not intersect it—Derrida argues that the operative mechanism is absence, while Eco asserts that the crucial component is presence."[16]

Baude gives the following example, "'Tree' and 'arbre' can be used almost, but not quite, interchangeably, and in neither case will 'tree' or 'arbre' be confused with aluminum foil," and concludes, "Following the implications of Eco's theory, we may not be able to say whether a certain reading or review of a book is the 'right' one or not, but we should certainly identify those that are wide of the mark" (p. 6). For Eco, the ideal reading would oscillate between a degree of Derridean openness and proliferation of meanings and the literal sense of the words on the page, making meanings and readings multiple but not necessarily all equal. It is out of such resistance and resilience and out of the differences this incorporates, out of the differences between the staged old autobiographies and the new autobiographies that emerge from this critical and creative staging, I will claim, that new conceptions of the self generated by the new autobiographical writing emerge.

◇

two

◇

THE ART OF THE IMPOSSIBLE

The chronologies of a life, descriptions of the places of childhood, and retrospective analyses of family relations appear concerned to establish origins and causes—the ghosts in the mirror, or rather their lack, or their problematic character. A loving father and mother, a happy home, the absence of violence, concludes Alain Robbe-Grillet. Why then sexual satisfaction in sadistic fantasies from a very early age? Was there something hidden in him that was not the product of his environment? Or was this the influence of his primary affective relations or of the images around him—in some sense the presence of the other in the self? Marguerite Duras begins her autobiography with a reference to her ravaged face, a face early "predestined" for the alcohol that replaces an absent God and for sexual pleasure. Her text evokes a surprisingly young and sudden aging at eighteen, and an early formative experience of fear. What are these predestinations or determinations or does the subsequent deconstruction of the fully self-knowing individual make such a project of self knowledge impossible? Nathalie Sarraute, more reticent about her private life and anxious to deny any relation between her life and her work,[1] is nonetheless also seeking traces of the origins of her writing vocation and the genesis of her preoccupation with tropistic psychological movements in the complexity of relations with parental figures. These relations can, however, only be explored with words. In all three works, it is in interaction with the other—the other of language, the other in the self—that the self takes shape. It is this otherness of the self's origin and formation that creates the impossibility of the traditional unified autobiographical subject present to itself.

It is not surprising, then, to find this late twentieth-century autobiography highly self-conscious, foregrounding the materiality of its conditions of existence (language) and the conventions of its genre by means of metatextual commentary. The double perspective, for example, is discussed as posing a major problem for the traditional autobiographical pact of "truth." Situated in the present, the adult writer is necessarily recounting from a present point of time and a point of view determined by intervening events, the young person he or she once was in the past. The intervening events cannot but alter any pristine memory. In the wake of Philippe Lejeune himself, Robbe-Grillet criticizes a classically traditional autobiography like *Les Mots* for its evocation of a rather odious little boy with literary pretensions that the adult Sartre (pretending to be in short trousers) manipulates. *Les Mots*, of course, undermined as it is by pervasive irony is hardly a traditional autobiography, but Robbe-Grillet is rejecting Sartre's attempt to reveal a true (and false) self through autobiography. Robbe-Grillet, Sarraute, and Duras are all explicitly at grips with the (im)possibility of recovering the past in the present; the imposition of their present knowing selves on their unknowing past selves. This impossibility (repressed by traditional autobiography in the interest of the realist illusion) has become part of the subject matter of their texts.

Recollecting the father's visit to Paris and her walks with him in the Luxembourg Gardens, a first narrative voice in *Enfance* recalls the question the child asks: "Est-ce que tu m'aimes, papa?" (p. 56) [Do you love me, Papa?]. It continues with the reflection that Papa detests words like love. The second critical voice remonstrates. "Tu le sentais vraiment déjà à cet âge?" (p. 56) [Did you really already feel that, at that age?]. Again, the first narrative voice remembers that in obedience to the absent mother's instructions, the child, not yet six, on holiday in a Swiss hotel with father, refuses to swallow her food until it is "aussi liquide qu'une soupe" (p. 17) [as liquid as soup]. Stubborn to all cajolement, a bad example to the other children, she must subsequently eat her meals alone, but she feels that she has remained loyal: "Je résiste . . . je tiens bon sur ce bout de terrain où j'ai hissé ses couleurs, où j'ai planté son drapeau" (p. 17) [I'm resisting . . . I'm holding out on this bit of territory on which I have hoisted her colors, on which I've put up her flag]. The second voice once again is critical of an evocation that is obviously a present construction in adult language and image. "Des images, des mots qui évidemment ne pouvaient pas se former à cet âge-là dans ta tête" (pp. 17–18) [Images, words, which obviously couldn't have come into your head at that age]. Philippe Lejeune interprets this minidrama as metatextual reflection on an aspect of the writing process in which it is, in fact, language that is worked on patiently and stubbornly or "liquified."[2] Such a linguistic reading of the childhood mealtime drama suggests hidden connections between the opening scene in which the child slashes the smooth silk of the sofa (of language) transgressively and this second apparently unrelated scene.

The traditional autobiographical convention of demarcating past time by using the past tense and marking the present of the narration with the present tense is undermined in Sarraute's new autobiography by the systematic use of the present and the blurring of the double time frame. The nature of memory itself, its gaps and imprecisions, already a problem for more traditional biography, adds to the difficulties of narrative choices and becomes, in its turn, food for the text. Nathalie's mother writes, suggesting she take the child back "Au bout d'un an et demi . . . ou peut-être de deux ans" (p. 164) [After a year and a half . . . or perhaps two years]. The child was seven and a half—or was she perhaps eight? Nothing remains of the thoughts of the child seen at play in the gardens. The first narrator refuses the impulse of the second narrator to "plaster over" this hole ("en tout cas rien ne m'en est resté et ce n'est tout de même pas toi, qui vas me pousser à chercher à combler ce trou par un replâtrage," p. 25 [in any case, nothing of that has remained with me and you certainly aren't going to push me into trying to plaster over that gap]). In similar fidelity to the uncertainties of memory, she ignores the demand for exactitude and verisimilitude made by the second voice. Wasn't the word for essay "rédaction" rather than "devoir"? (p. 194). Shouldn't mother's Russian friend be called "Uncle" in the Russian fashion? (p. 82). The difficulty of grasping memory, which is evanescent, indistinct, fragile, becomes instead a subject matter with its own linguistic difficulties and calls for its own metaphor and style: "C'est apparu, indistinct, irréel . . . un promontoire inconnu qui surgit un instant du brouillard . . . et de nouveau un épais brouillard le recouvre" (p. 74) [it appeared, indistinct, unreal . . . an unknown promontory which for a moment looms up out of the fog . . . and then, once again, a thick fog covers it]. The interlocution that for the linguist Benveniste is always implied by the use of "I" structures Sarraute's text. Exchange with the other outside the self or indeed inside is necessary for self-constitution. The second voice can slide between the personal, emotional form "Maman" to talk about the mother, the form used by the first narrator, and the distancing, analytical form "ta mère" [your mother]. The competing but unstable dialogic voices that sometimes overlap or reverse their roles are also figures of such internal differences necessary for interlocution.

Although Philippe Lejeune's interpretation of *Enfance* in terms of a "liquifying of language" is congruent with such textual operations and indeed with the whole text and is certainly a valid reading, I would suggest that even in the face of the (im)possibility of the excavating of the past and the (im)possibility of a truth of a dialogic (multiple, shifting, internally different) self, there is more to the art of *Enfance* than an account of the limits posed on self-knowledge by language and autobiographical convention. The striking device of a dialogue between a first person whose narrative voice is predominantly uncertain, emotional, and marked by feminine agreements and an unmarked (masculine or neuter) narrative voice stimulating memory, probing, analyzing, and correcting the memories of the first person voice, which it addresses as "tu," moves the text dramatically away from traditional forms. In a later chapter, I argue that this theatrical stylistic device creates a textual and sexual play not only within the narration in *Enfance* but also within Sarraute, the narrator.

Like memories, emotions cannot be exactly those of the lived experience. Time has smoothed them out, made them writable. Marguerite Duras' mother and her two brothers are dead at the time of writing. Sensation and identification fade. "Je n'ai plus dans ma tête le parfum de sa peau ni dans mes yeux la couleur de ses yeux. [. . .] Le rire, je ne l'entends plus, ni le rire, ni les cris. C'est fini, je ne me souviens plus. C'est pourquoi j'en écris si facile d'elle maintenant, si long, si étiré, elle est devenue écriture courante" (p. 38) [In my head I no longer have the scent of her skin, nor in my eyes the color of her eyes. {. . .} Her laughter I can't hear any more—neither her laughter nor her cries. It's over, I don't remember. That's why I can write about her so easily now, so long, so fully. She's become just something you write without difficulty, cursive writing]. In Duras' work emotion is inextricably bound up with language and the process of writing and has lost the primitive force of pure cry.

For the reader, too, the scene of the discovery of desire in the bedroom with the Chinese lover must modify the earlier image of the Mekong ferry crossing, the meeting between the young man in the black limousine and the white girl in her marked-down sale gold lamé high heels and man's pink felt hat. "Déjà sur le bac, avant son heure, l'image aurait participé de cet instant" (p. 50) [Already on the ferry, in advance, the image owed something to this moment]. This telescoping of scenes is less a pure effect of memory than an effect of interrelated text or process of rewriting or reading. *L'Amant* will itself be telescoped into or rewritten by *L'Amant de la Chine du nord* to become the story of a story. During the description of the return of the young girl on a boat to France, a young man drowns himself for love, perhaps, states the text, on "this" voyage, perhaps on another. The omniscient narrator seems to hesitate and the writer makes a correction. "Non, à l'écrire, elle ne voit pas le bateau mais un autre lieu, celui ou elle a entendu raconter l'histoire" (p. 137) [No, now she comes to write it down, she doesn't see the boat but somewhere else, the place where she was told about it]. However, the writing of the absolute character of the young man's gesture, fixed by a Chopin *valse* associated elsewhere in the text with Anne-Marie Stretter, and here flung out across the sea (memory, desire), under a brilliant sky, situates the "other" boat trip as essentially the "same" voyage. "Et une autre fois, c'était encore au cours de ce même voyage, pendant la traversée de ce même océan" (p. 137) [And another time, on the same route, during the crossing of the same ocean]. The death of the young man affects retroactively the sense of the affair with the lover which is "now" recognized as love—a "now" that is the moment of the boat trip and the moment of the writing, indeterminately.

In *L'Amant de la Chine du nord*, this love has become a fact of the text by its very repetition, but it is again traversed and made denser by references to other texts. The helplessness and shame of the lover from North China in the face of the intensity and impossibility of his love for the very young white girl, his interest in the little brother, and the financial indemnities from his wealthy father that he offers to the mother are developments of the memories in *L'Amant*. New scenes, in which the young woman recognizes the lover's desire to overcome love's mortality and his fear of losing her by killing her, derive from *Moderato Cantabile*. In this earlier novel, a *crime passionnel*, witnessed by the protagonists is reenacted ritually and symbolically by the protagonists as Chauvin "kills" a consenting and desiring Anne Desbaresdes. Duras claims to have transposed a real relationship and a personal experience into this account of fearful fascination with love unto violent death.[3] Both autobiographical *Lovers* operate a similar synthesis: a telescoping of affairs of text and of life, of memory as of the imagination, a present rewriting of both past text and of sex.

Robbe-Grillet insists in his text on the arbitrariness of his selection of a limited number of moments out of a myriad of moving fragments and the ordering and the setting of these moments in the concrete of a quasi-historical narration: "Les terreurs et les joies du petit garçon formant une base solide pour les thèmes ou les techniques du futur écrivain" (p. 59) [The terrors and joys of the little boy forming a solid base for the themes or techniques of the future writer]. He challenges the idea of formative moments or of "instants principaux" (p. 57) [central moments] selected arbitrarily out of the millions of moments in a web of life. Many of the memories he recounts, the visit of Count Corinthe to the family home on his prancing white horse, the child's glimpse through the red curtains of the shadows cast by his father and the Count in front of the flickering flames of the massive fireplace, for example, are described in the text itself as "forgés après coup par ma mémoire" (p. 8) [invented by my fertile memory] or as a passage that is "entièrement inventé" (p. 24) [a complete fiction]. It is the reader who is left to resolve the indeterminacy and to interpret

Corinthe, the white horse, the red curtains as (faulty) memory or fantasy or as myth, that is, as prefabricated literary stories.

The staging of the artifice in traditional autobiographical conventions is accompanied in all three works by the explicit questioning of the possibility of stable, single identity or presence. Of the portrait of his grandfather, Robbe-Grillet comments:

> Voilà donc tout ce qu'il reste de quelqu'un, au bout de si peu de temps, et de moi-même aussi bientôt, sans aucun doute: des pièces dépareillées, des morceaux de gestes figés et d'objets sans suite, des questions dans le vide, des instantanés qu'on énumère en désordre sans parvenir à les mettre véritablement (logiquement) bout à bout. (p. 27)

> [And so that's all that's left of someone, after such a short time—and that goes for me too, soon enough, no doubt: odds and ends, frozen gestures, disconnected objects, questions in the empty air, a jumble of random snapshots with no real (logical) sequence.]

In both Robbe-Grillet and Sarraute, there is a recurring theme of imposture or unauthenticity; he is a "false" agronomist writing a novel at his office desk; she is a "false" child, reciting a childish poem about her sweet pillow for adult approval. Both find the sentimental charge of the familiar world and its linguistic certainties and securities intellectually suspect. Both write for and against themselves ("on crée toujours pour soi," *Le Miroir*, p. 184) as they show the impossibility of the reproduction of the self for autobiographical analysis. This search for self among literary avatars takes the form of oscillation between the apparently unified subjective vulnerability of confession and the ironic deconstructive distance of internal splits and tensions.

Robbe-Grillet's first person organizing narrator, for example, is accompanied by a legendary third person character, Henri de Corinthe, fascist collaborator and sadist or war hero and victim. Corinthe is a figure of the father's wartime experiences, of right-wing histories of France, and of the son's sexual/textual contexts. This figure accedes to a shadowy existence that incorporates the rational and historical subject and the fantasmatic and the emotional subject; the logical ordering subject stands in apposition to the disorder and dubious sexual impulses of his double. In the later *Angélique ou l'enchantement*, the "I" or ego of the writer, refracted in the mirror in his study bedroom begins to float and tremble suggesting the incoherent monsters this "I" conceals—what Freud would consider to be the id as yet unassimilated by analysis. The "I," insisted Roland Barthes, following Lacan, cannot be written except where there is a *mise en scène* of the "imaginaire," an establishing of levels or topologies, and a dispersion of roles, the stage footlights being made to serve as an uncertain dividing line ("faire de la rampe une barre incertaine," *Roland Barthes par Roland Barthes*, p. 108). In its highest degree, the imaginary is experienced, says Barthes, as "tout ce que j'ai envie d'écrire de moi et qu'il me gêne finalement d'écrire" [everything I want to write about myself and that in the final instance, it embarrasses me to write].[4] The "I" then, as well as being multiple, is what is missing or unsayable. It is presumably for this reason that Robbe-Grillet claims to have formulated a new autobiographical pact in which such representations will function as the voice of the imaginary. "J'ai formulé un pacte nouveau. C'est l'imaginaire qui parle; l'imaginaire parle du souvenir" [I have formulated a new pact. It's the imaginary that speaks; the imaginary speaks of memory].[5]

The image of the ferry crossing over the Mekong River sweeping powerfully to the caverns of the sea, the photo that had never been taken of the girl of fifteen and a half in her sexually self-assertive dress, shoes, and hat beside an improbable luxury black limousine is Duras' imaginary speaking; her childhood self as the adult writer chooses (to see) it. The scene of the encounter with the lover on the ferry and the affair that is its sequel recur in *L'Amant de la Chine du nord*, but certain details are significantly modified. The "child" here is not fifteen and a half but barely fifteen; the transgressive aspects of the relationship are made evident as she is designated systematically as "la petite." For psychoanalytic theory,[6] the *"imaginaire"* is marked by the prevalence of the relation to the image of the other ("le semblable"); intrasubjectively by the narcissistic relation between the subject and the ego, intersubjectively by the relationship founded on and captured by the image of the other—erotic attraction and aggressive tension for example. Such a fracturing that makes the subject at once a monster and a hunter of monsters as in dreams is also clearly present in Robbe-Grillet's autobiographical alter ego figure of Corinthe.

This splitting, also articulated in the multiplication and displacements of the narrative voice, further disrupts the possibility of an "autobiographical pact" of identity between narrator and character or writer and narrator. Philippe Lejeune offers the following often quoted definition of the autobiographical genre: "Le récit rétrospectif en prose que quelqu'un fait de sa propre existence lorsqu'il met l'accent principal sur l'histoire de sa personnalité" [The retrospective prose narrative that a person tells about her/his own existence when this focuses particularly on the story of her/his personality].[7] But, in Duras' text, for example, the first and third person pronouns and nouns that indicate narrative point of view proliferate and shift in the same passages and even within the same sentence, creating a self that is both present and past, both subject and object of the narration.

> L'amant de Cholen s'est fait à l'adolescence de *la petite blanche* jusqu'à s'y perdre. [. . .] Peut-être découvre-t-il qu'ils ne se sont jamais encore parlé, sauf lorsqu'ils s'appellent dans les cris de la chambre le soir. Oui *je* crois qu'il ne savait pas, il découvre qu'il ne savait pas. [. . .] Il *la* regarde. [. . .] *Je* regardais ce qu'il faisait de *moi*, comme il se servait de *moi*. [. . .] Ainsi *j*'étais devenue son enfant. [. . .] Et parfois il prend peur, tout à coup il s'inquiète de *sa* santé comme s'il découvrait qu'*elle* était mortelle. (pp. 121–122, my italics)

> [The lover from Cholon is so accustomed to the adolescence of *the white girl*, he's lost. {. . .} Perhaps he realizes they never have spoken to each other, except when they cry out to each other in the bedroom in the evening. Yes, *I* think he didn't know, he realizes he didn't know. {. . .} He looks at *her*. {. . .} *I* used to watch what he did with *me*, how he used *me*. {. . .} *I* had become his child. {. . .} And sometimes he takes fright, suddenly he's worried about *her* health, as if he suddenly realized *she* was mortal.]

In this passage, the signified of the first person "I" moves between the writer "I" and the adolescent "I"; the adolescent subject "I," however, is also the adolescent object in the third person ("la petite blanche," "sa santé," "elle"). Toward the end of the autobiography, another third person, this time the writer as the object rather than the subject of the narration, takes the place of the first person writer. "Non, à l'écrire, *elle* ne voit pas le bateau" (p. 137, my italics) [No, now *she* comes to write it down, *she* doesn't see the boat]. Such pronominal shifts create a dissolution of unified self in an interchangeability between the narrator "je," the character "la jeune fille," and the writer "je"/"elle" within a nested Russian doll-like structure. This textual movement brings together different phases of Duras' work from the use of early symbolic or generative names which designate a more or less universal character type (Lol. V. Stein, Madame Desbaresdes), to anonymous pronouns of shifting reference and gender, *il(s)/elle(s)*, and finally to the individualizing "je" of autobiography. "Real" names, too—M.D. of *Les Parleuses* or Yann Andréa's collaborative biographical text; *MD*, which describes Duras' traumatic treatment for alcoholism; or Duras' 1992 *Yann Andréa Steiner*—are part of this process. In *L'Amant de la Chine du nord*, the experiments of *L'Amant* are continued: a third person generic character "l'enfant" or "la petite" is preferred here to the "I" or the "she," however, as the writer develops what might be seen as a maternal, protective relation to the young girl she once was in her early and absolute relations.

The overlapping, merging, and separating of the voices of the writer, the narrator, and the character (designated as "la jeune fille blanche," "la petite prostituée," "la petite vicieuse" [the white girl, the little whore, the depraved young girl] in *L'Amant* obliges the reader to accept multiplicity, nonexclusive contradiction and uncertainty and to participate in the production of identity and meaning. For example, in a sentence such as the following, "*elle* ne sait pas combien de temps après ce départ de *la jeune fille blanche* il [le Chinois] a exécuté l'ordre du père" (p. 140, my italics) [*She* doesn't know how long it was after *the white girl* left that he obeyed his father's orders], is the "elle" [she] of the boat voyage to France "la jeune fille blanche" [the young white girl] of the earlier love affair or the present narrator? Only the speaking voice in the present moment can constitute a unifying of the fragments of the different selves in time. As Gide had earlier put this: "Si je n'étais pas là pour les accointer, mon être du matin ne reconnaîtrait pas celui du soir. Rien ne saurait être plus différent de moi, que moi-même" [If I were not there to partner them, my morning self would not recognize my evening self. Nothing could be more different from me than I myself].[8] The shifting frames of reference complicate not only any autobiographical "pact" of identity, but also of sincerity, or indeed of comprehensiveness—the "je dirai tout" [I'll tell all] of Rousseau's *Confessions*.

Yet, these proliferating reconstructions of the past may also provide a way to move closer to personal obsessions and fantasies, to a hidden inner life, as in the germinal new autobiographical writing of Michel Leiris—particularly if the "I" is indeed what is missing or unsayable. Michel Leiris' construction of the self around the axes of sexuality and ethnography and heterogeneous bricolage of disparate facts are evident precursors of the forms of the new autobiographies. It is significant that his particular choices and configurations of mythological figure, the fascination with the fatal cruelty and strength of Messalina and the Medusa, and the pleasure in the woman wounded, tamed, and ritually sacrificed (like the bull in his metaphor of literature as sexual-sacred "tauromachie") have evident echoes in Robbe-Grillet's sexual-textual sadism and his dangerous/suppressed victim, Angélique-Violette.[9] The autobiographical works of Leiris condense allegorized (textual) figures, of Judith the avenger and Lucretia, the raped victim in Cranach's painting, for example, that derive as much from personal fears and fantasies as from the collective mythologies that both reveal and cloak the personal obsessions.

The questions raised by the splitting of the narrator into ego and alter, into multiple pronouns, his/her translation through mythological figures or a brico-lage of intertexts are both explicit and implicit. What is the "I" and what is its relation to the other? How can it be seen/known? Where is the line between memory and imagination? If past memories are only accessible in their present reconstructions in language, can memory really constitute a method that al-lows an account of life? As one of Sarraute's narrative voices asks: "Ne te fâche pas, mais ne crois-tu pas que là, avec ces roucoulements, ces pépiements, tu n'as pas pu t'empêcher de placer un petit morceau de préfabriqué . . . c'est si tentant . . . tu as fait un joli petit raccord, tout à fait en accord" (*Enfance*, p. 21) [Don't be angry, but don't you think that there, with that cooing, that chirrup-ing, you haven't been able to resist introducing something a little bit prefabri-cated . . . it's so tempting, you've inserted a pretty little piece . . . completely in keeping]. Might memories be the product of stories—the stories recounted to Robbe-Grillet by his parents or the "récits décousus qui circulaient" (p. 7) [the disconnected stories in general circulation]—that is, the products of other people's labels and definitions or of prefabricated language rather than of ex-perience?

Robbe-Grillet, Duras, and Sarraute all claim explicitly that the vehicle for exploring memories and language has an influence on the memories it inves-tigates. In *Enfance*, indicating that their full substance and meaning would be lost in their translation into French, Nathalie Sarraute uses a number of phrases in the original German, Russian, or English as the material for her work on memory. Duras, too, experiments with English phrases as "intertexts" in *Emily L.*, and Robbe-Grillet incorporates German phrases in his attempt to recon-struct an aspect of his wartime experience in Germany. Meaning, it would appear, derives from the complex network of interconnecting phonemic, syn-tactical, lexical, and cultural systems in which each language is distinctively inscribed and cannot be satisfactorily translated to another language system.

For all of the new autobiographers, the autobiographical "I" is a textual "I" and text can no more reproduce the lived experience with words than it can represent the world. Duras attempted to communicate the drama, the impos-sibility of this writing that is not life and not self during her interview with Bernard Pivot on "Apostrophes" in 1984 after the immense immediate success of *L'Amant*: "Je fais une chose impossible. On n'est pas là. La vie est ailleurs. On se double de ça, à coté de la vie. De quoi ça se procède? Je ne sais pas" [I'm doing something impossible. You're not there. Life is elsewhere. You con-struct a double with this, parallel to life. Where does this come from? I don't know]. It is because our language is structured as is clear consciousness, that is, according to the laws of the rational mind and of meaning, claims Robbe-Grillet in *Le Miroir*, because it is a reinvention of experience, that it is incapable of giving an account either of a world that is not us or of the specters that agitate within us. Although consciousness is indeed structured like a language for Robbe-Grillet and can therefore be written, he disagrees with Lacan's claim that the unconscious is similarly structured like a language and can be represented. (In this context, the word "consciousness," as used by Robbe-Grillet, refers to the Nietzschean collective and ready-made consciousness of language rather than to inner selfhood, awareness, integrity).

Despite the central role that Duras, Sarraute, and Robbe-Grillet claim that language as the other plays in their work, our first chapter demonstrated that there is also an insistence on the existence of realities outside language (life chronologies, geographies, family histories) explicit in all three autobiographies. This presents a problem for postmodernists who deny the existence of anything outside the internal relations of the text in the constitution of meaning ("le langage tout seul" [language alone] of Ricardou) and see the question of reference as inherently undecidable. But the Sarraute child's experience of joy is beyond words, claims her narrator. "Pourquoi vouloir faire revivre cela, sans mots qui puissent parvenir à capter, à retenir ne serait-ce qu'encore quelques instants ce qui m'est arrivé" (p. 64) [Why try to bring this back to life, without the words that might manage to capture, to retain, if only for a few more instants, what happened to me]. As she reconstructs in dialogue and narration the momentous decision of the child to remain with the father and not to return to the mother, Sarraute again comments both on the limitations of language and on her patient efforts to reconstruct feelings lost or buried:

> Mais cette reconstitution de ce que j'ai dû éprouver est pareille à une maquette en carton reproduisant en un modèle réduit ce qu'avaient pu être les bâtiments, les maisons, les temples, les rues, les places et les jardins d'une ville engloutie. (p. 165)

> [But this reconstitution of what I must have felt is like a cardboard model that reproduces on a small scale what the buildings, houses, temples, streets, squares, and gardens of a submerged town must have been like.]

In the words of Duras, the story of her life "does not exist"; there is never a center, no path, no line. Yet, beyond words, there is the circulation of force, of desire, a compulsion to write of what is forgotten, as yet silent. There is indeed a family "story" even if this escapes her understanding, ("m'est encore inaccessible," p. 34). This story is of the flesh itself: "cachée au plus profond de ma chair, aveugle comme un nouveau-né du premier jour" (p. 34) [hidden in the depths of my flesh, blind like a one-day-old infant].

> Elle est le lieu au seuil de quoi le silence commence. Ce qui s'y passe c'est justement le silence, ce lent travail pour toute ma vie. Je suis encore là, devant ces enfants possédés, à la même distance du mystère. Je n'ai jamais écrit, croyant le faire, je n'ai jamais aimé, croyant aimer, je n'ai jamais rien fait qu'attendre devant la porte fermée. (pp. 34–35)

> [It's the area on whose brink silence begins. What happens there is silence, the slow travail of my whole life. I'm still there watching those possessed children, as far away from the mystery now as I was then. I've never written, though I thought I wrote, never loved, though I thought I loved, never done anything but wait outside the closed door.]

Writing for Duras, then, stems from the wellsprings of a flow of desire that passes through the pre-Oedipal body into the textual body: "La mer, l'immensité qui se regroupe, s'éloigne, revient. [. . .] La mer, sans forme, simplement incomparable" (p. 50) [The sea, the immensity that regroups, withdraws, returns. {. . .} The sea, without form, simply incomparable], a force stronger than the clichés of social classification ("la petite prostituée de Sadec" [the little whore of Sadec]) and ready-made language. For her part, Nathalie Sarraute has always professed to be using language to explore a psychological tropistic reality outside constituted language. The unchanging, sparkling, Christmas-story image of the snow-covered wooden house of her infancy can however only be approached, perhaps touched, with circumspection by words, "j'ai envie de la palper, de la caresser, de la parcourir avec des mots, mais pas trop fort, j'ai si peur de l'abîmer" (p. 42) [I want to touch it, to caress this immutable image, to cover it with words, but not too thickly, I'm so afraid of spoiling it]. Even the iterative childhood dream of the stretch of fine sand, the holes, the rising sea of fascination and fear, claims Robbe-Grillet, is not represented by his text but set to function within it, to generate meaning. For, by pretending to express the world and the unconscious, the traditional text conceals its nature as construction and fails to leave the blanks, the gaps in meaning, that may allow the unknown senses of experience to emerge, according to the writer. Such a traditional text is the text of certitude and security that, for Nathalie Sarraute, is smooth and well rounded, with nothing that stands out, words in their best clothes and proper settings ("bien fréquentés," p. 197) where good manners are required. This text that produces the feeling that her mother is reading the bedtime story less to her daughter than "to someone else" ("c'est à quelqu'un d'autre qu'elle raconte," p. 21) is, for Sarraute, like the writing of Balzac and of Loti, a text that corresponds to the traditional collective rituals of reading and writing much as Sartre describes them in *Les Mots*.

The self-conscious new autobiography that declares its necessarily conventional and ritualistic origins and manifests the difficulty of directly mirroring what is not language and convention has been called an "autofiction." This term, for Doubrovsky, designates writing that, like psychoanalysis, takes place beyond the distinction between confession and invention.

> La "vérité," ici, ne saurait être de l'ordre de la copie conforme, et pour cause. Le sens d'une vie n'existe nulle part, n'existe pas. Il n'est pas à découvrir, mais à inventer, non de toutes pièces mais de toutes traces: il est à *construire*. Telle est bien la "construction" analytique; *fingere*, "donner forme," fiction, que le sujet s'incorpore. [. . .] L'autofiction, c'est la fiction que j'ai décidé, en tant qu'écrivain, de me donner de moi-même et par moi-même, en y incorporant, au sens plein du terme, l'expérience de l'analyse, non point seulement dans la thématique mais dans la production du texte.[10] (p. 96)

> [Truth, here, could not be of the order of the duplicate and for a very good reason. The meaning of a life does not exist anywhere, does not exist. It cannot be discovered, only invented, not arbitrarily but from all its traces: it must be *constructed*. It is the same as the "construction" produced by psychoanalysis; *fingere* "to give form to," a fiction that the subject incorporates. {. . .} Autofiction is the fiction of myself that I have decided, as a writer, to give of myself and by myself, incorporating the experience of analysis, in the full sense of the word, not only in the thematics but also in the production of the text.]

The analytical constructions of the new autobiographies may create a shiver of complicity in the reader but, as they turn around the traces of the self, the credulous reader has to take his chances, as Lejeune puts it. While Lejeune's concerns are for the safeguard of the "purity" of the traditional "pact" (honesty or sincerity),[11] it seems that in the new autobiographies, we are situated at the margins of the traditional, in the Barthesian realm of the trembling of uncertainties, where language is a nonassertive, nondogmatic, and pleasurable body, refusing closure and definitive single truth. In this new autobiographical space, the workings of the mind in the linguistic exploration of the *imaginaire* at the margins of the unsayable are of as much interest as any statement of meaning.

Fiction, as the construction effected by the experience of analysis, appears to have as much validity as fact.

Robbe-Grillet reiterates the assertion that appeared on the first page of the earliest work of the new genre, *Roland Barthes par Roland Barthes*: "Et c'est encore dans une fiction que je me hasarde ici" (p. 13) [And it is once again into a fiction that I venture here]. Just as the name of the author on the cover of Barthes' book is a fiction ("Tout ceci doit être considéré comme dit par un personnage de roman" [This must all be considered to be spoken by a fictional character], cautions the narrator) so indeed is the name of the writer, Robbe-Grillet, as the latter stands increasingly often before the microphone performing or in university lecture rooms, professor of himself, hardening readings of his polyvalent work. Quotations (characters, themes, and texts) from his earlier novels and films fill the pages of his new autobiographies continuing the intertextual assemblage operating in his fiction. Boris the Regicide and Jean the King are once again "complementary" figures (nonexclusive contradictions) of the writer. They are also rewriting; figures of the hero-villain of the earlier works *Un Régicide* and *L'Homme qui ment*. Fetish objects from his fictions—the broken glass, the old trunk in the attic, the heavy red curtains, the blue shoe stained with blood, Angelica in chains—are scattered across the surface of the new autobiographical texts. But many of these recurring fantasmatic intertexts become emotionally charged personal motifs—the rising tide that threatens to submerge the narrator, the devouring sea monster, the immemorial emergence of an action already accomplished (a crime?) that, effaced by the sea, leaves no trace.

In Sarraute's work too, the fragmented minidramas, the dialogue, the verbs (welling up, attacking, retracting), the metaphors (the soft, warm, smooth, inauthentic surfaces, the asperities that like Robbe-Grillet's holes, gaps, and monsters or Duras' blanks and silences reveal the violent movements eddying under the calm surface) are not different from those of her earliest work *Tropismes* or of her novels. It is indeed, she claims, only because the substance of the past and the nature of her family relationships appear to tremble, to palpitate beyond the words of the tribe and are not fixed once and for all that she gives in to the autobiographical temptation. For new autobiography may not require her to leave her "element" where everything fluctuates, metamorphoses, and escapes and she gropes toward more refined understanding somewhere between language and psychological movement.

The debate is continued within Sarraute's autobiographical text itself. The rational and "objective" voice in *Enfance*[12] attempts to push the emotional voice toward a clear understanding and expression of the pain of the mother's lack of understanding of her daughter and absorption in her new marriage or the stepmother's resentment toward her unwelcome and scholastically successful stepdaughter and preference for the new half-sister. But the "feminine" voice resists because her interlocutor's clear, well-rounded, logical formulations harden and fix fragile, moving relationships and feelings. Yet, for the child, already, the discrete ready-made phrase, the language of the other learned from the environment is a means of grasping and capturing the feelings that are experienced in their totality, beyond words, ("hors des mots, globalement," p. 18). The central memories of *Enfance* are, in fact, evoked and fixed by names or phrases such as "Ivanovo" (the fairy-tale house of birth), "Maman," "Kolia," "Papa," and the father's diminutives, "Tachok," "ma fille."

The text of Marguerite Duras is also largely such a constructional present of a writing that has its own emotional verisimilitude even as it deconstructs conventional "trueness to life." Like *Enfance*—"Look, Mother and Kolia are talking"—it involves an interlocutor or an audience intimately in a dramatic scene or, as in *Le Miroir qui revient*, "ta mort à toi, lecteur" (p. 28) [your death, O reader], invokes the reader aggressively. In Duras, the involvement of the reader has a more exhibitionist and intimate quality: "Sur le bac, regardez-moi, je les ai [mes beaux cheveux] encore" (p. 24) [On the ferry, look at me, I still have it {my long hair}]. The logic that the reader is invited to follow is less the logic of an ordering of the past than the emotional, imaginative logic of the local point of view the writing creates from moment to moment. "Ce jour-là je dois porter cette fameuse paire de talons hauts en lamé d'or. Je ne vois rien d'autre que je pourrais porter ce jour-là, alors je les porte" (pp. 18–19) [This particular day I must be wearing the famous pair of gold lamé high heels. I can't see any others I could have been wearing, so I'm wearing them]. In this last example the writer adds what may be an explanation of these present selections of a past, her own desire: "Encore maintenant, je me veux comme ça" (p. 19) [That's still the way I want myself to look today]. In fact, in other interviews, Duras will claim that she was wearing ordinary black pumps, raising the question of which version, the invented or the real, is the "truer" to her imaginative self-reconstruction.

The present of this new autobiographical writing has its own grammatical topologies. It can slip from the past into a dramatic emotional present or into an imaginary conditional in Duras' text—"Il a allumé une cigarette. [. . .] Il me dit que je me souviendrais toute ma vie de cet après-midi" (pp. 55–56) [He lit a cigarette. {. . .} He tells me I would remember this afternoon all my life]—

drawing on the traditional system of tenses not to reproduce a past temporal order but to create its own textual relationships and emotions. This desire or emotion, too, is articulated by the text. The insistent "encore" [again] that pervades the text, describing the Morris Léon-Bollée, for example—"Entre les chauffeurs et les maîtres il y a encore des vitres à coulisses. Il y a encore des strapontins. C'est encore grand comme une chambre" (p. 25) [Between drivers and employers there are still sliding glass panels. There are still fold-down seats. A car is still as big as a bedroom]—suggests the composite nature of Duras' present, tense of things in the present moment as of things past, what is absent as well as what is present. As we noted previously, between the elements of Duras' novels and her autobiography there is similar reversibility, what she herself has called "plagiarism."

In Robbe-Grillet's text, too, the present of the writing and its construction of a literary time demonstrates the nature of tense as an arbitrary relational system (one way among possible others of organizing time). *Le Miroir qui revient* is a mosaic of self-quotation that also inscribes pieces of prose resonant of a number of other writers including well-known fragments of Baudelaire ("O Mort, vieux capitaine, il est temps, levons l'ancre," p. 20) [O Death, old captain, the time has come, let's raise the anchor] or of Verlaine and Mallarmé.

In *L'Amant*, the shifting of time/tense reflects the shifting multiple point of view of a narrator who is at once omniscient and a point of view situated in the time that the writing and the evocation of the emotion of the writing is creating. From the photograph of the mother and her three young children the text can elaborate a historically past situation (that is, known to the writer already) in the future: "Il [mon père] sera rapatrié en France pour raison de santé. Avant, il changera de poste, il sera nommé à Pnom Penh. [. . .] Ma mère aura refusé de le suivre en France" (p. 41). Barbara Bray's translation chooses to use the conditional tense to render these future and future perfect tenses, in order to make the sense/tense less ambiguous: "He'd be sent back to France because of his health. Before that he'd go to a new job, in Phnom Penh. [. . .] My mother wouldn't go back with him to France." Tense, in Duras, inscribes present/past emotional intensity. The experience of physical love, "Et cela, en effet, avait été à mourir" is telescoped from a distant past; comes closer—"Et cela a été à en mourir" (p. 55) [And it really was unto death. It has been unto death]—in a repetition which insists, lingers, creates in the present a time and space of the emotion whose temporal reference is undecidable and clearly poses problems for the (English) translator.

The making of this new (chrono)logical textual order is presented as a correcting of another and also fictional account of the appearance of the would-be lover and his luxurious black limousine in the early novel *Un Barrage contre le Pacifique* (p. 195).

> Ce n'est donc pas à la cantine de Réam, vous voyez, comme je l'avais écrit, que je rencontre l'homme riche à la limousine noire, c'est après l'abandon de la concession, deux ou trois ans après, sur le bac, ce jour que je raconte, dans cette lumière de brume et de chaleur. (p. 36)

> [So you see it wasn't in the bar at Réam, as I wrote, that I met the rich man with the black limousine, it was after we left the land by the dike, two or three years after, on the ferry, the day I'm telling you about, in that light of haze and heat.]

Such an attempt at ordering of the "fictional" and the "true" creates inconsistencies and temporal contradictions. On the previous page, the scene on the ferry is described as occurring before the "abandoning" of the land grant ("Quand je suis sur le bac de Mékong, ce jour de la limousine noire, la concession du barrage n'a pas encore été abandonnée par ma mère," p. 35 [When I'm on the Mekong ferry, the day of the black limousine, my mother hasn't yet given up the land by the dike]). *L'Amant* derives as much from what has been written as from what has been lived, and evidently the writer herself is blurring the boundaries here between fact and fiction, memory and writing, or at the least, introducing uncertainty by using "abandon" in two different senses. Of course, as we observed earlier, all language as a mediating system is fiction and the truest autobiography, as Barthes pointed out, is affective, not civil code description. Ben Stoltzfus, for example, insists on the critical (rather than the "real") origin of these texts, arguing that they devalue the real in favor of imaginary constructions because "fiction as a metalanguage enables us to understand the autobiographical language of the self."[13] I would concur with this understanding of the analytical and ludic function—or deconstructive function, as you like it—that points to the impossibility of self/of representation. Yet once again, I suggest that it is, paradoxically, the art of evoking what cannot be described but only alluded to, the art of suggesting what is missing, the art "of the impossible" that is central to the new autobiographies.

Although some scenes are generated in part from photographs of the past, a representation of the central scene of the meeting between the Chinese lover and the little white girl on the ferry, cannot, indeed must not, preexist.

Elle n'aurait pu être prise que si on avait pu préjuger de l'importance de cet événement dans ma vie, cette traversée du fleuve. Or, tandis que celle-ci s'opérait, on ignorait encore jusqu'à son existence. Dieu seul la connaissait. C'est pourquoi, cette image, et il ne pouvait pas en être autrement, elle n'existe pas. Elle a été omise. Elle a été oubliée. Elle n'a pas été détachée, enlevée à la somme. C'est à ce manque d'avoir été faite qu'elle doit sa vertu, celle de représenter un absolu, d'en être justement l'auteur. (p. 17)

[The photograph could only have been taken if someone could have known in advance how important it was to be in my life, that event, that crossing of the river. But while it was happening, no one even knew of its existence. Except God. And that's why—it couldn't have been otherwise—the image doesn't exist. It was omitted. Forgotten. It never was detached or removed from all the rest. And it's to this, this failure to have been created, that the image owes its virtue: the virtue of representing, of being the creator of, an absolute.]

It is from this missing absolute image that the narration can proceed, "C'est donc pendant la traversée d'un bras du Mékong sur le bac qui est entre Vinhlong et Sadec" (p. 17, my italics) [So it's during the crossing of a branch of the Mekong, on the ferry that plies between Vinh Long and Sadec].

The text of The Lover is a means to approach the intense, emotional experiences of Duras' adolescence by reinventing them, and the reader is given the role of ordering what Barthes' might call "degrees of reality." These choices are not wholly aleatory, and Duras' own experiences probably did include the breaking away in transgression from the intense love-hate bond with the mother, the discovery of sexual desire, the passionate maternal (incestuous) love for the little brother and the ambivalent desire-hatred for the tyrannical older brother—all fairly commonplace situations of adolescence. The recollection of these relationships, like the affair with the lover, may be less a remembering than a fictional vehicle for a mature exploration of the unsayable of desire, repeated and intensified, once again, in the subsequent work, L'Amant de la Chine du nord. Taboo subjects, the masochistic impulses toward self-loss in drowning, or in domination, the voyeuristic desire to watch the lover make love to the beloved body of Hélène Lagonelle, the impulse to dominate in tenderness (the little brother), and sometimes in cruelty, the weakened other, subjugated by love evoke highly charged sadomasochistic structures of psyche and desire.

The central episode of *Le Miroir qui revient* (called the episode of "the returning mirror") is an obvious pastiche, not only of conventional narrative techniques but also perhaps of the ethnological tradition of autobiography, of Renan's dramatic and symbolic evocations of his regional origins in the Breton stories in *Souvenirs d'enfance et de jeunesse* for example. Robbe-Grillet's story presents the already well known "Comte de Corinthe"[14] crossing the lonely coastal moor on a prancing white horse with golden mane, the sum, claims Robbe-Grillet, of all the stereotyped white chargers of Celtic legend, of nineteenth-century painting, of the film "Missing," of the legend read during childhood of the "Schimmelreiter."[15] Henri de Corinthe adopts the posture of the cavalry officer of "La Défaite de Reichenfels," the painting that represents "débâcle" in European military history, and the defeat of 1940 in particular, and that is the "generator" of the fiction in the novel *Dans le labyrinthe*. In a playful game of extratextual reference, Robbe-Grillet also attributes the original of this figure of the cavalry officer to the protagonist of *La Route des Flandres* (Paris, 1960), the novel by Nobel Prize winner Claude Simon, and to Claude Simon's own ancestors. Approaching the sea, the officer stops his mount in the moonlight, alerted by a mysterious noise.

> Cela ressemble au *floc floc* répété d'un battoir vigoureux sur du linge humide. [. . .] Corinthe pense aussitôt à la vieille croyance paysanne relative aux "lavandières de nuit," jeunes femmes appartenant au monde des esprits et dont on ne peut guère attendre que du malheur, quelque chose comme les sorcières de Macbeth. (p. 90)

> [It's like the repeated slapping of a vigorous paddle on wet washing: *floc floc*. {. . .} Corinthe immediately thinks of the old peasant belief in "nocturnal washerwomen": young women from the spirit world, harbingers of ill-fortune, rather like the witches in *Macbeth*.]

The noise appears to be coming from the sea itself. The parody intensifies.

> Tiens, remarque en son for intérieur l'intrépide cavalier, cette laveuse nocturne ne craint pas non plus l'eau salée pour sa lessive! Et, plus intrigué que jamais, il pousse sa monture à travers la bande de sable découverte, jusqu'à la limite du flot. (p. 91)

> [Well, the intrepid rider remarks inwardly, this nocturnal washerwoman doesn't seem to mind washing in salt water! And more intrigued than ever, he spurs his horse across the strip of sand to the water's edge.]

A cataclysmic bluish light accompanies the following scene of flying spray and rearing white horse as the night rider recovers from the sea a heavy oval mirror that has remained afloat by some "miracle." This is clearly the returning mirror of the title. Reflected in the cloudy depths of its thick glass,

> Henri de Corinthe voit distinctement—et presque sans surprise—se refléter le tendre visage blond de sa fiancée disparue, Marie-Ange, qui s'est noyée sur une plage de l'Atlantique [. . .] qui le fixe de ses prunelles bleu pâle avec un indéfinissable sourire. (p. 94)

> [Henri de Corinthe distinctly sees—and almost without surprise—the reflection of the gentle, fair face of his lost fiancée, Marie-Ange, who drowned off a beach in the Atlantic {. . .} her pale blue eyes staring at him, a mysterious smile on her face.]

A number of these phrases and images, the mysterious smile of the drowned/drowning fiancée, for example, repeated throughout Robbe-Grillet's texts, are highly suspect. The rider, returning later to the beach to recover the "magic" mirror, that, utterly exhausted, he had abandoned on the strand, finds instead a scene of the sado-erotic category that has become familiar to those acquainted with Robbe-Grillet's texts. The mirror has gone, but in its place, situated by a sexualized description of a wide silken gently "curving" stretch of sand that is already "uncovered" ("une large bande soyeuse à la pente très faible, à l'accueillante concavité, se trouve déjà découverte," p. 99–100 [a wide, silky strip of sand sloping in an inviting hollow is already exposed]), freshly washed female underwear ("lingerie féminine") can be seen drying on the heath. These are silken garments of old fashioned refinement and charm spread out to dry by the faery washerwomen but, "Dear God, unbearably" ("Mon Dieu, ayez pitié") the little top is torn. And on the "tiny lacy triangle" of the panties and on the garter-belt flow stains of bright red blood (p. 101). What is the significance of these apparitions? When the white horse looks in the magic mirror that appears to reflect the beholder's deepest fantasies or disquiets, he sees, we are told, his own image, that is, his own death ("c'est à dire sa propre mort," p. 102). The mirror, the female body, and death are brought together, "at the seashore, once again." The phrase, itself, however, is intratextual, repeated from Robbe-Grillet's earliest fiction, *Un Régicide*, where it is a recurrent motif ("une fois, à nouveau, au bord de la mer").

Pastiche, intertext, language play, the fantasmatic subject appears to be an effect of language ("effet de langage") as Roland Barthes puts it.[16] Or, as Georges

Raillard suggests, is Count Corinthe, third person alter ego of the Robbe-Grillet autobiography, shifting, contradictory, mythical figure countering the autobiographical ordering, an effect of History, the return of "what has been repressed by a whole generation" ("le refoulé de toute une époque"[17]), that is, what is collective and belongs to the other in the text or in the self? Yet, beyond the ludic and critical stance and the concern with language, behind the collective representations of the French role during the period of Nazi power in Europe, and of the influence of parents, Corinthe embodies Robbe-Grillet's personal obsessions and explorations and inscribes the more secret, censored aspects of an individual imaginary. The multiple textual stances may signify compensatory fictions, invention, ruse, and a covering of deep traces. They are also seeking the return of the individually repressed, and a possible self-constitution. The writer's own metacommentaries declare that Corinthe represents his relationship with the sea, with sexual crime, and with fascist ideology. The reader must make her or his own determination.

In conclusion, in all of these works, while traditional autobiographical preoccupations may have been placed in parentheses by the accompanying metacommentaries, complicated by shifting pronouns or undermined by intertextual reference, the focus on childhood, homes and family relationships, historical contexts, the role of memory, and personal fantasies is still very much in evidence. The quest for origins and for the determining factors in the history of a personality and a writing vocation, however "impossible" (because effected by language) is still present. The autobiographical preoccupation is present also in the need of an individuated consciousness to leave traces of its feelings, experiences, and desires beyond death and in the desire to make manifest in text just what is distinctive or present only at inaccessible levels of consciousness, language, or desire.

There is also autofiction in these self-conscious texts, in the deconstruction of the conventions of traditional autobiography, the analysis of the problems of the textual reconstitution of memories, and in the openness and indeterminacy that allow multiple readings. Imagination speaks of personal fantasies but in a collective ready-made language; these writers create spaces traversed by the personal "imaginaire" and by the collective myths and representations, the materiality of the language that creates them.

Like the forms of the *Nouveau Roman*, the narrative forms of the new autobiographies generate multiple and contradictory decentered selves, self-consciously products of language and no longer present to themselves. Manifesting the impossibility of transcendence, the "impossible" origin covered over (but not erased) by Derrida's rereadings of Western metaphysics, *mise en scène* of the deconstruction of the traditional unified cogitating self now seen to be always already within discourse or its contexts, these autofictional forms nonetheless create new concepts of the self. The (im)possible self-knowledge that arises from the self's origins in the relation with the other and that creates interlocution in Sarraute, the alter egos of the imaginary in Robbe-Grillet, and intersubjectivity and rewriting in Duras begin to construct such new selves. The new 'self' cannot be known independently of the other. It cannot be known outside of its present selection and reorganization in the materiality of writing. Yet the pursuit of this other in the self, the other of the text, may provide glimpses of the unsaid/the unsayable in the world and in the old (traditional) rational self-present self.

We suspend the play of mirrors, then, as do the new autobiographies in question, in the textual movement between autoportrait and autofiction as childhood, sexuality, textuality, and self turn and return, in the contradictory but nonmutually exclusive new 'complementary' logic that gives them new meanings. This is art, seeking not Truth but truths and aware of the impossible nature of its enterprise. It is the art of the (im)possible moving between life and language, and toward a new autobiography (self/body/writing) out of (but not erasing) the old.

three

REWRITING HISTORY, STORY, SELF

The art of the impossible in the experimental new autobiographies has con-
tributed to a rethinking and a rereading of both autobiographical and fictional
writing. *Roland Barthes par Roland Barthes* (1974) signaled the new directions.
A number of works by Marguerite Duras, *L'Amant* (1984), *La Douleur* (1985),
Emily L. (1987), *L'Amant de la Chine du nord* (1991), and *Yann Andréa Steiner*
(1992), followed. Michel Butor's *Frontières* (1985), Claude Ollier's *Déconnection*
(1988), and Alain Robbe-Grillet's trilogy, *Le Miroir qui revient* (1984), *Angélique
ou l'enchantement* (1988), and *Les Derniers Jours de Corinthe* (1994), are situated within the new genre. Nathalie Sarraute's *Enfance* (1983) and *Tu ne t'aimes
pas* (1989) and Claude Simon's *L'Acacia* (1988) and *L'Invitation* (1989) can
also be considered autobiographical fictions.

The first chapter explored the features of three of the works of this experimental genre modeling new and self-conscious ways of reading autobiographical texts and new relations between the writer and the reader. Like the "new
novels" of the sixties and the so-called "new new novels" of the late seventies
and eighties, the "autofictions" unfold in a world of ontological and epistemological uncertainty; they provide only double (and contradictory) answers to
the investigation of origins and meanings. In Robbe-Grillet's texts, for example,
the detective invariably also turns out to be the criminal. The present chapter
argues that the most characteristic distinctive feature of the new genre is a
telescoping of personal story and history and a reversible movement between
inside and outside that is "complementary." In this sense, "complementary"
means contradictory but not mutually exclusive like matter in the new physics
or like the coextensive relationship between the so-called "laws of nature" in
the very different worlds of Newtonian and nuclear physics. In *Robbe-Grillet
and Modernity*, a recent study of Robbe-Grillet's work, I call this structure
"complementarity" by analogy with Heisenberg's theory of the "complementary" nature of matter and "uncertainty principle." This principle of contem-

porary physics derives from the dual or "complementary" nature of the ultimate base of the universe (elementary particles), both particle and wave, discontinuity and continuity, matter and energy, uncertainty and (statistical) predictability, according to the kind of observation effected. Uncertainty relations indicate that the measurement of speed (the wave) will affect the position (particle) and measurement of position alters the speed. These two parameters, position and speed, necessary for classical prediction and knowledge of the world are, in contemporary physics, never completely knowable, or knowable only with a mutually related uncertainty. The instrument of observation selected, the critical frame, becomes part of (and alters) the object observed; all observation, as Kuhn put it, in his *Structure of Scientific Revolutions* is theory-laden. The way of imaging affects the image produced.[1] In the new autobiographies, the self, imaged by language, is affected by the language that images it. As it redefines story and history and the relationship between them, such a complementary movement of the writing rewrites old conceptions of the self.[2] The new conceptions of the self, I suggest, introduce a wedge into the Derridean version of postmodernism.

The telescoping movement between story and history, fiction and truth, inside and outside takes the autofictions beyond the traditional retrospective autobiographical narrative of the development of a personality, a confessional narrative that observes a pact of truth and sincerity. The lack of unity between author, narrator, and character suggests the reader's own lack of a unified personality and requires her or him to examine the expectations or the knowledge of the law, of the others in the self, that she or he brings to the reading of the text. The transformed self of the new autobiographical fictions is both self and other. It is neither wholly fantasmatical—the imaginary speaking of memory, as Robbe-Grillet puts it—nor wholly referential. The text, for its part, is characterized by self-conscious literary strategies such as *mise en scène* or staging of its material and its processes, and the self-reflexive strategies of *mise en abyme* (story within a story) and of intertextuality, and yet it has an emotional power.

Knowledge of the self is always mediated by a sign system. The self is not the traditional single, centered Cartesian subject present to itself in thought (I think, therefore I am). Nor is it simply the postmodern, decentered play of linguistic signifiers or game of textual mirrors in which the person is endlessly deferred by the slippages between a system of signs where meaning inheres in the differences—phonemic, structural, semantic—between the signs of the system. Rather, in a new, logically contradictory structure, the autofiction walks an emotional and a logical tightrope between these opposites, seeking new forms better adapted to new visions of self, of language, and of world and venturing into boundary zones. Like the paintings of Magritte or the philosophical and critical writing of Baudrillard, these new autofictional forms raise the question of whether we can think in terms other than oppositional, whether we can find a ground between fiction and nonfiction.

As language, the new autobiography has connections with rationality, with historical moment, and with preexisting texts—that is, with the collective; with accepted ways of linguistic imaging of self. As textual creation, texture, interweaving of linguistic elements, images, and forms, the new autobiography is also "writing" in the most recent Barthesian sense. For Barthes, writing is both sensuous and semiotic exploration, a passionate, bodily, and individuated enterprise whose truth is finally affect identified. In *La Chambre Claire*, for the mature Barthes, love alone can decide whether the representation, the photo of an object (the mother) reveals its truth. Sarraute asserts the "truth" of the memory of an idyllic childhood excursion to the park with the mother recounted in *Enfance* because she can still "hear" the little bells and the whirling celluloid flowers. To authenticate her narrative, Duras invites her reader to see her adolescent self in her gold lamé high-heeled shoes and man's hat on the ferry crossing the Mekong river ("Regardez-moi" [Look at me]). Robbe-Grillet evokes the strong feelings aroused by the present crushing underfoot of a muskrat on his property at Mesnil-au-Grain in Normandy as evidence for the "reality" and the "truth" of the ambivalent but strong memory from his early childhood in which he steps on a wounded sparrow to put it out of its misery. His self-reflexive autofictional texts, characterized by ludic and intertextual play and self-conscious metacommentaries on their own linguistic functioning, *also* designate their origins as a bodily production of desire and of desire's concomitant pleasure/pain. But, like the traditional inner life of stream of consciousness, the inner (nonoptical) look that permits introspective sense perceptions immune from the confusion and doubt that accompanies observation of the physical world is itself an object of some suspicion. The report on the mind's activities—hearing the bells, seeing the young girl, feeling the body of the sparrow, desire, pleasure, pain—is, in any case, conveyed by language.

The new genre has become an individuated practice of writing (fictions) from the body that brings together or telescopes the "bios" and the "graphy," that is, both the local and particular life or sensation and the preexisting collective text. Robbe-Grillet's autobiographies, for example, like his fiction, continue to take apart the "natural," "human," "tragic" stories of literary convention and Sarraute's writing to press the coarse categories of traditional psychological event such as "love" or "anger," making language tremble and probing the ways feelings are fixed in and fix words.

In their preoccupation with a present of the writing and the suspicion of the representational fallacy (the illusion that the text adheres naturally to the world), that feeling can be "represented" transparently, in their questioning of common knowledge object as prefabricated by ideology, the new autobiographies, like the earlier new novels, initially appear resistant to History. Claude Simon's autobiographies, for example, continue to circle around the decomposing horse of *La Route des Flandres*, that is, around the gaping inadequacy of the lives of great men and public chronicled event to constitute a stable personal or Historical truth.

The earlier fictional work of these writers was interpreted persuasively as dislocating historical chronology and the causality and connective coherence this sustains. Yet although they have all spoken of their autobiographical texts as open, mobile, linguistic creations in the present moment, the inspiration for their multiple perceptions, sensations, and imaginings, as we have argued, also derives from memories of lived past events. And indeed, at the level of the metatext, Robbe-Grillet's *Le Miroir qui revient*, Sarraute's *Enfance*, and Duras' *L'Amant* probe the very questions of the distortions and limitations of these past events by the frames of the present that attempt to recapture them (the adult imposing her or his itinerary and present vision on the recreation of the child she or he once was). They note the way the past is altered by the often aleatory processes of choice and the uncertainties of recollection. They insist on the conventional nature of the strategies (fictional and narrative) by which the past is recovered and rendered coherent. In their texts, there is no longer any evident linear and causal relation between past and present, no clear line demarcating life and text. Although the direction of influence is unpredictable, the movements between the two are not random and form something resembling positive feedback loops. As in the new complex systems in far from equilibrium states described by chaos theory such as weather, cloud formations, market laws, turbulence (that is, "chaos" in the new scientific sense of orderly disorder), at the bifurcation points of sudden change or out of the orderly nonrandom patterns that emerge over time from unpredictability and disorder, such movement can be traced back through the text to detect the character of the tiny modifications, magnified by their repetition through the system, that suggest an origin. As in New History, concerned with the minutia and apparently minor events of the past or with those groups and persons traditionally without voice, the focus of the new texts is on the organic, the microscopic, and the unexamined. Time and history, then, are transformed but not eliminated as the reader is led by the metatext to ask not, "Is this really the true story of the writer's origins and history?" but "What does it mean to ask such questions?" or "What meanings do such questions have for these new indeterminate, reversible, looping, or telescoping literary systems?"

The concrete (textual) forms taken by the new conceptions of self and of history produced by the "complementary" and "chaotic" forms of the autofictions are individuated. Time/history in the work of Claude Simon has, of course, always been presented by his critics as what is unwritten by capital History—the wind blowing, the grass growing, and the old woman in black, bent beneath a bundle of firewood, passing. In the 1983 and 1987 autofictions of Nathalie Sarraute (*Enfance, Tu ne t'aimes pas*), time/history is constituted as in her earliest work of short sketches, *Tropismes* (1939), and in all her subsequent novels, by tiny protoplasmic, contradictory movements of the psyche seeking security and pleasure, attacking or fleeing to avoid destruction or pain, in psychological intrasubjective and intersubjective dramas whose origins are hidden from view. In Marguerite Duras, time and history trace their origin to the submerging seas, the desire for return to what Kristeva calls the Chora or original fusion with the mother (the homophonic mer/mère [the sea/the mother]). History takes form out of both the annihilating and constituting power of the violence of desire, out of the body, and the spontaneous fusion of the nonsocialized child with the natural world (the Lacanian presymbolic) as it enters the flat grey expanse of socialized ennui (the symbolic). For Robbe-Grillet, time is the precise, meticulously described swell of the wave, breaking and repeating at regular intervals, always already there, immemorially, along the same (or almost) line—as in the short text, "La Plage," in *Instantanés*— and yet slipping imperceptibly by the tiny imperfection into monstrous disorder, ready to suck the writer down to the green depths to drown. Recursive patterns of sexual violence emerge from Robbe-Grillet's selection and organization of the disparate debris (stereotypes, myths, events, fetish objects), the stories that mark both the strata of Western history and culture (Greco-Romano/ Judaic/Christian/Germanic) and from the topologies of the phantom cities of Robbe-Grillet's own imagination. Time, in Robbe-Grillet's new autobiographies as in his earliest novels, is at once the vertigo and repetition of libidinal obsession and the analytical deconstruction, the metatextual commentaries, that seek objective, ordered understanding of these disorders.

The past, then, in the new autobiographies, much as in the new novels, is the past telescoped with the confused and mixed multiplicity of the moment. It is a past that although no longer unproblematically an immediate apprehension of the real, is, at the least, a material remembered from the experiences of the past, reworked self-consciously and analytically in the present experience of the writing, mediated by the body and offering occasional glimpses of an obscure or unconscious origin. The new autobiographical texts also frame the metatextual questions of whether such a personal selection and literary reframing in the present of the writing is a betrayal of the experience of the past or, rather, the only possible bringing of its multiplicity to some clear and ordered consciousness of the "degrees of reality," to use Barthes' term, the only experience of the past knowable.

L'Amant and its cinematic rewriting L'Amant de la Chine du nord are exemplary in this respect. They can be read as a somewhat fragmented account, most often narrated in the sentient, passionate present, of Duras' childhood played out against the historical scene of French Indochina in the twenties and thirties. The grandiose tragedy of the widowed teacher-mother's purchase of a land grant that turns out to be regularly flooded by the sea constitutes both a central event in the emotional family saga that was the young Marguerite taking form and a criticism of a French colonial administration. The adolescent heroine's defiance of familial, social, and colonial taboos and racial discrimination in her passionate relationship with a wealthy Chinese is the projection of an individuated subjectivity and psychic life into a colonial history, a social situation, and an ideology that derive from the domain of collective experience and inherited text.

At first sight, there seems nothing particularly new in this apparently dialectical functioning of private and public spheres, of History and Self, colonial Indochina and Duras' life. But the collective and the individual have in fact become two "complementary" faces (contradictory but not mutually exclusive), virtualities of the same phenomenon. The Second World War, for example, the central event of the public historical experience common to these writers is re-presented/represented in Duras as a personal familial or sexual power struggle. It takes the form of a primitive scene of "masculine" domination and "feminine" submission, introjected and experienced in the material body. The war assumes the metaphorical face of the hated but seductive, bigger stronger brother, "invading," "occupying," and "destroying" the body (the territory) of the weaker, beloved "little" brother for his own pleasure and the affirming of his power.

Je confonds le temps de la guerre avec le règne de mon frère aîné. [. . .] Je vois la guerre comme lui était, partout se répandre, partout pénétrer, voler, emprisonner, partout être là, à tout mélangée, mêlée, présente dans le corps, dans la pensée, dans la veille, dans le sommeil, tout le temps, en proie à la passion saoulante d'occuper le territoire adorable du corps de l'enfant, du corps des moins forts, des peuples vaincus. (p. 78)

[I see wartime and the reign of my elder brother as one. {. . .} I see the war as like him, spreading everywhere, breaking in everywhere, stealing, imprisoning, always there, merged and mingled with everything, present in the body, in the mind, awake and asleep, all the time, a prey to the intoxicating passion of occupying that delightful territory, a child's body, the bodies of those less strong, of conquered peoples.]

As we noted in the first two chapters, there is both splitting and merging of a third person character "elle" [she] (now the adolescent girl, "the little one" of the past, and now the narrator-writer in the present) and proliferation of the first person narrator (now the young girl, now the aging narrator, now Duras, the writer). The third person pronominal reference in *L'Amant* also shifts continually between personal and social categories. "She" is the feminine self taking form, the poor "little *white girl*" or "the little *prostitute* of Sadec," or even *she*, the other woman, *elle*/L (Hélène Lagonn*elle*); "he" is masculine pronoun, "other" or the objectified "lover" or the member of a minority, "le Chinois de Cholen" [the Chinese man from Cholon]. In this process, fiction (self-exploration and wish fulfillment through doubles) and confession (self-explication and self-justification) are shown to be inextricably intermingled.

Writing is a function of life as self in these works is a function of the choice or the rewriting of self in the present, of fluidity between self and other and lack of clear boundaries. This may partially explain the many discrepancies between the various literary versions of Duras' life. Autofiction is a "complementary" (contradictory but not mutually exclusive) relation between the texts of the self of the past and of the present, between passion and the linguistic play that must double passion to bring it to consciousness, that is, between what Duras calls the "wild territories" of the unsayable (the presymbolic) and the (symbolic) linguistic order that constitutes the social self. Writing is also necessarily a linguistic cutting up, and a conscious "re-membering" and thus, paradoxically, a forgetting of these events. Sharon Willis's subtle study of the obsessive theme of desire and lack and its relation to violence in Duras gives voice to the reader's dual sense of familiarity and of loss in a world of deeply private fantasies that appear also to be the anonymous displacements and metaphorizations of collective sexuality. Such "desire" appears related to the Lacanian "lack" or absent Phallus or the Derridean absent transcendental signifier inherent in the very act of representation. The violence that inheres in the depths of the individuated psyche is present in writing, and in the "real," that is, in the "collective" or the symbolic where it creates turbulence.

In a collection of texts in the guise of newspaper articles on current events written in the summer of 1980, *l'Ete 80*, Duras gives an account of the historically situated impulse of the Polish people to freedom. The current historical events are filtered through a tenuous, inner story, the fragmented, unspoken drama of an affective bond that develops between an anonymous young woman summer-camp "mother" and a solitary and free-spirited "child" who appear daily on the beach in northern France overlooked by the writer's hotel. Madeleine Cottenet-Hage observes that in the second of the *Aurélia Steiner* films (1979), the character, spoken by Duras and identified only at the end of the film as Aurélia speaking from Vancouver, enacts at once a personal, a historical, and a universal story. This archetypal Durassian story of pain, for Hage, is at once the story of the loss of Aurélia Steiner's parents in a concentration camp, "the story of the Jews," "the story of humankind,"[3] and that writer's own history/story become legend.

The shame and pain inherent in the ethnically and socioeconomically mixed and taboo relation with the lover and the complex emotions aroused by the figure of the glorified and "abject" mother appear to have origins in Duras' own story. Abjection, here, can be understood both in its common sense of humiliation and poverty or in the specialized sense that Julia Kristeva gives it as a state deriving from the child's early ab-jecting (that is, the separating from the self with fascination and disgust) of primary bodily objects such as curdled milk, saliva, or feces and describing a stance in the mixed or "entre-deux" (neither one nor the other). The difficulty of her own mother's life, materially and psychically, and her periods of despair and perhaps madness, her preference and sacrificial suffering for her profligate son, experienced intensely ("beyond love"), the fascination and repulsion of the daughter's attachment, and the difficulty of the daughter's separation from the mother are at the emotional heart of the writer's recollections. As the final chapter will argue, the power of Duras' rewriting in *L'Amant de la Chine du nord* resides in the progressive reconciliation and even identification with the mother that it effects.

Pain as the other and chosen face of pleasure, already present in the scenes of the French actress-protagonist's passionate encounter with a Japanese lover against the backdrop of the historical drama of the dropping of an atom bomb on Hiroshima in *Hiroshima mon amour*, also marks the affair with the "autobiographical" Chinese lover. Both of these feminized, minority lovers themselves love and suffer. They experience passively, in the body, forces of historical injustice, racism, or nuclear holocaust as they participate in the pleasure/

pain of a self-affirming desire and a self-loss in the other that they do not resist. The ballet of bodily linguistic experience of pleasure and pain and of abstract collective forces—that is, of the drive for domination that is history and of the master-servant structure of the psyche—in Duras' work, appear to derive from monsters encountered in her own history. The humiliations, wild freedoms, and passions of her childhood in Indochina, like her experiences of the war or of the sufferings and joys of human bonding, reflect both a sociohistorical situation and an individuated psyche characterized by a fascination with, and fear of, domination and self-loss.

There is once again both historical reference and self-reference in Duras' autobiographical fiction, *Emily L.* History and personal story become abstract, represented in the appearance in the white spaces of the square of a town in northern France of a group of self-similar Asians, this time designated as "Koreans." Representing fear of difference and the tendency to see all difference as same, labeled "Koreans" out of ignorance, as Yann Andréa points out, this group nonetheless also serves to recall the unselfaware cruelty of the youths of Duras' childhood experience of Indochina who kill the starving dogs on the Kampot plain for sport. The alcoholic Emily L.'s inarticulate cries of fear and pain that, replacing words, elide the boundaries between the inner and the outer world, between self and text, between the presymbolic and the symbolic, like the Durassian text itself, are again a paradoxical literary articulation of a space of movement between preverbal experience and conscious historical text, between the individual life in the novel and the novel of life.

In this zone between what is apparently recounted inner story (hated, powerful, older brother and beloved, powerless, younger brother, victim of the latter's predatory oppression), and again within outside historical event (colonialism, the war, the emerging power of Asia), there are silences and contradictions. What Hélène Cixous has so deftly designated "a signifying artfulness,"[4] paradoxically appears to take Duras "further" than the conscious text, overtaken, says Cixous, by "her own unconscious."[5] The slippage between conscious and unconscious, pain and pleasure, masochism and sadism, between self and other, majority and minority, as between autobiography and history maintains these opposites while refusing their mutual exclusion in a movement of displacement. Such a telescoping insists on the virtuality of either aspect of the pair at any given moment.

Nathalie Sarraute's new autobiography *Enfance* is played out against identifiable historical backdrops that change from the absolutist prerevolutionary Czarist Russia of her earliest childhood at the beginning of the century to the middle-class France of her mother's remarriage and her father and stepmother's

later political exile. Natacha's story/history, like Marguerite's, is again generated out of the child's difficult relations with figures of familial authority and
affective power within a specific historical frame. This autofiction projects dialogic inner voices outside — or might it be the outside of the writing and the
feelings this generates in the author-narrator that produce the inner voices? In
the later chapter devoted to *Enfance*, I suggest that these voices introduce a
further "complementary" or telescoping movement, this time between the
masculine and the feminine. Although in the final instance, both "masculine" and "feminine" voices are controlled by the aging writer, Nathalie
Sarraute, who is consciously orchestrating the choices and order of the fragments spoken or remembered by both, the writing of the interchange between
masculine and feminine voices re-evokes/re-creates the feelings and tensions
in the child Natacha Tcherniak's life as she is pulled in opposite directions by
loyalties to divorced parents. The charming, silken, adored mother demands
absolute loyalty and devotion from her daughter but a number of the scenes
that portray her are implicitly critical. The calmer sketches of the responsible,
sternly moral, more cerebral, reserved, but loving and silently complicitous
father, curiously the only presence at the child's bedside during a severe reaction to a diptheria inoculation, also appear to be part of the writer's attempt to
understand the sentiments of those close to her by re-creating mini psychological dramas and by analysis. But like the child, the adult writer is re-creating feelings close to the child's trembling, listening still, as the child perhaps
did not, for the complex emotional movements that might lie beneath the
lieux communs of parental phrase or behind her own *énoncés*. She too is searching for love as well as for knowledge and seems to identify such empathetic
emotion close to the father as much as to the mother. At the level of the *énoncé*,
too, it may be the case that Sarraute identifies more closely with the critical,
investigative "masculine" voice of her own writing enterprise. Yet, at the level
of the *énonciation*, aware that words are flattening and inadequate and that
single, reasoned judgments are simplifying, it is the uncertain "feminine" voice
of seeking and emotion that seems to exemplify what is most characteristic in
Sarraute's work. In the polyphony of different voices that constitute the "we"
("nous") in the later autofiction, *Tu ne t'aimes pas*, it is finally the unselfloving
voice, on the side of guilt for the victims and for the outstretched hands it
must ignore that is preferred to the voices of self-love and self-satisfaction.

   Sarraute does not discuss the historical events of her father's exile under
the Czar, or the Russian Revolution, or the later Stalinist era that she experienced on a visit to terrorized relatives. Forced to live under an assumed name
and to go into hiding during the Occupation, narrowly escaping arrest by flee-

ing from the village of Janvry after being denounced as a Jew, she makes no mention of the war and the Holocaust that are central in Robbe-Grillet and Duras' histories. In all her texts, however, underlying the orderings of feelings and experience by cliché and dialogic social interactions, as yet dimly perceived and preceding dialogue, lurk "subconversations" which, I argue, are a form of reemergence of these violent, suppressed historical events. Perhaps, as the later chapter on *Enfance* will argue, all of Sarraute's works can be characterized by the piercing of the silken skin of the mother's femininity as of the mother('s) tongue, by the movement between the safety and belonging of her soft and glittering order and the impulse to resist such appearances, to question the authority of any such ready-made models.

However, Sarraute is as categorical at the beginning of *Enfance* as our other writers. Language, for her, is not life. It does not translate a plenitude of origins. It is a paper copy, a cardboard cutout of experience, incapable of representing the confused tropistic "real" of infrapsychological movement. At best, it is a remodelling through rhythm and metaphor of networks of signs in order to better bring hidden aspects of life to consciousness. History, too, is a rule-bound narrative, involving selection and exclusion and just such a ready-made doubling/linguistic suppressing of the real.

The admission of the relative powerlessness of the new language that creates linguistically mediated worlds but cannot clearly reflect the nonlinguistic world or the unconscious mind and the monsters of our being (drive to domination/desire for submission), explicit in Sarraute, is echoed by Robbe-Grillet. For the latter, in *Le Miroir qui revient*, all reality is "indescribable" as, for the later Barthes, the real is the "uncoded" and the autobiographical "I" a "character in a novel." As the following chapter will show, the figures of the war in Robbe-Grillet echo, if more faintly, Marguerite Duras' insistence on any knowledge of history being grounded in the experience of the gendered body, that is, in the felt reality of power and humiliation. In *Le Miroir qui revient*, this takes the form of a dissolution of clear boundaries between the external historical event and the unconscious impulse in the fantasmatic figure of the Comte de Corinthe — Resistance hero and Nazi collaborator, sexual sadist and victim of the (female) vampire. In *Angélique ou l'enchantement*, the historico-cultural myths of the cavalry officer, Simon, in the forests on the Franco-German frontier are inextricably interwoven with fantasmatic scenes of "feminine" bondage and sado-erotic "masculine" power. The suppression of woman's body seems to derive from a barely conscious anxiety (the anguish and fascination of death and disintegration) provoked by the attraction of the seductive and vulnerable "enchanting" feminine other in the self. Such an active sadistic suppression of the "feminine" is the other face of the fascination of the "rav-ishing" by the "masculine" in Duras. Even in these postmodern texts, then, differences persist. Whereas Duras and Sarraute introduce a certain degree of role reversibility, Robbe-Grillet fixes the female firmly at the very traditional cultural pole of "feminine" masochism.

Claude Simon's new autobiographies, too, attempt to capture history through personal stories and to explore the relations of power in sexuality and in soci-ety. For Simon, the linearity of traditional linguistic organization betrays the complexity of the simultaneously sensory, intellectual, and fantasmatic asso-ciations and memories of the writer. This traditional organization is a misrep-resentation of the discontinuity both of experience and of history. Yet, as Joan Brandt points out,[6] Simon too is aware that "all words cut up, set in concrete, and annihilate by replacing," what they re-present. Simon, says Brandt, calls upon the formal orders of art, the frame, the techniques and images of over-lapping and superposition, to seek out "that ideal perspective that would make an all-encompassing vision possible."[7] This is his art of the (im)possible. Simon, too, admits the impossibility of this art. His new text is "as lacking in depth and existence as a sheet of paper" ("aussi dépourvu d'épaisseur et d'existence qu'une feuille de papier" [p. 67]). For Brandt, the "effort to enclose the discontinuity of experience fails either because it leads to an annihilation of the real by sub-stituting its own flattened image or [because it] is undermined by the tempo-rality and the expansiveness of what it seeks to enclose" (p. 383).

Perhaps that is why the central event concealed behind Claude Simon's "impossible" ideal perspective is also inevitably absent. Already in the novel *La Route des Flandres* (1960) prefaced by the phrase borrowed from Valéry—"Two dangers threaten the world: order and disorder"—Claude Simon's cav-alry officer fictional protagonist-father-self circles obstinately around an ab-sent center/a disintegrating dead horse seeking orders in the chaos of the 1940 *Débâcle*. Like the "lack" in his own "signifying unity" that Robbe-Grillet pur-sues in *Le Miroir qui revient*, the hole at the center of the golden ring which gives the ring its form in the sequel *Angélique ou l'enchantement*, this void is not only absence, or degree zero, or disorder, but also the feminine principle of postmodern linguistic regeneration and emergence of new orders. The void is a recurring figure in all these works. In Duras' *L'Amant* (which was to have been called "Absolute Photography"), this degree zero takes the form of the imaginatively powerful photo that "had never been taken" of the adolescent self. In *Emily L.*, it is the missing unfinished poem, the "internal minimal difference" (p. 114) sensed but only imperfectly detectable, that lies at the heart of the poet's life and death. In *Angélique*, it is the crime that is always, already there, displayed as the absent center of the labyrinth, where the detective is also a criminal and the generative cell also a prison.

The void of self, as Keren Smith defines it in an article that compares the voyeur-criminal protagonists in Robbe-Grillet's *Voyeur* and Dostoyevsky's *Crime and Punishment*, is the lack of any unifying or transcendental principle (God, History, Man) that can give meaning to the self and to the world. This void of self distinguishes traditional writing—in which the void exists only in a binary organization of void or redemptive meaning, a binary of redemptive purity and criminality—from the postmodern. In the former, a mediation can be effected and a metaphysical or moral solution is possible. Dostoyevsky's protagonist, Raskolnikov, lost in the void ("If God were dead then everything would be possible") is redeemed from his crime by punishment and perhaps by female (self) sacrifice. The nondialectical, "complementary," "chaotic," postmodern void of self of the new autobiographies, does not permit such metaphysical mediation between opposites. It is, however, a site at which what is repressed by language and the social order—the monsters of will to power and will to self-dissolution of the narcissistic (sadomasochistic) psyche—can take form. A site at which authenticity might be sought.

As Niels Bohr interpreted the theory of complementary relations (matter as both wave and particle, continuity and discontinuity, and object modified by its perception), when you take the position of observing the particle, you hide the equally possible wave. Or put another way, the instrument or path I choose may hide/exclude another, just as valid. What is hidden when one takes up a postmodern position to observe or "read" the void?

A postmodern (or deconstructionist) position would be the denial of the ultimate Word—In the beginning was the Word of God (Divine Law) or of the Father (Social Law)—denial of an independently existing objective Real, of any unifying principle, or of any Platonic Ideal that would transcend language and guarantee the meanings of self and world. A postmodern text that knows it looks through a textual mirror, through our relationships with language rather than directly at the real or the self implies acceptance of the void created by the absent logos as a positive generative principle.

Returning to the question of what is hidden when one adopts a postmodern position, this would seem to be the equally possible stance taken by the text of tradition and its denial or conquest of the void, the denial or conquest of the absence of the logos, in the name of relations with the "divine," with heroic, inner being, or with common humanity and human rights, that is, relations with the self, the world, with fellow man or woman (love) and with death (destiny, tragedy). Here, even if God is dead, everything is not permitted for the traditionalist or for the humanist. In the story of Camus' archetypal modern "outsider" (*L'Etranger*), meaning comes flooding back; the text, as Robbe-Grillet puts it in his critical reflection on *L'Etranger* in *Le Miroir qui revient*, implodes. Meursault's flattening of appearances (filial affection, career ambitions, friendship, romantic love), his refusal of imposed social and linguistic codes becomes, in the final pages, Camus' affirmation of certain positions—of lucidity in the face of death and the absurd, of the aesthetic of refusal (I was right), of the value of each moment of being alive. Camus moves from the void and an incipient deconstruction of linguistic and narrative codes (the *passé composé* replaces the *passé simple*, the tense of narrative or historical truth), from a deconstruction of human emotions to the affirming of existential humanism and freedom. His later protagonist, Doctor Rieux of *La Peste*, commits himself to fight against everything that diminishes man—thereby covering over inhumanity, disease, death—covering with commitment and with human "solidarity" the void or lack of necessary relationship between man's desire for meaning and the world or God who remain silent.

What does the assumption of such a traditional or existential humanist position conceal in its turn? Concerned with producing meaning, with reflecting a human nature, condition, or rights, this text largely ignores the ideological production of these meanings and the productivity of the sign. In Keren Smith's comparison of Robbe-Grillet's *Le Voyeur* and Dostoyevsky's *Crime and Punishment*, both Mathias and Raskolnikov move beyond the habits, the social functions, and the common humanity that give life conventional value. They are both outsiders in the community, dissociated from ordinary reality, and have difficulty relating to others; both voyeurs, and both in the void. For Mathias, the words of others, in the bar, for example, become uncertain, without clear meaning, and on a number of occasions, he succumbs to vertigo. In a church, Raskolnikov has a similar experience.

In the skeptical thinking of Dostoyevsky, the increasingly obsessive idea of an elite breed of men for whom everything would be permissible, an obsession that culminates in Raskolnikov's gratuitous murder of a moneylender, derives from that writer's exploration of the idea of the death of God. Given his nineteenth-century contexts and public, Dostoyevsky, however, could not but write to defeat the void. Sonia's compulsive compassion, her ability to identify with the pain of others, suggests the possibility of Raskolnikov's redemption, narrative resolution, and closure. A little girl, sacrificial victim, perhaps raped and murdered may also pay for Raskolnikov's crime. The void, here, can become a source of redemption and of ultimate spiritual renewal.

The void in Robbe-Grillet's *Voyeur*, on the other hand, is a central generative principle; the missing hour in Mathias's itinerary that generates a series of imaginative reorganizations of events to create Mathias's alibis and ultimate "innocence." The objects that constructed Mathias's crime (cord, cigarette ends, figures of eight, iron rings, the limbless mannequin in the shop window, newspaper cuttings and cinema billboards and their representations of sexual violence) are washed away, erased, lost, or replaced, that is, "unmade," and the text can begin over again. The creative play of the linguistic imagination that issues from the void, the *Voyeur* seems to conclude, is the only freedom and commitment possible in the postmodernist era of the productivity and openness of the sign.

But although Barthes could write ironically as early as the mid-sixties that the void had almost become a positive principle ("Jamais le néant n'a été si sûr"), Robbe-Grillet's mother, as the writer repeats twice in *Le Miroir qui revient*, was perspicacious in a different way from Barthes about her son's text. "'C'est un beau livre,' m'a-t-elle déclaré quand je lui eus confié le manuscrit, 'mais j'aurais préféré qu'il n'ait pas été écrit par mon fils'" (p. 80) [It's a fine book, she told me when I gave her the manuscript to look at, but I would have preferred it not to have been written by my son]. For void in Robbe-Grillet is a complementary thing. It is also the vortex of the fantasies and obsession of the unconscious, a presymbolic disorder of the monsters of the deep. Mathias's possible torture, rape, and murder of the adolescent Jacqueline/Violette in *Le Voyeur* or of Angélique von Arno also found drowned in the sea in *Angélique ou l'enchantement* links him to the sea-monster devourer of little girls and to the obsessive staging, interrogation, and suppression of the body of "the beautiful captive." In Robbe-Grillet's textual/sexual "cérémonial immobile de la violence et de la représentation" (*Topologie d'une cité fantôme*, p. 43) [immobile ritual of violence and representation], the void seems to function as a vortex or strange attractor for the fatality of passion, to become a topos of violent fantasy. It is the red hole between the paving stones ("le trou rouge entre les pavés disjoints") of the strange "feminine" other, the "feminine" organic or presymbolic silence that constitutes a zone of shadow at the limit between the consciousness of language and the unconscious drive. Situated at the intersections of the Freudian pleasure principle and the Freudian destructive compulsion to repeat, this void, then, appears to encompass not only self-loss, chora, flow, but also violence and destruction and the secret of the origin of the sado-eroticism that colors the selections among the ready-made representations or generators used by Robbe-Grillet to construct his work.

For Claude Simon, too, the war/history is the story of military father figure and ancestor, the story of Simon's own participation in the French *Débâcle*, and an exploration of the hidden origin of stories. In the recent "autobiographi-cal" evocation of an invitation to Soviet Russia, History takes the form of the personal assemblage of the fragments of the disparate official and private dis-courses overheard. Meaning, like the text itself, is produced in the infinitely branching interactions of the syntagmatic and paradigmatic axes of the work-ing of the language that create effects of the mind and of the emotions. Yet the war, like the visit to Russia, is grounded in Simon's own lived past/presently recalled experience, generated by perception, memory, and desire as well as by the ready-made texts of history including those of great men (the father, the great General). The encounter with Gorbachev described in *L'Invitation* is overlaid by these personal and public pre-texts. The new textual/physical body in Simon again models fields of complex interaction between biology and his-tory, language and the unconscious.

The new autobiographical fictions do not lead to classical self-knowledge, nor do they remain limited to modern self-consciousness. They involve a cir-culation of selves marked by the foregrounding of pronominal shifts, from I to he or Corinthe, from I to she or the little white girl (Duras), from I to you, or to we (Sarraute). According to Lois Oppenheim,[8] they slip from the focus on the anonymity of collective forms to forms of individuation. The opposite can also be argued for a number of these works. Barthes' early (1975) new autobi-ography *Roland Barthes par Roland Barthes*, for example, centered on a joust with *l'imaginaire*, taking over the term that Lacan used to describe an aspect of his "mirror-stage." For Michael Sheringham, Barthes' broad appropriation of the term "imaginaire" to autobiography encompasses the realm of the "Moi/je," the domain of the self or of all statements we make about ourselves, the categories we use to describe others, the statements of the truth of different disciplines. As Sheringham interprets Barthes' use of this notion, the imagi-nary can be seen rather as a prison, and language as the escape route. "We remain trapped in *l'imaginaire* as long as we attempt to latch on to our illusory ego, resisting the open play of intersubjective desire through which we have access to the superior realm of the symbolic."[9] The challenge of autobiogra-phy, "quintessentially an activity which reeks of *l'imaginaire*," or of "the apo-theosis of the adjectivized self" is its "rehabilitation." One's images are trans-formed into a *mise en spectacle*, a theatrical representation, "a therapeutic and ethical activity, a form of inoculation in which, by taking large doses of *l'imaginaire* in the practice of autobiography, one hopes to move towards a certain liberation, lessening one's entrapment in its nets" (p. 29). What Sheringham analyzes here as Barthes' desire to neutralize or deny consistency to the "*imaginaire*" (what is mistakenly taken to be real) in that writer's practices of new autobiography, Robbe-Grillet himself comments on at length in *Le Miroir qui revient*. He sees in Barthes' own case, less a catharsis than an evading of the monsters that lie concealed in Barthes' own life by twisting and turning between images extraneous to the individual. Again, both the Imaginary and the Symbolic, both self-creation and self-expression, can play hero and villain. Sheringham remarks that Barthes "who exposes his confessional, autobiographical avatar as a victim of the Imaginary is just as much a fiction as he is" (p. 71).

Once again, it is the telescoping of opposites creating "complementary" forms of self and writing, history and story, masculine and feminine self that intimates the revolutionary interest of these new intergeneric, biographical autofictions. In the new autobiographies where the theoretical "death" of the author as origin and finality is scrutinized by a competing concern with what might constitute the specificity of an individual style or preoccupations—what Duras calls the adorable monsters of the unconscious and we have called the void of self. As in the new Historicism, History is indeed story, narrative forms and strategies, but it is also, as Veeser has shown, the specific social, political, and personal contexts out of which the story arises. The specificity of these contexts will be examined in the following chapters in relation to particular individual works. Finally and to conclude on a more theoretical level, the new autobiographies, beyond the text all alone, or consensual, artificial signifying chains that run parallel to the world, shift ground in relation to Derrida in the postmodern debate. They are closer to the more qualified openness of the sign, and the occluded transcendental that Eco, for example, postulates. The questions of how we interpret the world remain central, but the void as absence of Phallus or transcendental signifier, as generative linguistic principle and creativity of the sign, is also sign of what Eco would call the original language.

We noted that the experiences of twentieth-century French history (the Second World War in particular) serve as a pre-text for the fictions of a returning if altered and constantly splitting self in many of these new, individuated, and ground-breaking histories/stories. The following chapter will look more closely at the nature and meanings of the writing of the war in the new autobiographies, particularly in Robbe-Grillet's *Le Miroir qui revient*.

Alain Robbe-Grillet

THE SECOND WORLD WAR AS HISTORY AND STORY, TEXT AND PRE-TEXT, ORDER AND CHAOS IN *LE MIROIR QUI REVIENT*

The previous chapters began to examine the uncertain relations between fact and fiction and between history and story and to delineate the new "complementary" structures that characterize the most recent and perhaps final phase of the French *nouveau roman*. This phase is marked by the interest in the relation between the collective and the individual (between History and personal history) and by the production of a new literary "autofictional" genre. This chapter looks again, this time through the lens of a single new autobiographical work, *Le Miroir qui revient* (1984), at the apparent contradictions between an approach seemingly grounded in biography and History and the insistence on language as the glue that binds the latter together in a self-conscious metabiography, metahistory, or indeed metafiction. As Michael Sheringham puts these questions in his study of the return of the "ego" in the new autobiography,[1] what kinds of relationships are being negotiated between the old teleological properties of narrative and their complicity with a causal vision of reality and the formidable advances of narrative theory? What is the relationship between a fullness of subjective experience and a postmodern vision that replaces selves by subjects placed and displaced by discourses and desires, and ordered by politics and history? What is the part in this process of critical renegotiation being played by the rehabilitation of narrative effected currently by new historiography? For this new history is rewriting History as personal history, local detail, and narrative.

Despite the absence of any immediately recognizable chronological thread, historical events play an evident role in *Le Miroir qui revient*, Alain Robbe-Grillet's first autobiographical novel, which evokes a coming of age during the Second World War and a writing career that is a complex response to the experiences of this period. The war lies at the heart of the life as at the crisis point of its political and social contexts. The stories that it generates, this "autofiction" among them, appear to be still mediated by changing context over historical time in spite of their spatialized and discontinuous forms. The crucial question is whether the temporality of traditional History has returned to French texts of "modernité" to argue against Derrida's provocative formulation: "Il n'y a pas de hors-texte" ["There is nothing outside the text" or "Everything is context"]. This chapter argues, once again, that a new sense of history emerges from Robbe-Grillet's self-professed revolutionary work.

First to figure in the fragments that have a clear and sustained historical reference in *Le Miroir qui revient* is an account of the unexpected French *Débâcle*, the shocking collapse of the French armies in 1940. This is, significantly, experienced predominantly through the stories recounted by the father. Finding himself on the road in a chaos of fleeing civilians and disorganized military units after burning useless plans of defense systems in the courtyard of the Paris Ministry where he works, the latter reaches the Loire Valley to discover the bridges destroyed in front of him, detours in confusion and finally abandons the uncertain military adventure, deserts, and returns unheroically home to protect his family in Brest. The responses of Robbe-Grillet's parents, at least their shock and confusion, do seem, in retrospect, to have some measure of correspondence, if not with canonical French History, at least with other individual accounts and with recent scholarly rewritings. R. J. Young's reassessment of the *Débâcle*, an event still largely mythological in the collective French consciousness, suggests, for example, that the Blitzkrieg, the unexpected crossing of the Ardennes, the unconventionality of certain military tactics, the tempo of armored air warfare, took not only the Allies by surprise but also the German command itself, disquieted as it saw its rapidly advancing units surrounded by Allied armies.[2]

The *Débâcle* initially vindicates Robbe-Grillet's parents' strong antirepublican and basically antimilitarist positions, aspects of their right-wing, monarchist, anglophobic, and anti-Semitic beliefs, and their abhorrence of the disorders of the Popular Front. The armistice and the elevation to authoritarian power of Maréchal Pétain, along with the end of the Third Republic and the disorder of the thirties, meet with the approval of these supporters of Maurras. The values of Vichy (order, work, country, family, morality, a certain elitism) echo the values of the Robbe-Grillet family and, as such works as Amouroux's *Quarante Millions de Pétainistes* suggest, those of a majority of the French. Even François Mitterrand, as recently surfaced documents and rewritings of history suggest, is not exempt. Pierre Péan's biography of the former president

Arbois 1924. Alain Robbe-Grillet and his sister Anne-Lise with Grandfather Robbe. Photo from Editions de Minuit, Paris; courtesy of Alain Robbe-Grillet.

traces his itinerary from right-wing positions through support for Vichy to resistance. His life-long friendship with René Bousquet, former head ("secrétaire général") of the Vichy police and recently convicted of (war)crimes against humanity, is documented again in Eric Conan and Henry Rousso's astutely named *Vichy, un passé qui ne passe pas* [Vichy, a Past that Does Not Pass]. In 1994, the magazine *Le Point* published photographs of Mitterrand with Pétain at Vichy and with Bousquet at Latché.

Other disconnected snapshots of the *Débâcle* and the Occupation evoke what appear to be the adolescent's own experiences. These include the departure of the French fleet from Brest (to be attacked by the British and "never to return"),[3] the Paris streets strangely "empty" under the Occupation, the father-provider's single-minded devotion to the family's physical survival, the student political divisions and the occasional indications of Resistance activity that, to the young Alain, hardly seem real. Finally, there is the confession of his own compulsory departure along with thirty or so others of the National

School of Agronomy and a number of young Frenchmen born in 1922 to work "voluntarily" in Germany. According to the words of Maréchal Pétain, they are to bring "our" imprisoned soldiers "home" to their families by this act of patriotism. A few of his classmates did, however, take to the "maquis," joining the Resistance or going into hiding with relatives in the countryside rather than accept this mandated "work service," that is, STO, or *Service de Travail Obligatoire*.

The reality for the young Robbe-Grillet in Germany bears little resemblance to the rhetoric. The gap between Pétain's words as mirror of a unified and meaningful shared real, and the incoherence and complexity of the lived experience of self and world begins to emerge. The absurdity of life for this intelligent agronomy student as a fitter and turner in a Nuremberg arms factory (the Maschinenfabrik-Augsburg-Nürnberg) is described at length: its rigors, the surprisingly general adjustment by the workers to the orders of their new and alienated existence, the vague signs that only retrospectively indicate the existence of other camps more horrifyingly strange than Fischbach. Robbe-Grillet's claim that there was no common knowledge of the mass extermination camps until near the end of the war, received with cynicism by some, is surprisingly echoed by Marguerite Duras' recently published pseudodiary of the period, *La Douleur*. In spite of working actively for a Resistance group that she claims was led by François Morland (alias François Mitterrand) and her own husband's imprisonment and deportation, in August 1944, harassed and played with by an agent of the Gestapo (Monsieur X), Duras' fear for her husband is confined to general fear about the war. "On ne sait pas encore pour les camps. On est en août 1944. C'est au printemps seulement qu'on verra. [. . .] Rien n'a encore été découvert des atrocités nazies. [. . .] Nous sommes au premier temps de l'humanité, elle est là, vierge, virginale, pour encore quelques mois" (p. 118) [We don't know yet about the camps. It's August 1944. It's only in the spring that we'll find out. {. . .} Nothing has yet been discovered about Nazi atrocities. {. . .} We're still living in the first age of humanity, pure, virginal, for another few months. Nothing has been revealed about the Human Race].[4]

Nuancing negative memories of privations and illness, and the occasional evidence of discrimination against the Poles and the Jews, Robbe-Grillet recalls musical concerts in the beautiful baroque church of the neighboring German town during the early "apprenticeship," good nursing care received in the local hospital, and Allied bombing, not of the arms factory, but of the workers' camp itself and of the irreplaceable medieval town.

Claude Ollier's new autobiography or autofiction *Déconnection* (1988) is an account of that writer's STO experience working for the German war machine in the same Nuremberg factory, also toward the end of the war and a similar attempt to exorcise a ghost. (The two men met in the factory and participated together in an experience for international youth in another kind of work camp, this time in Bulgaria, where Robbe-Grillet found a similar duplicitous, but this time Communist, discourse on freedom and authority.) Arrested for the simple foolhardiness of being on the Paris streets after curfew and narrowly escaping an even less enviable fate, Martin, Ollier's protagonist, reconstructs Ollier's experience as a deported worker under French law in terms of entrance into the flattened strangeness, contingency, and isolation of another universe. Strictly regimented yet disconnected, situated in precise, personally observed detail of Nazi Germany yet curiously timeless, this wartime experience that presents the appearance of reality is also a fantasmatical one. Martin too attends a concert in the noble old church, but, alienated by the huge swastika above the musicians and the Aryan discourse that annexes their music to National Socialism, he leaves, unlike Robbe-Grillet. He too is shocked by the old city reduced to smouldering ruins by Allied bombing. Caught up in the irrationality of the apparently logical discourse of power that surrounds him, the narrator is not in a completely meaningless universe. The evocation of occasional gestures of human solidarity and the portrayal of the mental resistance of a German co-worker suggest some awareness of responsibility and reaction even in the face of the irresistible and tragic loss of German and Western civilization. But the shared values that might have allowed identity, criteria for truth, and single meanings, in Ollier's work as in Robbe-Grillet's, have disappeared. As Colin Nettelbeck argues in his meticulous study "Robbe-Grillet and Friends in Nuremberg: Exorcizing the *Service de Travail Obligatoire*," the disconnectedness of both narratives is an indication of the difficulty experienced by both writers in coming to terms with any individual responsibility for their compliance with STO (as part of the minority of 40 percent of students who did not default), their participation, polishing tank axles, in the German war effort, and their acceptance of an amoral world drifting relentlessly toward a skepticism and an abstraction that could themselves be seen as alibis.

The examination of the apparent making of the writer, Robbe-Grillet, by his historical contexts is completed in *Le Miroir qui revient* by a negative picture of the hypocrisies of the Liberation, a glimpse of the personal shock that the fall of the apparently strong and ordered Third Reich and the simultaneous revelation of Nazi horror constitutes for this child of right-wing parents, the account of the break with the clearly inadequate family ideology, and the decision to write in order to explore the contradictions and inversions that the war and the liberation had revealed.

This "break" with parental ideology may not have been quite as clear-cut as Robbe-Grillet's account indicates. During an interview with me in his Neuilly apartment in July 1991, Robbe-Grillet himself, somewhat surprisingly, brought up the recent reopening of the debate on the existence of the extermination camps and the gas chambers, arguing for their nonexistence at least inside Germany itself. My own sense of his surprisingly passionate need to discuss the question was of a movement between a still uneasy conscience and a deep desire to vindicate his and his family's positions (his mother's words?) in the light of certain contemporary and dubious revisions of history. During the same discussion of history, Robbe-Grillet also pointed to Duras' little-known work of 1940, *L'Empire français*, to suggest that he was not the only one of the now well known *nouveaux romanciers* to have held problematic and presently politically incorrect positions at the beginning of the war.

The apparent confession-expression of a right-wing personal history in *Le Miroir qui revient* is, of course, sufficient for Robbe-Grillet's critics to find their worst convictions vindicated, the "fascist" background explaining and convicting this sadistic, cerebral writer and his dehumanized "nouveau roman." But in the writer's remaking, by selections in the present, of the text of his past, History does not serve to seal an autobiographical "pact." The returning mirror of Robbe-Grillet's title is not the Lacanian mirror, not the mirror that unifies even while rendering "other" the hitherto dissociated fragments of the self. Clearly, there are vast gaps between the adolescent's fragmented and mostly indirect encounters with incomprehensible events and the official histories. The meanings that his parents read in the stories around them and into their experiences in the thirties—the importance of King and Country and Tradition, the strength of Order and Excellence and Honor threatened by Communist and Popular Disorder, dangerous Jewish Internationalism, and the chaos inherent in Liberal Democracy—and those that Gaullist History, for example, will later write, diverge greatly. The questions of the power that inheres in the control of discourse and in knowledge, and the various orderings that the latter can effect, begin to entwine themselves around the lines.

Like the Gaullist censorship of collaboration that sustained for more than a decade the myth of a Resistant France, the stories of heroic Resistance to Nazi brutality, of the majority of the "right" and the minority of the corrupted "wrong" that characterize so much of the traditional representation of the period, have

The wine harvest at Arbois, 1925. Alain Robbe-Grillet and his sister with their parents (center) and workers. Photo from Editions de Minuit, Paris; courtesy of Alain Robbe-Grillet.

themselves "become history." That is, in popular idiom, they are no longer exclusively true or relevant for the modern scene. The long-censored documentary, *Le Chagrin et la Pitié*, which shows collaboration as much more than the crime of the ambitious or misled few, Resistance as politically complex and divided, and preoccupation with individual material survival as a norm, can be screened today on all television channels. The present decade is becoming that of the return of the repressed, with the commemoration of the round-up of Paris Jews including children at the "Vel' d'Hiv." in Paris and their subsequent fatal deportation, and the screening of *L'Oeil de Vichy*, a 1993 documentary on Vichy propaganda and power. Writers and politicians from Louis Malle (*Au Revoir les enfants*) to Simone Weil and documentary films like Pierre Sauvage's autobiographical *Les Armes de l'esprit* and *L'Oeil de Vichy* seek to bear witness to an experience of Occupation before it is too late. A set of collaborationist texts has emerged to stand in apposition to the old Resistance stories (their second face), both sets highlighted by the trial of Klaus Barbie in Lyon and the documentary film *Hôtel Terminus*, along with the assassination of Bousquet, the first Frenchmen to be charged with crimes against humanity, and the recent trial of Touvier. Other less polarized texts also challenge heroic official versions, and this decade has also seen an exploration of the excesses of the left-wing purges of right-wing intellectuals in 1945.

The courage of many of the resistants is not necessarily denied or the importance of opposition opinion underplayed. Yet a novel like Jean Dutourd's *Au bon beurre* — part of the ever-growing vogue for war novels in France, and recently subtitled *Scènes de la vie sous l'occupation* — is typical in its portrayal of the profiteering on the black market and, like the more recent film *Uranus*, of the self-interest and petty rivalries that could culminate in the denunciation of neighbors and that cut completely across official political lines.

The postwar stories of the Second World War, identified explicitly in *Le Miroir qui revient* as the ten-year myth of unanimous Resistance, and the subsequent recent opposite and equally excessive myth of the nation as a "troupeau de lâches et de traîtres qui a vendu son âme et l'ensemble du peuple juif pour une bouchée de pain noir" (*Le Miroir*, p. 47) [pack of cowards and traitors that sold its soul and the whole of the Jewish people for a single crust of black bread], had been staged by Robbe-Grillet in his 1968 film *L'Homme qui ment*. Here, already, they pose the question of the part of fantasy and myth in History; the question of the writing of History as a rewriting or a writing "against." In the film, these myths are deconstructed in the interchangeable figures of Jean (Trintignant), true Resistance hero because his name is inscribed on the war memorial, and the collaborator or imposter, his Don Juan double, Boris, who kills the father('s Law). These opposing characters, investigator hero and criminal traitor, neither one but both, are also names and figures of the narrator throughout the work. As Robbe-Grillet himself points out, these figures have a real referent. The war memorial in the village of Slovenia where he was making the film, a coproduction with a Czechoslovakian group, contained the names of "resistance" heroes chosen by the Communist party, many of whom were known locally to have been traitors.

The issue of the "collaborationist" writings of a Maurice Blanchot and more recently of a Paul de Man and the fierce debate in France in 1988 over the profascist sentiments of the philosopher Heidegger (who had exerted a profound influence on the thought of Derrida among others), have raised the question of the need or the competence of the literary academies to monitor the moral and political "rightness" of those who produce its canonical texts. In Germany, "revisionist" or "new" historians have been attempting to normalize the movement from the weakness and disorder of the Weimar Republic to the support of the silent majority for the Nazi drive for strength and authoritarian order and an improved economic situation. The remarks to this effect of Philipp

Jenninger, President of the Bundestag, marking on 10 November 1988 the fif-
tieth anniversary of Kristallnacht, articulate a surprising public emergence of
a movement away from the unique and absolute German responsibility demanded by the post-1968 generation toward a relativizing of the Nazi Holocaust. This would now be situated within a collective human history of repeated attempts to impose "new" and authoritarian "superior" "orders" (of class
or race or ideological conviction) and accompanying genocide. Stalin and Pol
Pot might come to stand in our time alongside Hitler. Uniqueness, we can
suppose, would come to reside in questions of degree of horror and "efficiency."
Like the revisionist interpretations of a Francis Fukayama, these rereadings
are, of course, also fiercely contested; Jenninger resigned his position on 11
November amidst what seems to have been a predictable furor.

History's recent rewritings, however, now make it necessary for the reader
to consider seriously Robbe-Grillet's claim that Maréchal Pétain, the victor of
Verdun, was, in June 1940, a symbol of hope for almost everyone. The son is
also anxious to note that his parents, supporters of Vichy, admirers of German
manners, discipline, and efficiency (his father, a veteran of World War I, taught
himself to "translate" the works of Schiller; his mother had held a teaching
position in Germany), refused any contact or collaboration with the enemy.
Anglophobic and anti-Semitic, they were, he claims, nevertheless incapable
of denouncing or harming any human being. Only on the day of the Liberation does his father hang a portrait of Pétain in the house as a gesture of independence and of scorn for the collective coat-turning of that event and, at a
time, claims the son, in *Le Miroir qui revient* when the "nine-tenths" of French
households that had displayed such portraits during the Occupation were discreetly disposing of them.

It is the collapse of the Third Reich and the revelation of his parents' and
his own profound self-deception that the writer identifies as marking his own
story more than the fall of France or the collaboration of Vichy. The discovery
of the enemy within determines his decision to write.[5] (Perhaps also in this
perversely polysemic and multi-layered work, Robbe-Grillet is paying "homage" to the tradition of the Bildungsroman where a major insight into one's
experience leads to the decision to write a book.) The fall of the Reich and the
revelation of the disorder of Nazi horror behind the ceremonies of an ideal-
ized and seductive pure order and the popular ideal of National Socialism
(work, country, sport, nature, cleanliness) was "celui d'une certaine idée de
l'ordre, qui avait pu nous paraître grandiose, la faillite dans le sang et la folie
d'une ordonnance rigoureuse devenue totalitaire" (p. 46) [the collapse of a
particular idea of order that might have appeared awe-inspiring, the failure of

a rigorous system that had become totalitarian, a collapse into blood and madness].

All definitive orderings or Truths subsequently become suspect, including Robbe-Grillet's own literary enterprises in which only local, relational, provisional, and moving orders survive. Hitler and Stalin were not accidents of history, the writer claims, but the logical conclusion of the systems that they operated. For Robbe-Grillet as for Kristeva,[6] ethics and morality come to reside not in the respect for, or repetition of, a code but in its shattering by the play of negativity and desire, its reassemblage in lucidity, distance, and impermanence. For Kristeva, too, Fascism, Stalinism, and anti-Semitism have a connection both with orders of representation in power and with the anguish and "horror," the "abjection," present in the psychic spaces that our culture has repressed.

Robbe-Grillet's rewriting of France's sociopolitical history from his own social and inner experience and the project of placing flowers on his parents' grave are clearly inextricable. It is not evident to the reader whether the writer's "coming out" is an assumption of responsibility for his/their relationship with history or, rather, the case for his/their defense. It does seem that in these achronological fragments, the reader is weaned away from the ordered march of the Hegelian world spirit through sequential historical time toward Sartrian lucidity and the concomitant freedom to choose one's actions and self of existential humanism. Robbe-Grillet's mother, for her part, the writer tells us, simply refused, until she died in 1975, to believe that Nazi genocide could have taken place.

Le Miroir qui revient is shaped by the early influence of the "stories" transmitted by the parents (right-wing parents who were, as the writer sees it, "himself taking form") and the historical context of place and ideas in which they moved, as by his own personal encounters with history; that is, by culturally determined collective discourses and specific conditions. But, like Robbe-Grillet's earlier texts, it is also forged out of what the writer describes as a life of stubborn, solitary experimentation with the limits and the revolutionary possibilities of the literary text. It is a work of his stories on Story(telling), of his writing on Language, his histories on History and his characters and narrators on Self.

Moving by linguistic associations from fragments of past childhood events (often unsure whether these are personally experienced or recounted stories) to the writing situation re-creating that event in the present, across blank spaces from "impossible" fragmentary portrait of long since vanished soldier or sailor ancestor or "loving" mother to characters in his novels, leaping from literary

*Alain and Anne-Lise
Robbe-Grillet in
Brittany, 1927. Photo
from Editions de
Minuit, Paris; courtesy
of Alain Robbe-Grillet.*

criticism of founding texts, his own works as well as those of Balzac, Dostoyevsky, Flaubert, Sartre, Camus, Barthes, to early dreams, fears, and fantasies and revelation of possibly generative, concealed, transgressive, sexual impulses, the text insists on the random, discontinuous, factitious, seeking character of its own elaborations. Reality is not immutable across time. Affective memory reconceptualizes past images in the present and thus transforms them. Discourse (Language, History) fabricates an intellectual memory and recovers the past according to its current rules. Nor is this past unchanging across space. The language or world of the observer, the process of the observation, modifies the object observed. For the reader, the text is necessarily a persuasion—to be understood or resisted.

As Robbe-Grillet himself points out in the text, the autobiographical genre, which selects in the present a limited number of imprecise memories usually as a function of the desire to explain the present in terms of the past—the old army general reorganizing the movement of his troops in his imagination to justify the outcome of the battle — is conventional and artificial. Conforming necessarily to a novelistic model, to conventions of what is worthy of autobiography, to presuppositions that there is a hierarchy of "principal" moments, these "memories" are usually "logical" and "moved." Traditional History might equally be seen as a set of coded, conventionally based, discursive (narrative and linguistic) practices of control; as a desire to explain the present as a function of the past and thus establish sequence and causality. The unforeseen defeat of 1940, for example, subsequently gave rise to the establishment of simple causal relationships between the defeat and the (presumably weakened) society that suffered it. Some contemporary rereadings no longer see either the *Débâcle* or this relationship as natural and inevitable. Young's study of military planning and foreign policy in France between 1933 and 1940 finds no great imbalance in the military strengths of Germany and the Allies and no clear, single explanation for the fall of France. He looks critically at the idea of military unpreparedness or failure to rearm and at the myth of defeatism, and situates both as postdefeat and largely unjustified elaborations. Any predictability or order in the complex global historical event seem to emerge only statistically and from chaotic, contradictory, aleatory, individual movements.

Le Miroir qui revient is not the Stendhalian mirror: not an innocent representation of childhood, a clear mirror of history that returns to dawdle along a Breton road alongside a family home bombed by the Allies, or reflect a difficult year (1943–44) spent laboring in a German arms factory until hospitalization made possible a return to France. Like the transparent mirror, History is undermined from within, is upturned, re-turns. An apparently realistic autobiography, the text describes the "strangeness" of the intrusion on personal success at the High School at Brest in the "superb" summer of 1940 of an external and collective disaster, the feeling of "void." ("Je venais de terminer brillamment, au lycée de Brest, ma classe de mathématiques élémentaires" (p. 34) [I had just done brilliantly in my math course at the Brest lycée].

Such a feeling of void or strangeness, akin to the existential awareness of the hole at the heart of existence (or the postmodern lack of any unifying principle that would transcend language and guarantee the meanings of self and world), the hole in the golden ring that gives the ring its existence, later discussed in the sequel autobiography *Angélique ou l'enchantement* (1987), is illustrated in the descriptions of explosions of the fuel supplies set alight by the departing French Navy. The floods of burning bitumen drowning stream and meadow, the formidable rising columns of red flames and black smoke fall on the family garden as "vapeurs chaudes, suffocantes, chargées de suies épaisses et lourdes comme des flocons de neige, au goût âcre de lampe à pétrole mal réglée, le goût de la défaite" (p. 34) [hot, suffocating fumes thick with heavy soot, like snowflakes, and permeated with the acrid stench of a smoking kerosene lamp—the taste of defeat].

Apparently this is a continuation of the careful detail of the realist description and a use of the "incontinent" metaphor that Robbe-Grillet's theoretical writing had once so castigated, now present in the cause of representing objective images of his experience of war. Yet these snowflakes are curiously reminiscent of the repetitive snowflakes of the decor of *Dans le labyrinthe*, also a novel of *débâcle* and military defeat generated by a military painting, *La Défaite de Reichenfels*, that makes a reappearance in *Le Miroir qui revient*. In *Angélique ou l'enchantement*, the snow falling on the "Maison Noire" (the Dark House that is both the Breton home at Ker-an-dû and Robbe-Grillet's stately home at Mesnil-au-Grain in Normandy) comes to symbolize the nature of the writing environment. Some critics have read the snow as symbolizing the writer's solitude. It has also been argued that snowflakes, so intricately patterned but never identical to one another, show the fractal dimensions, the infinitely recursive, self-resembling patterns, the positive feedback mechanisms and the sensitive dependence on initial conditions—as it falls, no snowflake meets with exactly the same conditions—described by the new science of chaos. The snowflake shares the disordered order and nonrandom unpredictability of a "chaotic" system in far from equilibrium states. The flame and smoke of the description, for their part, recall the fire, revolution, and rape/destruction of the female sexual/textual body that culminate in a satirical sadistic scene at the end of *Projet pour une révolution à New York*. In *Topologie d'une cité fantôme*, or *Souvenirs du triangle d'or*, smoke and fire from the "smoking mountain," Vesuvius, are generated by the meanings of the name of Robbe-Grillet's American pop-artist collaborator, Rauschenberg. As for the kerosene lamp, it would seem to derive from that last precarious bastion of light against the disorder and darkness of the tropical night encroaching on the narrator's desperate ordering of the world, the lamp described at length in the 1957 novel *La Jalousie*. We are as much in the realm of intertextuality and in metaphors of creative endeavor as in a lived reality.

On the fifth day of the cataclysm, Robbe-Grillet saw his first German soldier rattling along on a motorcycle with a passenger in the sidecar:

Par le chemin creux qui montait depuis l'arsénal jusqu'à la plaine de Kerangoff. [. . .] Leur visage était fatigué, les traits creusés, le teint plombé de poussière. Entièrement du même ton verdâtre et minéral que leur peu

spectaculaire machine, ils ont ainsi traversé la plaine en biais vers le cimetière
de Recouvrance, secoués par les inégalités du terrain, solitaires et dérisoires:
nos vainqueurs. . . . On peut les retrouver à présent dans le *Labyrinthe*,
avec leur véhicule archaïque et leur air exténué, avant-coureurs de l'armée
ennemie qui investit la ville prise. (p. 35)

[on the sunken {creux} lane that led up from the arsenal to the Kerangoff
plain. {. . .} Their faces were tired and drawn {creusés}, livid with dust. Exactly the same greenish, mineral color as their far from spectacular machine,
they went diagonally across the plain towards the cemetery at Recouvrance,
jolting along on the uneven ground, solitary and ridiculous: our conquer-
ors. . . . Today they can be seen again in *Labyrinthe* {*In the Labyrinth*}, dead
tired in their archaic vehicle, vanguard of the enemy army that takes over
the besieged city.]

The tragicomic description appears "realistically" convincing: an image from
the past that respects Lejeune's autobiographical pact of sincerity and truth
and the identity between the narrating and the narrated "I." Yet, once again,
the direction of the causal relationship between the "real" event and "fiction"
(the "real" naturally inspiring the fiction) is reversible. In *Le Miroir qui revient*,
this description is a rewriting of the earlier fictional text *Dans le labyrinthe*.
The words *"ville prise"* recall Jean Ricardou's so-called "new new novel" *La
Prise de Constantinople* in which there is ludic play between *"ville prise"* and
"fille prise" (the sack of the town/the rape of the young girl) and a demonstration of the generation of meaning from the differential relations within a system of sounds (or sex). Ricardou's "fille prise" evokes the figure of the omni-
present "beautiful captive" in Robbe-Grillet's work, Angélique/Violette, the
relation of domination with the female "other" at the heart of both phantasm
and text. A "portrait" of Robbe-Grillet's maternal grandfather is seen to be reminiscent of the character Old King Boris in the novel *La Maison de rendez-
vous*. Was grandfather, too, inspired not by the memory but rather by the text?
    Writing, declares Robbe-Grillet, is always a rewriting. The autobiographi-
cal text, as Roland Barthes had declared before him, is a fiction. ("Et c'est
encore dans une fiction que je me hasarde ici." *Le Miroir*, p. 13 [And it is once
again into fiction that I venture here].) The writer is a character in a story. And
History, like Fiction, is a discourse, framing, imposing linearity on simultane-
ity and complexity, ordering rather than transparently reflecting, a function of
the present. Representation may have a relation to the orders and disorders of
perception and biological and social experience but it is predominantly self-

reflexive. The details of the text refer not to outside events but to similar details elsewhere in the text or to other texts. The passage concludes:

> Maintenant il n'y a plus de plaine de Kerangoff. A la place de la route en terre incertaine, sinueuse, il y a une rue rectiligne et goudronnée, avec des trottoirs, qui porte le nom d'un maréchal de la précedente guerre contre l'Allemagne, celle que mon père a gagnée, dont les récits d'héroïsme trouant l'interminable cauchemar boueux avaient hanté d'une crainte obscure (tu seras soldat, toi aussi) la moitié parisienne de ma trop imaginative enfance. (p. 36)

> [Kerangoff Plain no longer exists. The uneven, winding road has been replaced by a straight blacktop street with sidewalks, named after a field marshal of the previous war with Germany, the one my father won; his stories of heroism punctuating {trouant} that interminable nightmare of mud haunted the Parisian half of my over-imaginative childhood with a nebulous fear (you'll be a soldier too).]

There is indeed traditional History here, a legitimizing reality, that is, an apparent documentary or neutral empirical reference, a material, geographical base of personal experience and indications of the working of time. But there is also a concentration of the myths of War in a dialectical organization (heroism and nightmare, glory and holocaust, victory and defeat), that is, a reference to the products and processes of the collective imagination and to practices of the historiographic institution. There is metaphor in the above description as well as myth, and for Robbe-Grillet metaphor is intentional, not innocent. The Great War with its rectilinear road under the sign of a Marshall and the celebration of its "victory" replaces the complex, painful memory of the Second World War "defeat."

Just as complex situations are replaced by simple military and social myths, the straight line of historical certainties and clear positions replaces the curve of doubt and the complexity of the old road. We note that the straight line of Euclidean geometry and of Cartesian rationality and the curve of the multiple geometries of the new sciences are central and "complementary" (contradictory but not mutually exclusive) metaphors throughout Robbe-Grillet's work. History, it is suggested, moreover, is always a manipulation of signs; a story told by someone who cannot stand outside the story she or he tells.

Once again, for the practiced reader of Robbe-Grillet the sinuous, rutted road is a sign but not only of the complexities and holes of history. The recurrence of the sinuous ("sinueuse"), siren, serpent, seduction, sexuality, curve, compliance, and complexity, as it winds from text to text, has produced at least one book-length study (Vareille) seeking in the traces of this S, communication with the working of Robbe-Grillet's subconscious. The word "*creux*" and its insistent repetition links this text to the proliferation of other fissures, holes, invagination throughout the writing, figuring the monsters (of sexuality, of violence), the disorders, the dark spaces that have been made to disappear and of which our texts can render so little account.

At the "corners" of the phrase, in the "hollows" ("*creux*") of the sentence, Robbe-Grillet sees these monsters lurking to threaten the flattest surfaces, the most resolute narrative voice. Structured like our "lucid consciousness," that is, according to the laws of meaning, "articulated" language, claims the writer, can account neither for an exterior world that is precisely "not us," nor for the ghosts that agitate "within us" (p. 41). The text designates its inability to mirror anything other than the conscious mind and thus the ready-made (that is, cultural meanings, the subject's implication in social and discursive practices already in place, historical significations). Yet it is also the only instrument at hand to explore and break down both these limitations and the insistent desire for meaning itself. Robbe-Grillet's autobiographical wartime experience and its collective context is pre-text for this attempt. It provides the grids, the material that *Le Miroir qui revient* uses to construct its textual forms, while it designates the ideological nature and interrogates the universality of the "historical" or common knowledge "real" that this wartime experience appears to represent. History, like Autobiography, becomes the material of the fiction and the instrument of its own deconstruction.

Such a deconstructive fiction is not reduced to linguistic play or structural sterility. It may carry with it powerful traces of originary event. Out of the infinite unweaving and weaving of the web of language, the speaking, desiring subject can spin unique new configurations. Roland Barthes thus sees style as individual rather than cultural in *La Chambre claire*,[7] born of drive and the body and a linguistically unknowable, ahistorical, material (genetic) core.

The historical material, the pre-text, is often identifiable as itself quotation or (inter)text. The representations of the war re-presented in *Le Miroir qui revient* are those on "the walls of the city" to use Robbe-Grillet's phrase: the innumerable political newspapers the mother consumes daily, the unacceptable text on the beam of the factory roof, "Du bist eine Nummer und diese Nummer ist nul" [You are a number and that number is zero]. The 1940 poster of Paul Reÿnaud, French Président du Conseil, declaring, "Nous vaincrons parce que nous sommes les plus forts" [We shall conquer for we are the strongest], is rapidly replaced by "Faites confiance au soldat allemand" [Have confidence in the German soldier], accompanied by the image of a blond, clean, smiling National Socialist soldier helping children cross the road. Like the poster in front of the Nuremberg station depicting scenes of fire, rape, massacre, bathed in an apocalyptic light and titled in Gothic characters "La victoire, ou bien le chaos bolcheviste" (p. 125) [Victory or Bolshevik chaos], these texts present as reality what are ideologically based constructions. *Le Miroir qui revient* itself points the moral Robbe-Grillet found in 1984 in these inversions of signs: "Ce n'est pas le chaos qui règne en U.R.S.S., bien au contraire. Dans le régime soviétique aussi, c'est l'ordre absolu qui engendre l'horreur" (p. 125) [It is not chaos that reigns in the USSR; quite on the contrary. Under the Soviet regime too, it is absolute order that breeds horror].

The suspicion of language as ideology and as instrument of power that the choice of these texts makes evident (Robbe-Grillet refers to Barthes' provocative formula that all language is "fascist" in his text [p. 64]) is doubled by the intuition of the misleading nature of the dialectical functioning of meanings of signs. Robbe-Grillet interprets this historical period as the ordering of the world in terms of the mutually exclusive opposites of rational thought that sets up Germanic Order/The Law versus Jewish Disorder/Freedom/Lawlessness. Yet the very awareness of the limitations of language, which does not describe but instead frames and constructs "reality," an awareness that underscores all of Robbe-Grillet's work, obviously has a base in those representations that produced him as a subject within History, or at the least, in the personal history constituted by the opinions of family and friends.

Robbe-Grillet's histories/stories of the Second World War, plural in function, slipping uncertainly from history to fiction, from past to present, experience to text, from self-realizing in his own new text to self-dissolution in the language of the tribe always already there, conjoining these disconnections while insisting on their difference, thus do have a clear and immediate historical interest. They are, as their critics have suggested, an important overt staging of ghosts still partly locked away in the cupboards of the French past. *Mises en scène* of certain mythologies of the war (and of the Third Reich) revealed now as constructions, they are nonetheless grounded in the aspirations, beliefs, and social organizations, the strong and complex Franco-Germanic connections of the time.

Le Miroir qui revient is both an unmaking of those collective myths that do not designate their origin in history/story/relations of power but pretend to have a natural and eternal origin, and a staging of the unnoticed functioning of myth and metaphor in language. What is made manifest in this text is the danger of a natural and eternal History that returns, and of unnoticed and intolerable inversions and manipulations of signs of the kind that occurred in the representations of 1939–45 and turned so many people into quasi-indifferent or unwitting collaborators of the persecution of millions of innocent victims. The threat of the evacuation of story from history and thus the return of totalitarian and definitively ordered History (the need to learn to read deconstructively the texts that surround us) remains a central message of Robbe-Grillet's textual War.[8]

Yet, once again, the medium that pretends to be competent to re-present and consider history is a reconstruction of this history, somewhere between experience, guilt, metatextual reflection on the functioning of history and text, and the creative freedom of form or style. The war is the reference, the object, the unmaking of a certain knowledge, and the return of the past through the subject and the play of his text. What is perhaps played out here, once again, is the Freudian or Barthesian dilemma of the necessity and the impossibility of infidelity to the authority of the Past/the Father. And in the text, a strange, recurring, and shadowy third person character unsettles and negates the first person histories and their meanings as they are elaborated, through his contradictions as fascist and as revolutionary, his mixed historical and fictional character, his transgressive excesses, his combining of aspects of the father and of the son.

Corinthe is both the shadow of the benevolent and eccentric father-provider ("Papa"), and the imaginative fantasy of heroic and powerful aristocratic or political paternity ("mon père"). Whether childhood memory or once again recounted story ("Je pense—ai-je déjà dit—ne l'avoir jamais rencontré moi-même," p. 7 [I've already said I don't think I've ever met him]), the Comte de Corinthe is a ludic, legendary figure perceived only in the "play" of the parental door, outlined against the flickering flames of the "monumental" fireplace. The night rider of folk memory and of the ancestral Breton legends of the godmother's telling, galloping through the mists on the lonely cliff paths, he is also the romantic cavalier on rearing white steed venturing into tumultuous seas in order to recover the returning representational/magic mirror which has, it seems, undergone a sea-change.[9]

As Georges Raillard and, after him, Pierre Brunel have pointed out, Corinthe returns seven times. Brunel[10] sees the variants of Corinthe as generated by Hoffmann's nursery story of the Sandman (l'homme au sable) and issuing from stories of double paternity, the two fathers of Oedipus, Laios and Polybus in *Oedipus Rex*, for example. As other sources for Robbe-Grillet's figure, he identifies Rossini's *Siège de Corinthe*, Wagner's wounded Tristan and Flying Dutchman, and Lucius in Nodier's *Smarra*, who leaves his companion on the battle-field of Corinth.

This eminently fictional character has previously appeared in a number of Robbe-Grillet's own works, in passing references to the Rue de Corinth in *Les Gommes*, in *Souvenirs du triangle d'or* (1978), and in the film *La Belle Captive* (1983) where he is victim of a female vampire bite, source of the "two small red holes a centimeter apart" ("deux petits trous rouges espacés d'un centimètre," p. 226) on our Henri de Corinthe's neck. Intertextual self-reference, Corinthe also derives from Phlégon de Tralles' early Roman story *La Fiancée de Corynthe* and its theme of the weakening of the male by his commerce with his pale virgin bride. More directly, he is borrowed from Michelet's nineteenth-century rewriting and Barthes' retelling of Michelet's story.[11] Corinthe, Robbe-Grillet's text informs the reader, is also generated by an engraving in the journal *L'Illustration*, seen in childhood, of a cavalry officer on a rearing steed turning to urge on his following troops toward his double dying on the ground. The engraving may be an intertextual reference to the generative painting "La Défaite de Reichenfels" in *Dans le labyrinthe*, once again; it refers also to a story by Kipling read in childhood and telling of a "dead" officer ever-haunted by the fear of being trampled by his own men. The lieutenant-colonel that, as a child, Robbe-Grillet believed his own father, wounded veteran of the Great War, to be, is not only autobiography but intertext. In the sequel "autobiography," *Angélique ou l'enchantement*, Corinthe is the expressionist German painter (Lovis Corinth), the Captain who saves the father from death on a day in 1914 in the First World War, and a younger Second World War version, Simon, escorting the spy Carmina-Angélique through the perilous forest. Simon is also the cavalry officer, de Reixach, in Claude Simon's Nobel prize-winning novel *La Route des Flandres* and the love-stricken protagonist (Simon Le Coeur) of Robbe-Grillet's *Djinn* (1981). All these figures are both doubles of the writer and figures of the writer's paternity, both past and text. Corinthe, claims Michael Sheringham, is not only playing a kind of "wild card" (Raillard's "signifiant flottant") whose function is "to maintain the play of fantasy within the text," he is also "partly a displacement of a desire to unmask one's progenitor and understand one's genius."[12]

Offering the narcissistic writer the possibility of self-generation (generation from same) and self-containment, omniscience and omnipotence, in the tradition of the Romantic creator, Corinthe is compared in the text to literary models. Like the fictional Rollebon of Sartre, explains Robbe-Grillet, he goes on mysterious journeys to Russia and Germany. As is also the case for Dostoyevsky's Stavroguine, information on him is fragmentary, conveyed by unreliable third parties and always uncertain. Nor is it impossible that Corinthe has taken on characteristics from right-wing historical "heroes" of the 1930s and 1940s: "Henri de Kerillis, François de la Rocque, or even the Count of Paris, who was also called Henri and was the pretender to the throne of France" (p. 103). Count Corinthe thus sets in play the Maurassian sympathies of the father (a member in the thirties of the Croix de feu, Colonel de la Rocque's right-wing organization), and the diversity and complexity of often warring attitudes and behaviors of the right-wing factions of which Weber, and the autobiography of Henri, Comte de Paris, give an account.[13]

In September 1938, asserts the text, Corinthe is in Berlin ("this is a fact that seems incontestable"), where he meets "two important personages very close to the Chancellor." At the beginning of October, "just after the Munich agreement on the Sudetenland, he is in Prague where he arrives on the evening of the 7th (coming, it is believed from Crakow by train), that is, barely hours before the explosion of a train from Germany" (p. 174). A letter from Corinthe in the archives of the secret police in Dresden, found after the war, contains a detailed report on the damage to the railway system. In 1940, Robbe-Grillet's text continues, with all the detail that conventionally signifies the "true," Corinthe fights on horseback and with panache against enemy armored divisions suggesting a Polish connection (the massacre of the Polish officers in the Katyn forest is subsequently mentioned — massacre for which the USSR first accepted responsibility in 1990).

Is Corinthe a Nazi collaborator or an agent of the Resistance, a traitor or a hero? Is Corinthe an "imposter," as the text also suggests, leaving France hastily when the American troops entered Paris, rumored to be in Buenos Aires or Uruguay "trafficking in women, drugs, light arms, art work." Involved in politics, a spy, this fantasmatical Nazi may equally be an avatar of the Mengele history, or the story of Robbe-Grillet's spy-hero-artist Manneret/Manet/Man Ray in *La Maison de rendez-vous* (1965). The movement between History and Fiction becomes vertiginous. (Is Corinthe simply Robbe-Grillet playing games, "rien de cohérent" as the anagram invented in Parisian literary circles suggests?)

Toward the end of *Le Miroir qui revient*, Corinthe becomes not only a complex fantastic figure of biological, historical, and literary paternity remembered and subverted, embraced and rejected, but increasingly Robbe-Grillet's own face in the mirror, a self-portrait of the writer as the other of the self, shivering and ghost-like, a living specter, at his bedroom desk in Robbe-Grillet's house at Mesnil-au-Grain. Humorous excessive *mise en scène* of Robbe-Grillet's own idiosyncrasies, obsessions, and fears, he incorporates both the latter's passion for classification and order and (in his response to Wagnerian opera, for example) Robbe-Grillet's own contradictory propensity for emotionality and romantic heroism. These are, of course, and not coincidentally, the commonplace notions of the characteristics of the Nazi psyche.

Wadja's film *A Love in Germany*, for example, situates the origins of the event on which its story focuses—the hanging of a young Polish worker prisoner in a German village because he breaks the "law" by having a sexual relationship with a married Aryan woman—in just this insistence on order. The precise and "scientific" Nazi taxonomies and prescribed measurements for determining racial categories, the detail of the laws regulating sexual interaction of the women of the master race with other ethnic groups, appear to find an echo not just in self-interest but in a psychological need to respect the "law," to impose its rules on others, and to suppress whatever threatens the categories of established order.

The splintering of the protagonist (need for order, sentimental romanticism) brings to consciousness the contradictions of the unconscious as the writer pursues those monsters by whom he is pursued. Suspected of the violent drowning of the very young, blond Marie-Ange van der Reeves (whom the writer confuses with the beautiful siren Angélique von Salomon or Salome), possessing the possible SS connections that would qualify him as a stereotype of sadomasochistic representations, and recalling the documented sexual experiments on the bodies of young girls by Nazi "scientists," Corinthe also puts into play the question of the hidden monsters in the self, and the links between sexuality, history, and power.

Just as new history, it is claimed, no longer provides us with heroes, with clearly continuous and meaningful traces, or with single irreversible judgments, Corinthe/Robbe-Grillet, assemblage of the commonplaces of our representations as of the writer's material existence and his desiring body, is not an objective knowledge of an essence, or a subjective awareness of an "existence" free to determine a self in *Le Miroir qui revient*. In his proliferating, contradictory, fleeting doubles, he is the staging of the historical determinations and the mythologies and stereotypes of discourse, of the psychological structures and the discontinuities that constitute a splintering of the old stable and unique ego, at once present and in question. He challenges the authenticity or freedom of the authorial self and the continuity and coherence of History. Narcissistic and self-conscious, he explores the more theoretical self-loss in ironic distances and infinite reflexivity that Linda Hutcheon (*Narcissistic Narrative. The Metafictional Paradox*) and Jean-Francois Lyotard (*La Condition post-*

moderne) have respectively identified as the "metafictional" and the "post-modern" condition.

I argue that in the demonstration of Corinthe's origins in Robbe-Grillet's own distinctive contexts (historical and psychological) as well as in the new analytical and skeptical practice of writing, in the "complementary" nature of this character—neither Robbe-Grillet himself nor an arbitrary construction—Corinthe takes the conception of the self in the autofictions beyond the post-modern condition and the unmotivated nature of the sign.

Comte Henri dies, a recluse in Finistère where he lived alone at the bottom of an old gun emplacement that dates from the time of Vauban and is built into the cliff. The significance of this final passage is curiously uncertain, and although much is pastiche and intertextuality, there is some historical reference: "Mon père est allé à son enterrement, un enterrement civil, avec une fausse messe dite en plein air par un prêtre interdit, devant la porte fermée de l'église. [. . .] Il était donc excommunié? Depuis quand? Pour quelle faute?" (p. 226) [My father went to his funeral, a civil funeral, with an illicit mass celebrated by an unfrocked priest, held in the open air outside the closed church door. {. . .} So he had been excommunicated? For how long? Why?].

The allusion to excommunication would seem to refer to the historically documented *Action Française* movement, supported by Robbe-Grillet's parents. Representing a desire for the old aristocratic values, elitism, authority, and order, it signals here, once again, the return of the "Seconde France" of Robbe-Grillet's childhood based on the material conditions as much as on the myths (the myths of Apocalypse and Purity among them) central to this period. Condemned by the Vatican in 1926, and disavowed by the Pretender in late 1937 for its integral nationalism (Tannenbaum), the excommunication of the *Action Française* is evoked in the present perhaps as evidence for the anarchistic, anticonformist positions of its supporters, Robbe-Grillet's parents, positions that their son espouses still.

If there is closure of a sort in the death of the "historical" figure Corinthe in this ironic passage and perhaps some absolution for Robbe-Grillet's parents' right-wing discourse of the thirties, staged here as a discourse of misguided finalist opinion[14] (all discourses it would seem are not equal), in the final instance, Corinthe, like the war, is himself textual and without closure. Alive once again and writing his memoirs in Robbe-Grillet's study-bedroom at Mesnil-au-Grain in *Angélique*, where his death is announced for a sequel to be entitled *La Mort de Corinthe*, this figure of the writer brings together the generators and the mechanisms of the creative Robbe-Grillet text. He enables the text to slip between the time narrated and the time of the narration, from histories to fiction, personal life history to life story transformed by the "imaginary," product of and producer of proliferating jagged fragments whose edges, as the writer declares, do not match.

In the *Returning Mirror*, "histoire" (both "history" and "story" in French) as pre-text prefigures a new text through the nondialectical forms that dislocate both traditional narrative forms and traditional historical orders. This new text exceeds the stories/histories in which we are enmeshed, or, at the least, makes manifest the new "complementary" and "chaotic" structures underlying recent transformations of these orders. These, I have contended, are the mobile, plural, nonlinear structures that appear at the level of the infinitely small in the probabilistic leaps of quantum mechanics where matter is both particle and wave and the observer, like the teller, part of the observation and the tale told. The manner of their detecting demonstrates that no metatext and no viewpoint is uncontaminated by its object; no object/history is free of its viewpoint. These new structures have analogies with the objects of the new science of chaos and its discovery in tiny deviations from a system in perfect order of the seeds of monstrous irregularity and unpredictability, yet in entropy and in complex disorder (turbulent flow, transition states of matter), in "chaos," curious pattern and new self-organizing, self-similar forms of order. Since James Gleick's book *Chaos: Making a New Science* became a best-seller in 1988, chaos has become a major topos of contemporary thought.

A summary retracing of the configurations of the war in the work of other writers of *nouveau roman* practice reveals a preoccupation with the rewriting of the traditional dialectic between history and story, order and chaos, not dissimilar to the figures apparent in Robbe-Grillet's work. In *La Route des Flandres* (1960), a novel prefaced by the phrase borrowed from Valéry, "Two dangers threaten the world: order and disorder," Claude Simon's cavalry officer protagonist circles obstinately around an absent center (the disintegrating horse) seeking patterns in the chaos of the *Débâcle*. In *Les Géorgiques* (1981), text which is itself constructed, in a now familiar postmodern strategy, from other texts of Western tradition (from Virgil and from Michelet's *Histoire de la Révolution*, for example), the disordered ("chaotic") yet strangely self-organized, self-similar, patterned, and recursive overlapping circles of military defeats and victories that constitute Western History/Text take form around a sexualized void or matrix of birth and death. The polysemous title of the novel *Histoire* (1967) evokes the public history and private story telescoped in that fiction. A "textual" aesthetic is central in these works and yet the war is grounded in Simon's own sentient present experience. The textual/sexual body and the reversible topological spaces of the Moebius strip where inside and outside, cause and effect become indeterminate constitute places of interconnection between biology and world.

Nathalie Sarraute, narrowly escaping arrest after being denounced as a Jew, does not use Historical event or discuss the War and the Holocaust directly. Yet in the "subconversations" that underlie social discourse lurk disordered but precise tropistic movements revolving around the reactions of aggression and fear, the desire to control, and the need to build defenses. The impulse of the baker of Janvry to denounce her, derived, she claimed in a rare interview with Marc Saporta[15] from just such movements, the baker's fear of disorder, his desire to be "right," to impose the rule of law, and suppress the hidden threat. These tropistic movements of aggression, the fear of disorder, the attempt to impose an absolute order, are both at the heart of the History that Sarraute lived and the hidden source of her own "autofictions" that explore the strength and weakness of the authoritative "masculine" voice of certainty, and the ambivalence of the piercing of the silken skin of the "feminine." Sarrautean "subconversations," then, consist of disordered but precise contradictory affective movements (tropisms) centered around the "masculine" desire to master and control and the "feminine" instinct to submit, flee, or build defense. The writer's own first voice in *Enfance* with its queries, quibbles, and desire to correct the imprecision, uncertainty or inaccuracy of the second seeking "feminine" voice, participates in such a process.

Robbe-Grillet's explanation of anti-Semitism in *Le Miroir qui revient* is formulated similarly in terms of the need to suppress a spirit of liberty, a ferment of disorder; his parents are anti-Semitic, he claims, because they fear the "dangerous" internationalism that is an aspect of this spirit of liberty and disorder. The Berkeley theorists initially explained the "prefascist" personality psychoanalytically in terms of repressed desires, Hitler's hatred of Jews being seen as rooted in displaced hostility toward his severe father. Subsequently examined in the light of the Berkowitz hypothesis of frustration—the fact that frustration and subsequent anger increase aggression against scapegoat minorities—the authoritarian personality is currently seen to be also illuminated by social learning theory. Bob Altermeyer[16] identifies fear of change and disorder and self-righteousness as the two single traits which consistently correlate highly with the "authoritarian" scale. Fear of disorder arouses hostility, and self-righteousness (perceiving the self as morally superior) disinhibits social taboo against aggression. In this theory, the targets of discrimination are those seen as "causing trouble" and are identified with the threat of a disintegrating, chaotic world.

In Duras' pseudodiary *La Douleur* (*The War*), the global, objective, or outside events that constitute Resistance and Holocaust are refracted through the textual mirrors of the local inner experiences of feminine waiting and emotional pain: the pain of the loss of her unborn child or, later (and somewhat problematically for this reader), the pain of childbirth. Knowledge of History here also emerges through the other; from Marguerite's waiting for Robert L. (Robert Antelme, Robert L/il/elle), her husband, deported in 1944 for his activities in the Resistance. The intensity of this emotionally and physically experienced waiting holds center stage and not the events of Robert's dramatic rescue, claimed to have been orchestrated by François Morland, alias François Mitterrand, from the barracks for those dying of typhus in Dachau. Marguerite's own timeless, careful nursing vigil over the pain of Robert's slow return to the living is given precedence over any account of heroic sequential external events of war or rescue. Duras' presumption in speaking in the place of the victims of the Holocaust has been criticized as an unjustified appropriation of a pain that she herself experienced only vicariously. Her defense might be precisely that she does not give voice to the other or indeed to History but rather to a history that can be, for her, only ever a face of her own story; she can begin to know the other's pain or loss (the pain and sorrow of the modern world) only through her own.

A similar "knowledge" of history through personal pain (pain as the other and often chosen face of pleasure) is present in the diffuse suffering of the protagonists in Duras' earlier fictions. In the "holocaust" film text *Hiroshima mon amour*, the shorn victim shut away by her shamed family in a cellar at Nevers for sexual "collaboration," the young German soldier she loved assassinated at the Liberation on the local Quai des Arts, is linked to the grieving mother of her adolescent lover by their shared pain. Such a figure of the Mater Dolorosa has, of course, drawn the multiple images of the violence and suffering of history together in an apparently timeless personification from Michelangelo's Pietà to twentieth-century war memorials in village squares in France.

Duras focuses on the inversions of signs operated by the "Liberation" and the Gaullist period, the ambiguities of revenge. In "Albert des Capitales," a short fragment in *La Douleur*, the ritualistic humiliation and torture of a (middle-class) collaborator-traitor that the narrator (Thérèse) herself directs in the name of the (proletarian) Resistance to obtain "knowledge" of his guilt through confession is seen as a form of collaboration with oppressive orders of power.

For Duras, what can be known of history or holocaust is not through knowledge or classification of the past or from the power that control of historical discourses brings but through the powerless "feminine" body. There are pitfalls here in taxonomies, margins of uncertainty between pain and pleasure, between strength and weakness, between self-loss and self-assertion, resistance and attraction to the German soldier. The territories of the war are in the body, beyond language; in a presymbolic desire that may be (sado)masochistic in character.

Robbe-Grillet's personification of the war in the figure of Corinthe echoes Marguerite Duras' insistence on any knowledge of history being grounded in the nonordered, immediate experience of the body, in the felt reality of power and humiliation. In Corinthe, the imaginary of the war hero/traitor as self-possessed and tough, identification with the Law of the father, and sexual fantasies of control accompanied by an anxiety-provoked suppression of the seductive, vulnerable, dangerous feminine other are inextricably interwoven with historical event.

The narrator of Simon's *La Route des Flandres* has lost most of his war comrades including his friend Blum and his cousin and commanding officer, de Reixach, and as Lynn Higgins points out, he is a disillusioned veteran of the decomposition and animality of the *Débâcle* rather than part of a traditional "warrior elite" "glorifying war as a means to masculine self-affirmation."[17] He seeks "knowledge" of the chaotic events of the past by spending a night with Corinne (de Reixach's wife). Why, asks Higgins, is Simon's war narrative and his epistemological quest embedded in an erotic one? Her reply is that the myth of "Woman" is "a ritual" of the male solidarity shared for example by Georges and Blum; Corinne is the object of the sexual stories the two tell, indistinguishably, to reestablish their status as (male) human subjects. But Simon's discourse that depends on and originates in Corinne, a return to the womb or melting-pot ("matrice le creuset originel," p. 42), or to the maternal ("le lait de l'oubli," p. 261) [the milk of forgetting], that is, to the origin of life, also identifies her with the dead horse, the earth of the grassy ditch or the eternal wound ("l'éternelle blessure," p. 191), that is, with the fascination and fear of death. In the final instance, argues Higgins, Simon's war narrative silences Corinne/Woman and constructs itself (her) as a means of dialoguing with the dead (Blum) "through suppression of the feminine."[18] As in the texts of Robbe-Grillet where what that writer calls the "guard-rail" of geometrical precision, scientific objectivity, and ordering does not prevent a moving, liquid universe of desire and death from encroaching upon the domains of both story and history, the multiple, mythological, intertextual perspectives that disseminate the figures of Corinne throughout Simon's texts (*La Route des Flandres, Histoire, Triptyque*) return us toward what we have called the "void."

In *W, ou le souvenir d'enfance*, a new autobiography that is significant in respect to the centrality of the war but that the scope of this book does not allow us to analyze in any depth, Georges Perec attempts to trace details of his mother's existence and probable death at Auschwitz through his own childhood memories. A narrative that assembles and footnotes memories and facts alternates with a second fictional narrative reconstituted from his adolescent writing that appears to have operated substitutions and displacements of this early experience; the two kinds of narrative are connected in significant ways (in particular by the quest for the mother) at dimly perceived intersections. Neither version, however, proves complete or satisfactory in what is yet another new autobiography constructed around the impossible search for a missing center and/or a monstrous void out of a central war experience.

The authoritarian narrative tradition of connections (beginning, middle, end), whose underlying images the critic Edward Saïd[19] has characterized as those of paternity, succession, and hierarchy, like sequenced, encyclopedic History, has been partly undone. It is no longer possible to fix an origin, to order a top and a bottom or ranking order, or even to impose a definitive rational taxonomy that escapes the body. Within Robbe-Grillet's chessboard itself, within the grid, there is the labyrinth, and in the labyrinth the monster lies somewhere curled, a minotaur of self and of history—the Comte de Corinthe, that "marine monster" who, in *Le Miroir*, is said to devour little girls.

And yet, as History is shown to be also story and pre-text (for the construction of the autobiographical fiction) arising from sociopolitical contexts and prior knowledge of the functioning of History, or from void, pieces of something for which there are no other working terms than history or self nonetheless emerge from individual contexts and styles. Although a Derridean subject, divided, decentered, deferred, and existing in the differential play of signifiers, predominates, although History as an object outside of the subjective contexts that construct it is in question, selves and histories still function at least as working stories in and beyond the text.

There is no internal consistency in this open, self-reflecting, and contradictory work where the sign remains multiple and shifting in its reference, in degrees of fact and fiction, and textual/sexual and historical practices are conflated in a miscellany of styles, nor is there any clear and single meaning that surfaces as it puts History and Story, Self and Text, Order and Disorder into play. The "meanings" that emerge from this staging of the pre-texts of *Débâcle*, War and Liberation, lie in its "complementary" and "chaotic" forms; in a returning human/humanism that is also a structure/structuralism. This is the "mixing of every language" of Barthes' final writings, akin to his "imposture" or the "tricks" that displace history/self/literature to make these at once always already there in the constituted laws of discourse and continuously changing; both histories and stories, Hegel's diachronic fixed coherent sequence and Foucault's synchronic relations. It is Stephen Greenblatt's trick of displacing what Derrida describes as the "circulation" of discourses within the autonomy of the text by the mutual constitution of material conditions and language and negotiated reciprocity between social and aesthetic discourse. It is Wolfgang Iser's "dynamic oscillation" from History to Fiction.[20]

Meanings also inhere then in the questions that continue to circulate, undecidable. We cannot say how far History is story, its writing a rewriting or intertext. Nor whether it can escape ideological manipulation or take account of its own origins and ends, its distance in time and space from its objects, in a deconstructive mode. Changing historical contexts appear to articulate our cultural constructions, our selves. Yet might it be rather our cultural texts and our unconscious selves that articulate History? What is the relationship between Holocaust, discursive practices of ordering, and power-play in the narcissistic, sadomasochistic structures of self?

The Second World War serves as a pre-text for the exploration of the contexts of a returning and individuated self and its relation to past and present and to power in a new and ground-breaking text. Yet in an interesting slippage, it is the collective texts emerging at other cultural sites, postmodernisms of various kinds (quantum physics, chaos theory) that appear to organize this individuated self around a rethinking and a subversion of the poles of order and chaos and the binary oppositions and categories that these poles subsume. The war is the material for an individual writing project that explores *both* the limitations of ready-made language and History *and* their power; the (im)possibilities of individuated self-reinvention, of the reinvention of history, through new collective novelistic forms.

◇

five

◇

THE ANGEL IN ROBBE-GRILLET'S MIRROR
Writing, Power, and the Feminine in *Angélique ou l'enchantement* and *Les Derniers Jours de Corinthe*

In an earlier study of *Angélique ou l'enchantement*, I argued that Angelica, pure angel and devilish enchantress, helpless prisoner and powerful Other, is the hidden founding myth and the underlying structure whose metaphorical transformations, organized along a metonymical axis, construct the meanings of Robbe-Grillet's second autobiographical fiction.[1] Similar in function to the figure of Corinthe who attracts and at the same time relativizes "the fantasmatic currents at large in the text," as Michael Sheringham describes that figure of "disordering subjective fantasy,"[2] Angélique is used to "augment the fictional dimension, but also to alter its alignment with the other material"—the discourse about the self, the discourse about earlier texts, the discourses of and about fantasy—"creating a topology whose surfaces are never securely mapped" (p. 32). The work's densely packed generative title announces a syntactic and a semantic ambivalence; both an apposition and an opposition of characters and of functions. Angélique and Enchantment can be read as single paradigm, as synonyms organized along a syntagmatic axis; that is as appositional, identical doubles, one mirroring the other. A second edition in 1988 added a comma to the title, now *Angélique, ou l'enchantement* to give this reading weight. Yet these doubles might equally be oppositional and mutually exclusive; two poles in a battle of the sexes necessary for the establishing of difference and subsequently of identity.

Angélique-Enchantement is both the enchantress and the enchanted, both fatal entrapment and beautiful captive, both the sadist and the masochist of a bipolar, narcissistic, structure of the psyche. I suggest that the use of Angélique goes beyond the dialectical thematic movement between opposites that she organizes. The strategies of the text situate her in a "complementary" relation to Corinthe in the Heisenberg sense—that is, contradictory but not mutually exclusive. This Angel in the mirror is the locus of Robbe-Grillet's exploration of the relations between his writing, power, and the feminine. At the same time, she may constitute a rewriting of these relations.

In the first pages of *Angélique ou l'enchantement*, Robbe-Grillet claims he is incapable of writing what is there before his eyes, whereas he never writes anything without seeing it in an almost material fashion. He cannot see himself directly but only in the mirror of his writing. In the opening immobile designs of the things around him, the crack in the ceiling, the faded flowered wallpaper, the knots and veins "on the walls of my room," that is, also in descriptions that recall those in his previous novels (*Dans le labyrinthe, Projet*), the narrator detects the distorted fragments of human faces that are him and yet not quite him. The text derives from Robbe-Grillet's "imagination speaking of memory,"[3] but imagination is simultaneously inspired by the sensory objects that surround him and interacts with the writing process. The reader is indeed drawn into a game of textual mirrors but a game that implicates a particular textual and sexual body (Robbe-Grillet's). Seeking a path in the epistemological and ontological forests of indeterminacy that characterize the postmodern text, the reader is moved by the strategies of this particular text between literary characters and narrators (Count Corinthe, he, I) who are substitutes one for the other, and a sentient, creating, thinking author(ity) — "desacralized" and "decentered," as Ben Stoltzfus argues,[4] but neither dead nor substitutable. There is no unified theory that would, as the physicist Stephen Hawking sees it in his *Brief History of Time*, reveal the mind of God, and yet the characters (or worlds), although contradictory and complex, are somehow commensurate; that is, share common units of discourse.

The changing and contradictory aspects of the "fairground freaks" and "war-wounded" whose refracted reflections embody the monstrous character of the narrators and the narrative give way (too infrequently, regrets the narrator) to another fugitive figure, who, like the writer, is at once coextensive with and through the looking glass of writing, both inside and outside, both in life and in text. She is at once a projection of the narrator and his "other" who will help him to image the self. As he inscribes the "trembling name of Angélica" ("le nom tremblant d'Angélica," p. 8), the manipulating and moved narrator catches a glimpse of a pretty blond woman smiling at him among the curving foliage and uncertain garlands of the indeterminately real and intertextual wallpaper flowers. Angélique (the angelic Marie-Ange or the diabolical charm of Carmina/Manrica, as you like it) is the textual/sexual body who pursues him and whom he pursues throughout the writing of this text, once again, as in a recurring, if curiously well organized, waking dream. The trembling name

Alain Robbe-Grillet in his Paris apartment, Boulevard Maillot. Photo by Catherine Robbe-Grillet; courtesy of Alain Robbe-Grillet.

of Angélique generates present emotional and poetic invocation and, simultaneously, ironic past quotation as a passage from *Le Miroir qui revient* re-turns. "Pourquoi me poursuit-il encore? . . . Pourquoi m'as-tu quitté, petite flamme, me laissant transi, solitaire, au milieu de la pluie et du vent?" (p. 8) [Why is it still pursuing me? . . . Why did you abandon me, little flame, leaving me frozen and solitary, amidst the rain and the wind?]. This passage pirouettes between pastiche as alibi and indirect revelation of secret (Robbe-Grillet himself publicly identified this allusion as reference to a mistress who had left him)[5] and the investigative intent that continues the quests of Robbe-Grillet's earlier metaphysical detective fictions—*Les Gommes*, *Le Voyeur*, and *Dans le labyrinthe*.

A second trace of Angélique appears fleetingly in a similarly suspect "adjectival" but also enchanting prose poetry of this autofiction among the insubstantial and disparate cohort of ghostly knights in white armor that follows the first angelic vision. What the writer describes as the inner vision and the violence of memory, that is, writing as a mixed function of imagination, fantasy, memory of lived experience and of past writings reforming in the present moment, is staged self-consciously in the evocation of fair unbound feminine hair swirling among the cloud visions.

Textual mirrors operate similar reversals that encourage non-Cartesian passage from inner to outer vision, as from writer to narrator, or narrator to the character of Corinthe and back again at all levels of the functioning of *Angélique ou l'enchantement*. The text slips by semantic play with the multiple meanings of words from the "carpet" of rough drafts ("tapis de feuilles") on the writer's desk to the "carpet" of dead leaves ("tapis de feuilles") on the tree-lined approach to his vast stately home. It moves imperceptibly from the first person "I," the writer at his desk, to the third person character, "he" or Henri de Corinthe, who has left his worktable to observe the weather outside and from Robbe-Grillet's "real" home at Mesnil-au-Grain in Normandy to the legendary Dark House ("La Maison Noire" or Ker-an-dû) of childhood memory at Kerangoff in Brittany. For example, from "le comte Henri" standing at the window with his disparate and incomplete writings on the bureau behind him, the text passes to a description of the murky depths of the mirror on the door made of mahogany recovered from shipwreck at sea and indirectly evoking another recurring Robbe-Grillet character, "le marin péri en mer" [the sailor lost at sea/in the mother]. In the mirror, partially opened and therefore at an unusual angle, "my" face is reflected, resembling, in the half-light, that of a stranger who had slipped silently into the room "while my back was turned towards the window" (p. 13). Similar splitting and passage occur between the bearded face of Robbe-Grillet in the mirror, marked by the scars and dark patches of life and aging, and the child whose name and face are similar but whose problematic existence appears to the present narrator to have been lived by some other.

The writer's names and alter egos from earlier works proliferate, splitting, merging, procreating, Jean Robin, Simon le Coeur (Jean Coeur, Joli Coeur), Henri de Corinthe, Henri Robin. A metacommentary accompanies the splitting process to showcase the illusion of single identity or centered inner self. "L'auteur, c'est l'être qui n'a pas de visage, dont la voix ne peut passer que par l'écriture et qui 'ne trouve pas ses mots'" (p. 30) [The author is he who has no face, whose voice is transmitted only in writing, and who "cannot find his words"]. The writer cannot find his words because these are not his own. They are, he claims, the words of the ideology in place that conditions him. His own anti-ideological discourse is caught within a linguistic law and meanings that Derrida has claimed are always-already there. It would seem then, as Foucault argues in *Power/Knowledge*,[6] that power and knowledge are necessarily a product of the Law. Even in rebellion, in revolt against the law, the writer remains within its power that is everywhere and nowhere. In this frame, the rebellious or detective son and his investigation of the secret room of the enchantments and metamorphoses of the angel in his mirror might simply underscore traditional paternal, divine, or linguistic authority.

But, at the least, Robbe-Grillet's effractions against laws of genre, subversions of narrative conventions (the telescoping of first and third person narration, life and text, history and fiction, in particular) and sado-erotic thematics force his readers into examining their own often unconscious expectations or their naturalizing of the Law and its taboos. The sometimes strikingly beautiful images and textual rhythms, heroic and enchanting myths and the thought-provoking metacommentaries exercise other kinds of seduction. Transgressions of genre overwrite the boundaries between the diary that traditionally focuses on the time of writing, the descriptive self-portrait, the memoirs that put emphasis on the contexts of a life and the autobiography with its traditional double perspective (the aging writer remembering in the present the story of the development of the child in the past). They transfuse poetry, drama, critical literary theory, self-conscious metacommentary, proliferating intertexts, and, most noticeably, fiction and myth into a traditional autobiographical narrative to create (meta)fictional autobiographies. In a fashion characterized by the text's own metafictional critic (or superego) as both uncertain and excessive, the topologies of the new texts allow, simultaneously, an exploration of possible selves in the form of fictional protagonists and a confessional catharsis. This catharsis, however, is less a traditional tragic "purging" than an exposing, exaggerating, becalming, and defusing of hidden impulses through their *mise en scène*.

I have argued that in their contradictory but not mutually exclusive telescoping movements between exploration and confession and past and present and their abolition of dualities, these "new" texts, necessarily inside power (that is, within language, narrative conventions, and traditional stories) might nonetheless challenge received power/knowledge through the "complementary" and "chaotic" forms they elaborate; forms that work against the power of the traditional text from within. The attempt to produce precise taxonomies and orderings to create a totalizing table of contents, for example, serves, in the final instance, to indicate the very limitations of this ordering. The proliferation of the diverse contents obscures rather than reveals the text's (the life's) origins and meanings.

Local, even individuated situations, too, as Foucault himself suggests in *Power/Knowledge*, can come to modify global collective power and its product, common knowledge (what Robbe-Grillet labels stereotypes) rather than vice versa. Or as Teresa De Lauretis argues in her rethinking of the feminine,[7] "differences" between the sexes or between individuals or between groups in different contexts, differences not clearly accounted for by constructionism or by Foucault's models, might have their own revolutionary force. In this modified form, essence, no longer necessarily an immutable nature or biological destiny but the product or interiorizing of specific situations, could coexist with constructionism. We noted that differences between languages—between "you've been abandoned" in Russian ("tiebia podbrossili," p. 172) and in French ("on t'a abandonnée," p. 172), or "I'm going to tear it" in German ("Ich werde es zerreissen," p. 13) and in French ("Je vais le déchirer," p. 13) in Sarraute's *Enfance*, for example—suggest that from one language to another words are almost interchangeable yet not quite. This specificity may open a small window of escape from the prison house of language and nonmotivation of the sign.

Robbe-Grillet writes self-consciously out of the collective, out of the intertexts familiar to a nation, a generation, and a gender of which he is part, but also out of the specific. In the second part of this chapter, I argue that even as he chooses, unmakes and remakes his prefabricated collective thematics, his work may indeed reflect a sadomasochistic structure of the psyche, the struggle for domination between the ego and superego and between the ego and the alter that is also a particular, personal preoccupation. Robbe-Grillet's thematics insistently bring to text that Hegelian master-slave dialectic of History to which

Feminism's investigations of the power relations between the sexes has brought new perspectives. It may be the case that his sado-erotic thematics derive in part from male biology, programmed, he claims in *Angélique*, like the dog or the stallion, for acts of violent penetration. But these are also a product of the sociosexual revolution of the time and of its peculiarly French contexts. The inspirations of the sadomasochistic thematics would include the rehabilitation of Sade and diverse other libertine writers currently considered to be liberators of love. Robbe-Grillet has shown considerable interest in this particular body of writing.

At the same time, individuated selections are operated among this underground erotic material, explained often as the collective "erotic clichés," the "dull and decadent mythology of the society in which we live"[8] and sometimes as the material of a ludic and individuated textual/sexual revolution. The content, tone, and structures of borrowed fairy tales and medieval or operatic romance from Ariosto to Wagner, the proliferation of references to classical, romantic, and impressionist-expressionist painting (Ingres, Delacroix, Lovis Corinth) are colored with the marks of Robbe-Grillet's own distinctive sado-erotic universe and Lolita syndrome. Angélique figures a specific incestuous father–very young daughter relation. She is also "enchantment," that is, a seduction that is not only a game but also the intense fascination with (and fear of) the feminine prey, Carmina as violent (violated) pleasure and danger. In interviews and talks Robbe-Grillet has often analyzed the enchantment of the young and beautiful feminine body, smooth, unlined, and eternal as being the fascination of immortality. And yet the enchantment is also danger and death.

Although the relation Robbe-Grillet sustains with his choices and with the "material" that he privileges appears to derive from ironic distance and freedom (analysis, knowledge, power), his texts also manifest anguish and a fear of impotence. These are present both explicitly and in the repetitions of certain distanced, common, but obsessive images (of self-loss in the forest; of death by drowning, siren song, or vampire bite; and of the captured, punished false angel). It is the case that the scythe of the "Ankou" (the Breton Grim Reaper) and virile knightly combat also threaten the protagonist's life but Angélique as the handmaiden or instrument of Corinthe's betrayal or death is never far.

The new autofictions (*Le Miroir qui revient*, 1984, *Angélique ou l'enchantement*, 1988, and *Les Derniers Jours de Corinthe*, 1994) may not be a return to the mimetic mirror, that is, to the illusion of the direct reproduction of the real. They are, however, a turn away from the linguistic as onomastic play of signifiers or the scrambling of narrative conventions that marked the *nouveaux romans* and a turning toward the ghosts in the mirror, the unconscious inner shadows, somehow reflected in the text. Self remains a function of the writing and a projection of the heroic stories we tell or do not tell about ourselves (a function of a novel of a life), but this no longer excludes the opposite claim that writing is a function of self-exploration (of the monstrous life in the fiction).

Using the autobiographical genre against itself to explore its own limits and artifices, that is, as Calle-Gruber claims, subverting autobiographical narrative with fictional narrative and vice versa,[9] the criminal son, according to the narrator's own metaphor, takes on the hydra-monster of ideology from within, wearing its skin as a mask, seeing with its eyes. This is a disguise, he claims, a subterfuge, to avoid being swallowed up by the devouring sea monster, an avatar of the swarming forest-sea of invasive metaphor evoked in Le Miroir. But the choice of entry point into ideology, of disguise, may, in fact, provide the opportunity to do a little devouring. Grandmother dressed up as wolf has more legitimate access to the tender, forbidden, little Red Riding Hood/Angélique and Corinthe/Robbe-Grillet may himself be the devouring monster.

Angélique returns in the theoretical discussion of the Kojève lectures on Hegel taking the form of the void that gives the golden ring its form. The golden ring is femininity as both lack or castration *and* as opening, nonself-reflecting center and new possibilities. The Angélique motif, the vertiginous seduction and subsequent punishment of the very young and fragile feminine—or punishment and seduction as the text invaginates to make relations of cause and effect reversible—recurs both directly and indirectly. It is present in the metaphors of the female sexual organs, for example, in the descriptions of the hollows and faults ("creux") in the burning logs of monstrous origin ("la monstrueuse souche de chêne qui brûlait dans l'âtre," p. 31) in the monumental hall of the paternal house where Corinthe meets the father.

Other intertextual and/or Freudian references (from Les Gommes, Le Voyeur, Djinn) are brought together in the description of the mobile bridge crossed on the adolescent's cycle route to school. The two halves of the oscillating mobile platform of the drawbridge create a turbulent empty space or opening (a "faille houleuse," p. 17) "plunging" toward the water and forming disturbing parted metallic lips that recall the red hole of the subtitle of Djinn ("un trou rouge entre les pavés disjoints" [a red hole between the paving-stones]) and the various holes and mouths that gape with dangerous fascination throughout Robbe-Grillet's work. This description may be also an ironic "homage" to the work of the critic Ricardou, who has characterized the quay that "plunges into the water" at the beginning of Le Voyeur as a generator of the hidden sexual crime. Robbe-Grillet has recently adopted the metaphor of a bridge to describe himself and his position in the world, ever moving forward—if toward decline—and refusing to look back on a past that would, thereby, like Eurydice, turn to ruins.[10] However, Proustian red holes between the paving-stones cause the walker to stumble as memory looms up through the mist. We recall, that the assassin and the rose are brought together on the paving-stones of a bridge in the night city in a description of a Magritte painting that serves as intertextual generator in Robbe-Grillet's *La Belle Captive*—a work consisting of Robbe-Grillet texts generated by reproductions of Magritte's paintings, the text of which is reproduced in *Souvenirs du triangle d'or*. In these factitious or intertextual scenes, there is often a self-conscious staging of the stereotype of brutal or criminal virility that, however distanced, is nonetheless not without affective or sexual charge. This is the case, for example, of the description of the father's heavy boots pacing the fragile hollows and holes in the paving-stones in the "hall of weapons" (the "salle d'armes"). This is a secret room of virile fraternity of monumental and Oedipal dimensions with its monstrous log/origin burning in the fireplace, a hall from which the son is excluded by the father. The violence implicit in the stereotyped symbolism of the dichotomous and arousing difference between the sexes (force, fragility), prepared for by the description of Angélique as "little" flame, also underlies the subsequent "confession" of the narrator who recalls the rag doll-victim the child carries up the monumental staircase to bed "soumise et molle à souhait" (p. 31) [as submissive and soft as could be desired], who will struggle, but only a little, like "undulating" seaweed "abandoned" to the waves. The assiduous reader of Robbe-Grillet will hear the textual echoes (from *Un Régicide* and *Un Voyeur* among many other novels) but may also see this doll as posing the question of the truth of the two porcelain dolls, victims of various tortures, that staged the young Alain's sadistic anal stage in *Le Miroir qui revient*. Is the childhood doll a "real" porcelain or rag doll? Is this doll perhaps a variant of the toy or "plaything" ("le jouet") "who submits to all my caprices" ("jouet, petite souris frémissante entre les griffes d'un chat, tendre poupée de chair soumise à tous mes caprices, sans défense, ne s'animant que pour mon plaisir," p. 58 [a toy, a little quivering mouse between the claws of a cat, a tender flesh and blood doll, submitting to all my whims, defenseless, coming to life only for my pleasure]), that is, the Spanish Republican female spy captured by the army and commented on by Robbe-Grillet's parents ("She deserves what she gets") who plays both an autobiographical and a fictional role in the textual *Angélique*?

In the theoretical metatext, Robbe-Grillet articulates pretensions to freedom and absolute and transgressive power. He makes the claim that the writer is the only god of this universe, and the monstrous ego ("son moi propre," p. 35 [his own ego]) is the unique possible source of meaning. The artist whose self is "singular, monstrous, solitary" ("singulier," "monstrueux," "solitaire," p. 35), an incomparable creative source of meaning, is the "last man." His "criminal" project is one of information rather than of meaning, that is, it signifies, for Robbe-Grillet, by means of the unexpected, by interior distances, shocks, and contradictions. It also creates information through the metacommentaries that break and frustrate empathy with the narrative and the metalepsis or sliding between levels of real and represented, or between (reversible) cause and effect that disrupt traditional reading practices. At the level of the fiction, Robbe-Grillet manipulates the competing narrative voices and assumes omniscience "Et voilà maintenant que je porte sa faux . . . se dit mon père," p. 47 [And now I'm carrying his scythe {. . .} my father said to himself], referring, in this case, to the grim reaper. His is the power to select and orchestrate the correlatives of the feminine—the little flame, the frail feet, the bent neck, the reddish-gold hair streaming like seaweed floating in the water—and the masculine—giant size, lance, prancing stallion. He justifies his violent or sado-erotic elements metatextually as the liberating freedom to expose and play with those images that enchant him. Yet even at the level of the metatextual commentary where his analytical critical voice is most often uncontested, the narrator discovers certain limits to his omnipotence. He confesses that he does not know where his text originates, where it will take him, or just how his tapestries will play out to construct, for example, his table of contents.

The questions of origins and ends and of the power or impotence of the writer and reader are posed most dramatically by the recurring presence of Angélique. She reappears in the guise of the Princess Aicha in a textual animation of an illustration of the rituals of capital punishment practiced in seventeenth-century Turkey. The long, dramatic account of her torture, deflowering, and quartering is justified as originating in a book of historical documentation. Again, a "true" story told to the adult narrator by a friend returning from the Atlas Mountains in Tunisia, a story of a young bride punished for her apparent nonvirginity by quartering, provides an external origin and alibi for these suspect stories of the beautiful, innocent, and guilty young victim. Brunehaut, another avatar of the punished maiden, dragged radiant through the primitive forest tied to the tail of the wild stallion, "alabaster among the flames," originates, it is claimed, in a childhood reading of Henri Martin's *Histoire de France*. The young woman pursued and devoured by dogs (bitten on the thighs, raped, and served at dinner in Uruguay in the exaggerated version in which the suspected fascist Henri de Corinthe is implicated) comes from a tale by Boccaccio discovered in the childhood attic at Kerangoff and from Robbe-Grillet's own previous version of this story in his film, *Le Jeu avec le feu.* The story of the capture of the young woman spy by male army officers has its origin in an illustration in a work on the Spanish civil war seen as a child in a bookstore on the Boulevard Saint-Michel, an illustration commented on by the twelve-year-old Alain's parents. The gentle father's unexpectedly savage recommendations for the treatment of the young Republican by her captors both suggest the unconscious violence against the female other lurking in all "men" and serve, once again, as an outside and collective origin for the variations on the theme of the "seductive" female as natural male plaything deserving her punishment. Other intertextual sources cited or referred to within the text include the operas of Wagner and Verdi, Claude Simon's novel, *La Route des Flandres*, Delacroix's *Massacres à Scio* and *La Mort de Sardanaple*, Ingres' *Roger délivrant Angélique*, a romantic painting in the writer's room of a knight on a white horse piercing a piece of bloodied gossamer fabric with the point of his lance, an abstractly violent impressionist-expressionist painting by Lovis Corinth, and Flaubert's massacres at Carthage in *Salammbô*. Robbe-Grillet's metatextual commentary claims that these are, indeed, the outside "generators" of his work, evidence for the stereotyped character of his sado-erotic thematics and of Angélique as everybody's fantasies.

Yet even if the abstract violent red triangles of Lovis Corinth's artistic creations were to be superimposed on the insipid illustration of a white horse that actually hangs in Robbe-Grillet's study-bedroom,[11] the image would still be very different from those that proliferate in the writer's universe. The suspect fascination with absolute barbaric cruelty and power on the one hand, with submissive suffering on the other that Robbe-Grillet detects in Delacroix, that painter's fascination with the odalisque or sex slave or the voluptuous sequestered spaces of the harem that mark the Western imagination of the Orient are considerably transformed again in the writer's reworking of these textual generators. This is also the case in Robbe-Grillet's use of Ingres' painting "Roger Freeing Angélique." Here, once again, he alters what he interprets as the unconscious seduction exerted on the painter by the voluptuous curves of the sacrificial victim. In Robbe-Grillet's versions of this painting, the hero's piercing lance is clearly turned less toward the monster than toward the "guilty" young female victim. And in a second (in)version or invagination in his stories, the monster's fascinating devouring mouth is simply another side of Angélique.

In the father's story of his secret wartime mission on 20 November 1914, just before he is seriously wounded in an ambush, he catches a glimpse of a young blond woman on a cart, marked with a cross. This story is transformed by the imagination of the twelve-year-old son and, "in another version" (or inversion),

in order, apparently, to ward off or protect himself from "the wound" the father suffers, the diaphanous and innocent young angel is made the prisoner
and victim, her "frail" wrists bound and her "delicate" feet "cruelly" wounded
at each jolt of the cart by a bed of thorns. The Christian references suggest
that Angélique is a mediating sacrificial victim, a heroic scapegoat in René
Girard's sense,[12] protecting certain necessary social distinctions and limits by
her death. But all women (Angélica and Carmina, the fair, diaphanous angel
and the flaming witch) turn out to be angels of death and to deserve their
punishment. They are shown to be justifiably at the mercy of the voyeur (writer
or reader) or potential executioner fearing feminine enchantment.

Other assemblages still modify the fairy story to make it one of the innocent
soldier Simon escorting the dangerously seductive prisoner Carmina through
the forest on 20 November, or of Corinthe, who setting out in pursuit of the
soldier becomes lost in the labyrinths of an enchanted forest that has neither
center nor exit where he is led by the songbird to rescue the false sprite,
Manrica/Carmina, imprisoned in the spring. The narration of the sequel adventure slips from third to first persons, from masculine Corinthe, galloping
on his white horse pursued by the triangular pack of Freudian wolves in a
dreamlike snow-stained landscape, to a pretended feminine first person,
Manrica, frozen with fear in "my" arms, clinging to "my" breast, and repeating a patchwork of ironic intertextual invocations to the father-reader ("Ayez
pitié, Seigneur" [Have pity, Master]). These derive from Goethe's poem, the
Erlkönig, but, more particularly, evoke Robbe-Grillet's own distinctively sado-
erotic thematic complex. "Ne reconnais-tu pas la morsure des loups, le sang
qui coule sur ma triste chemise blanche, ma chair déchirée contre toi?" [Don't
you recognize the bite of the wolves, the blood that flows on my unfortunate
white shift, my torn flesh against you?]. The now familiar Freudian/Lacanian
text connoting incestuous impulse makes another appearance to end this passage: "Et ne vois-tu pas comme je brûle?" (p. 120) [Don't you see I'm burning?]. Are these indeed "feminine" fantasies? In any case, the apparently female voice speaks a traditional Freudian masochistic identification with her
own Oedipal desires for the father. In Les Derniers Jours de Corinthe, Angélique/
Marianic, the pubescent beach-ball-playing seductress is hired out to Corinthe
by her own father, the Professor Van der Reeves.

At the end of Angélique, a final spellbinding and virtuoso narrative weaves
similar thematics together—the very young virgin captive at the mercy of the
hero's lance and/or perverse seductress, dominating the sado-erotic sexual game
even in pretended vulnerability and shed blood and finally punished by death.
The story, it is claimed, is the tale of the "real" seductress of the innocent

young Alain, Angèle/Angélique von Arno; a story of childhood sexual initiation told by Robbe-Grillet to his editor and friend, Jérome Lindon. Angélique's story recounts games of Roman master and Christian slave, initiated, in fact, by the adolescent girl, who projects her responsibility for sexual transgression on her manipulated male partner. An apparently formative scene in which menstrual blood imagined to be the blood of a forbidden deflowering stains the young girl's thighs, arousing the adolescent male, would provide a "real" origin for the proliferation of images of wounding, of red blood on the white bodies of young mannequins or young women that occur in almost all the films and fictions after *Projet*. However, the exhibitionist scene at the Opera at the end of *Angélique* in which Corinthe, surrounded by S.S. officers, publicly stages the wounded bleeding pubis of his partner among the inevitable shattered glass fragments of symbolic penetrating violence and before the cultural elite of Parisian society casts a similar scene as fiction. This fantastic assemblage seems, once again, to be an ironic and literary self-staging, a simultaneous self unmasking and masking (one Robbe-Grillet hides another) as much as a revelation. Elsewhere, the reader is informed that Angélique von Arno is a historical personage, the fourteen-year-old mother superior of Port Royal.

Like the Breton cart from *Angélique* that carries the knowing, manipulating young heroine to her final resting place, Angèle's suspicious death from drowning (the naked body discovered along the Léon coast) recalls other texts. Earlier textual/sexual victims of the monstrous seaman or marine monster ("le monstre marin") who "devours little girls" in *Le Miroir qui revient* include the punished and drowned Violette in *Le Voyeur* (flower/woman/little rape, virgin-victim thrown to the sea monster for the rites of spring or witch with the devil in her), the innocent and diaphanous Marie-Ange van der Reeves, the fiancée-spirit (or vampire) who disappeared during an underwater harpooning expedition organized by Corinthe (*La Belle captive*), the spirit Djinn, victim of Jean/Simon le Coeur (*Djinn*), and once again, the drowned Angélique whose reproachful face appears in the returning mirror of *Le Miroir qui revient*.

The counterimage is the male fear of being made impotent, of being the enchanted, devoured, or drowned victim of the siren, the songbird, the sylphide, the precocious child-woman. This is linked in *Le Miroir* with the nightmares of the child caught in the sinusoidal waves and deep rock pools, sucked down to drown while his mother watches from the other side of the red curtains, or with the image of the seaman lost in the mother/the sea ("le marin péri en mer") at the end of *Angélique*. The scene of the barely adolescent boy cursed by the bleeding and controlling young Angèle is a variant of these scenes. In *Les Derniers Jours de Corinthe*, both the treacherous sea and the seductive and manipulative child-woman recur in a number of such vertiginous experiences.

Beyond language game and intertextuality, such selections, repetitions, and variations are both the writer's accounts of his own (individuated) "coming out," his fears and fantasies, his implication in a very specific sadomasochistic "battle of the sexes" and also the staging of the ideology in power, including its hidden fears of the apparently dangerously sexual female body and of feminine takeover. The narrator-Robbe-Grillet contends, however, that the question "Who am I?" turns out to be a question of structure and not a question of meaning. And if there is a confession, claims the metatext, it is without guilt or repentance: "Je connais mieux que la plupart des pervers les monstres sanglants qui m'habitent, et je n'en éprouve ni culpabilité ni repentir" (p. 192) [I'm better acquainted than most perverts with the bloody monsters that dwell within me and they cause me neither guilt nor repentance].

Robbe-Grillet seems to be insisting that this self-conscious knowledge enables him to be a player rather than a pawn in life's game. Is Angelica/Enchantment, then, merely a ludic double metaphor? Or is there a meaning to this "complementary" apposition? Why do figures of the detective or questing hero in Robbe-Grillet turn out to be doubled or replaced by the imprisoned or threatened criminal? Why does the fascination and fear of being victim of a charm, submerged or lost in the rhythms of the caressing or swelling sea, have the second face of the defensive punishment and suppression of the female body? Might it be that although the writer fights to stay within the symbolic, in control, at some level, what tempts him is the limen, regression and loss?

The battle that Robbe-Grillet stages is characterized by what Jessica Benjamin in her study of the master-slave relationship calls "rationalized violence."[13] Rationalized here refers not to the motive for the violence but to its calculated, ritualized form of expression. The fantasy of erotic domination and control and of its opposite, ecstatic self-loss in absolute submission (even unto death), pervades the texts of Western culture, the Mystico-Religious text, the Political text, female Romance Fiction, and the Pornographic. Violence is, for Benjamin, a derivative of the desire to achieve the differentiation that derives from both necessary autonomy, and the recognition by the other necessary to achieve this autonomy.

In Hegel's analysis of the master-slave relationship, selfhood, existing for oneself, desiring, is an effect of existing for another, of the other's desire, and of being able to affect another by one's acts. To attain this recognition and to obtain the sexual gratification dependent on the other, the self gives up its earliest Freudian fantasy of self, that is, of omnipotence, and accepts dependency in return for connection with and recognition from the (m)other or earliest caregiver. Benjamin argues that, in an individualistic society, the developmental and psychological process of recognizing the Other as real, of connecting with another erotic being in order to feel erotically alive oneself, is paradoxically more difficult and can create a sense of isolation and unreality.

"Violence acquires its importance in erotic fantasy as an expression of the desire to break out of this numbing encasement."[14] Sadomasochistic ceremonies of the control or devouring of the other are not then an apology for male violence in general, claims Benjamin, but an attempt to replay ritually the never totally relinquished desire for omnipotence, or the desire to remain safely autonomous by substituting subjugation of the other for connection. At the other pole, the need for recognition leads to the obliteration of self. To escape from this conflict, the Hegelian desire for omnipotence (the self-consciousness that wants to be recognized by the other in order to make itself the world) and dependency on the other for recognition, says Benjamin, "It is all too tempting to imagine that one can become independent without recognizing the other person as an equally autonomous agent. [. . .] One need only imagine that the other person is not separate — she belongs to me, I control and possess her."[15]

The rituals of consenting domination and submission serve, as Benjamin sees it, to allow one partner to uphold the limits of rationality and control and allow the other to risk her/his separateness and approach self-loss and psychic death. And some vicarious identification with this limit, visibly experienced in the body by the other, is possible from the position of control. Sexual eroticism, or the fantasy of rational violence, as heirs to religious eroticism, offer, for Benjamin, a controlled form of transcendence, the promise of the real thing.

What might be most likely to be concealed in such a contemporary mirror are the earliest and symbiotic relationships of the child to the "mother," the pleasure of absolute protection and dyadic fusion in self-loss; the simultaneous unpleasure, humiliation, and rage of complete dependence or the disappointment with the mother who cannot meet the child's absolute demands. Or, perhaps, again, the later anxiety of separation, the necessary renunciation of the powerless preferred loved object in favor of the father's powerful law. Such a classical duality of the relation with the feminine, the love-hate of an intense affective bond with the angelic-diabolical mother could provide an interpretive frame that would account for much that appears both as experiential and as sociohistorical in the Robbe-Grillet autobiographical mirror. This reading would consider that the thematics of violence against the female body (the suppression of the mother's parts in a bid for autonomy or self-engendering), like the texts of Sade, constitute an act of revenge on the first mother. There is, of course, no clear reading of the scenes in which Robbe-Grillet depicts a mother silently censorious of brute male sexuality and of her son's emerging sexual (sadistic) orientations, no single reading of the curious scene of the (vampire?) mother sheltering a tame bat under her blouse. Within the frame of the close-knit and devoted family of childhood, the mother (whom the son suspects of secret lesbian preferences) may have indeed posed the questions of sexual difference and sexual identity and aroused a need for self-assertion in the child. The power of the mother's words, her fervent right-wing convictions strengthened by an experience of teaching in Germany, and her misguided readings of history and subsequent refusal to admit the existence of the Holocaust may have led to a certain ideological reaction. Yet, as in the textual relation between the fantasmatical figure of Count Corinthe and the "real" father, Angélique turns out to be a creature of very different stuff from the real-life mother, Yvonne Canu.

The splitting of the ego in the compulsion to repeat takes one of two directions, sadistic or masochistic. The sadistic child uses omnipotence by identifying with his original other (mother) and actively directing the same treatment at another, thereby repressing his original, dependent, impotent position. The masochistic child achieves this repression by actively seeking a repetition of his passive position in relation to the original other. At the deepest unconscious level, however, these conflicting structures coexist, ungendered. Melanie Klein's elaboration of the Freudian thesis that the sadist is also a masochist insists that this conflict is ultimately played out between Thanatos and the ego; Lacan's concept is of consciousness that becomes fascinated by the image of the ego reflected by the other and no longer sees what the ego is. Indeed, seeing (the self or the other), in Robbe-Grillet, turns out to be more complex than we thought. We are in a postmythical paradigm, after Adam, Actaeon, and Psyche, where seeing and knowing are no longer necessarily loss and death, in an Eden after the Fall. It is the void of self that makes the look problematical; the look organized by the sadist to freeze the siren, to know her, is victim of its object, is the object. No one, claims Lacan, possesses the gaze (the Phallus); the look is necessarily castration and lack. Consciousness is constituted as in phenomenology as consciousness of its object. And all that is left on the side of the subject-observer is the intentional part of intentional consciousness, intent in this case to maintain distance and separation and resist enchantment.

Robbe-Grillet's representations of aggression against the opposite gender, like Marguerite Duras' violence against the feminine self are both clearly modeled by the ideology in power. Yet Angélique is an exploration of the traces that suggest imprisonments within formative and surrounding texts and within early "experiential" knowledge and the unconscious.

The golden ring in *Angélique* represented by the half-opened lips of Carmina is also the O shaped by the mouth of the writer himself as he creates distortions of his own image before the narcissistic mirror in his study-bedroom where everything begins. The negative heroes, usurpers, criminals, and narcissistic subversives that he projects himself into, most often through the figure of Corinthe, are, in the final instance, themselves shaped by this O that circumscribes a void in which the masculine and feminine coexist.

Angélique, ethereal angel, virgin sylphide, songbird, and flower-child, Justine, exerts the enchantment of difference on the narrator. But enchantment is feared as dangerous identification, or as a doubling, or as incest, and finally seen as perfidious. Angelica is also Violette, "fauvette" (little wild animal), Dalila or enemy agent poisoning the wine, fatal Carmen, flaming witch, for whom the knights do battle and die. Consequently, she is made to assume guilt for her own penetration, wounding, and suppression. And as in the classical dualistic sadomasochistic relation, it is the sadist who believes "he" is the cruelly persecuted or manipulated victim, the masochist who believes "she" is guilty, in an inversion.[16]

Only the "masculine" narrators see ("dérobent") and speak of enchantment. Neither Angèle nor Angélique nor Angélica has a voice to tell her own story or to situate herself outside this nonreversible sadomasochistic duality where she stands inevitably at the masochistic pole. She can only plead for mercy ("Ayez pitié"). The long portrait of the bloody "grande Catherine," it is true, is situated at the sadistic pole in hyperbolic sexual appetite and cruelty, but this is a curious and jarringly unpleasant hyperbolic portrait with obvious references to Catherine Robbe-Grillet's role as a dominatrix and to the monstrosity of women who assume power. "La grande Catherine" shares the devouring sex mouth of the female victims who elsewhere deserve punishment; she is, however, no longer enchantment and does not call for her own suppression. It is perhaps not without significance that Robbe-Grillet wrote the preface to his wife's first novel, *L'Image*, a staging of masochistic fantasies but did not contribute to the account of her later experiences as dominatrix in *Cérémonies des femmes*.

In any case, although there is complicity between the feminine masochist character in Robbe-Grillet's works and her masculine aggressor-narrator, this does not seem to be true of the relation between the masculine narrator and "La grande Catherine." The androgynous figures of Frédéric de Boncourt, blond "angel" and gentleman-soldier, or indeed, of Angélique, disguised daughter-soldier, breasts bound and member of the Waffen S.S., do not appear to offer serious alternatives to Enchantment, that is, to the seduction of the feminine side of the self. However, this feminine side can be approached only as the dangerous other, as duality, held by the text at a protective distance or seen as chaotic nature to be suppressed by the orders of culture. What does emerge in Robbe-Grillet's textual fragments in both autofictions is the underlying assertion of a distance, the defense against absorption by this fascinating and needed other, this parent who is "myself taking form," inevitably introjected and absorbed.

However much Robbe-Grillet's text is reluctant to consciously relinquish a certain control within existing (male) orders, however fraught with contradictions the problems of the relation between feminine text and male author, something in the writer is carried beyond himself in the process of the staging of his fantasies and their reorganization in new complementary and nonlinear, recursive forms. In both the content and the structure there is a movement between text alone and something carried by the text that derives clearly from the body. In *Angélique*, the writer, lost in "the eternal maze of organs," realizes that in spite of his strong theoretical positions and his lucid deconstructions, he is incapable of really knowing the import of what he writes.

Marx shifted emphasis from Hegel's philosophical and static ahistorical master-slave dialectic to a more dynamic historical model permitting change. While the surfaces of the Robbe-Grillet text situate Angélique as object of control and the male narrator as controlling, a position that corresponds, not coincidentally, to women's socialization to censor resistance or competition in favor of self-sacrifice and connection, the mobile complementary structures suggest the necessity of movement beyond any model of gender-specific psychic structures fixed at opposite poles.

At the level of the metacommentaries, Robbe-Grillet's analysis of his myth of the feminine as the triumph of the young and beautiful, smooth, female face over the wrinkles of time and anguish (virility is worn marked, and femininity smooth) seems to be, indeed, close to cultural stereotype. His declared personal preference for what he calls Latin vines ("lianes") over German "Walkyries" and for the smile of feminine eternal youth over the grimaces of masculine time again seems close enough to cliché to leave the reader confused. Yet the defensive or strategic character of these ratiocinations is, in fact, explicitly admitted by the metatextual commentary and thereby defused/excused.

However, the writer's defense of his collaboration with Guido Crépax' comic-book version of *Histoire d'O* or his preface to Garnon's *La Nouvelle Justine* on the grounds of the modernity of their aggressive, discontinuous frames and antirealist freedoms and his interest in the pornographic as subversive ignores the questions of self-loss in cold, glossy, infinitely reflecting postmodern surfaces or, indeed, of the sadomasochistic dualities in their thematics. At the level of the énoncé in *Angélique*, the apparently transgressive and subversive staging of the angel in the mirror simply makes existing orders of sexual power manifest with the masculine at the pole of domination or power and the feminine (only apparently powerful), subdued or fixed at the pole of powerlessness. Like Corinthe in *Le Miroir*, if the writer sees himself appear in the returning mirror in the guise of Angélique (the feminine), he also sees his own death, the death of the rearing white horse, that is, of the powerful male sexual principle. At the level of the thematics, he therefore refuses the risks of reversal of the masculine and feminine poles or of their telescoping, and chooses to suppress enchantment. At the level of the metatext, he proclaims the inevitability of the battle of the sexes and sustains the dualistic relations of power in place.

At the level of the textual structures, however, it does seem the case that Robbe-Grillet's criminal art subverts old textual orders (of genre and of narrative) and introduces new nondualistic "complementary" forms and "chaotic" structures (similar to the disordered order of complex systems that chaos theory describes). And, in the final instance, the self explored/staged through its own fictions and histories turns out, like the angel, to be both a textual and a sexual production; both "essence" in the De Lauretis sense (individual difference) and ideological construction (ready-made text), both autobios and graphy, and potentially, both masculine and feminine. These selves in the self may be different or contradictory but not mutually exclusive. The mirror (of writing) alone permits cathartic recognition of the nature of the enchantments of Angélica by turning these to stone, that is, to representations (text is not life) that manifest imprisonments and fear of impotence. At the same time, breathing life into these representations, it opens up the possibility of the coextensive assumption of more than one position, permits a movement back and forth, in a space at the uncertain margins between the *énonciation* and the *énoncé*. In this contradictory but not mutually exclusive space where enchantment, that is, the power or powerlessness of Angélique, represents a possible position even for the male and not a trap of usurped occult fatal power, enchantment (Angélique, the feminine, the new hybrid autofictional text) might come to embody the transforming power of writing rather than the rewriting of power.

Nathalie Sarraute

six

VOICE(S) IN NATHALIE SARRAUTE'S *ENFANCE* AND THE SEX OF THE TEXT

Enfance stands at the intersection of autobiography and novel, in what Sarraute describes as a "more spontaneous, more direct and freer"[1] form, between speech and writing and in close relationship to drama. The "grain" of Nathalie Sarraute's own voice, to borrow Roland Barthes' striking term, is physically present as pitch, stress, intonation, and color in the talking book version of the work the writer herself recorded. In the Barrault Company's stage adaptation at the Théâtre du Rond Point, Paris, in 1985, the play of the voice of the actress evoking childhood again held center stage.

These audible voices in the text that call upon the sounds and rhythms of the human voice and of textual syntax are metaphors at once of being and of language. They can be situated theoretically somewhere between textuality and Derrida's phonocentrism (deriving from Western logocentrism, phono-centrism, for Derrida, erroneously assumes an absolute proximity or congru-ence of voice and being). History is not completely erased in a pure play of anonymous present text as the voices of the past, of mother, father, and step-mother, of books read, are recalled to life through dialogic interactions in a distinctive text/texture. Yet the speaking voices and the voices in the text are those of the actress and of the storyteller, that is, of personae with masks and selected tones of voice rather than of persons. Sarraute's writing is situated over the threshold of that modernity[2] in which "words ceased to intersect with representations and to provide a spontaneous grid for the knowledge of things,"[3] and where, in a crisis of metaphysical philosophy, the narrative function loses its foundations, "the great hero, the great perils, the great quests, and the great goal."[4]

Nathalie Sarraute claims no allegiance to the theoretical thought (Derrida, Lyotard, Lacan, Barthes, Foucault, Deleuze) that has been labelled postmod-

*Nathalie Sarraute as a
very alert baby. Taken in
Russia around 1903. Photo
from Editions Gallimard,
Paris; courtesy of Nathalie
Sarraute.*

ern in the Anglo-American literary world. Nonetheless, the major topologies of postmodernism, as defined by Alice Jardine, for example, in her study of French "modernité" (*Gynesis*)—the breakdown of the conscious Cartesian subject, the deconstruction of mimesis (the text as a copy or representation of an original experience) and of dialectical thinking, the questioning of man's Truth, the denaturalizing of our "master" narratives and the interest in what eluded them (their nonknowledge)—correlate closely with the new narrative strategies practiced in the Sarrautean *roman* and in her new autobiography.

To begin then close to the conclusion, it is evident that these audible voices reading a text are not simply the elderly woman, Nathalie Sarraute, speaking in her own voice in any naive fashion. Nor are the dramatic voices in the text, the "characters"—who in this autobiographical work are also "implied" authors if the classical autobiographical pact of identity between writer and character is considered to be operative—an unproblematical demonstration of a complex but ultimately unified authorial self. At the level of the structural organization of *Enfance*, the curious splitting of the narrator into two different dialoguing "voices" makes this manifest.

Some definition of the literary notion of "voice" is called for. Aristotle's classical idea of the "ethos" that enables an orator to establish a personal and convincing image could serve as a starting point. In modern critical thought, Pound's "persona" and Yeats's "mask" imply self-conscious, distanced, and dramatic or lyric voice. Booth's use of the term "implied author," defined as an ideal, literary, created version of "the real man," both conveys a sense of a human presence and insists on the separation between the character and the actual author. Such an implied author, according to Paul Kane, is closest to "that sense of authorial presence which helps shape our response to the work" that is "generally what is meant by voice"[5] in current idiom. Without the speaking tones of such voice and the implicit (real or ideal) audience that addressing voice creates, literature would lack the drama that brings it to life. As an indispensable critical term to describe certain dramatic properties of texts and of reader response to sensed presence in texts, a notion that critics are unwill-

Nathalie Sarraute as a young child. Photo from Éditions Gallimard, Paris; courtesy of Nathalie Sarraute.

ing to give up without resistance, voice continues to be generally if somewhat idiosyncratically employed in literary criticism despite the questions posed by postmodern critical theory.

For voice as transcendent self-presence, as a moment of consciousness when speaking and thought, language and meaning, knowing and being, seem one ("presence of the object, presence of meaning to consciousness, self-presence in so-called living speech and in self-consciousness") has been powerfully put into question by Derrida.[6] Postmodern theory has rendered this conventional metaphor of a Western tradition preeminently based on a metaphysics of presence problematical. Voice is a founding metaphor of Western thought but in the postmodern idiom (where metaphor is never innocent), voice can no longer be self-evidently a form of presence, or an organizing center. Presence itself, for Derrida, is always already self-divided, a matter of "différance" (that is, of the mechanisms of difference and deferral of the sign system that mediates it).[7] Nathalie Sarraute's voices, products of her situation in what she was to proclaim well before Derrida as "the age of suspicion,"[8] are unlikely to be innocent guarantors of traditional authorial unity and presence.

Two gender-marked voices speak in *Enfance* to create an oppositional self-divided, but shifting and sometimes merging dialogue. An analytical and critical speaker marked by masculine grammatical agreements ("grandiloquent" and "outrecuidant," p. 10) comments on the incompleteness and possible falsifications of the second voice; questions, quibbles, and contradicts. Was the memory really accurate? Did the parents or the child really feel that way? This self-assured voice is characterized by Cartesian rationality, exactitude, and critical distance most particularly in the analysis of the mother's verbal behavior. The second first person voice that moves between the responses of the writer-interlocutor in the present ("je me suis un peu laissée aller," p. 21 [I allowed myself to get a little carried away]) and the words of the young Natacha of the past ("elle m'a vue venir," p. 24 [she saw me coming] and "je suis morte," p. 29 [I'm dead]) is marked by feminine agreements in both roles. What we will call this "feminine" voice, despite Sarraute's own reluctance to accept that her texts are in any way gendered, evokes the welling up and irruption of tropistic psychological movement. Seeking to recover buried memories and feelings in the present of sensation, it attempts to reconstruct the child's passionate childhood desire for the mother's warm and soft presence, the huge prestige and power of the mother's words, the fear of rejection by both mother and stepmother and the simultaneous attempts at self-affirmation and separation from this fascination.

The judgmental and interruptive character of the first voice is most evident in its prompting of this second interlocutor, addressed by the familiar form "tu," to impose definitions, make judgments, push her investigations to clear conclusions, and heed his more rational arguments as a means of arriving at knowledge. This logical and incisive "masculine" (or, at the least, universal or neutral, that is, not marked for the feminine) voice appears to have less sentient knowledge than the "I" ("je") and to stand at a greater distance from the events evoked. It is not without significance that the adjectives that reveal his grammatical gender are "presumptuous" ("outrecuidant," p. 10) and "grandiloquent" ("grandiloquent," p. 10). Nor is it clear whether this attribution derives from the resistance of the second voice to his interrogation, or from the author herself as she oversees and organizes the debate between the two voices. In spite of his probing and apparent rightness as he urges the narrator toward lucid judgments of the mother's indifference, the stepmother's neurosis, and the child's fear of abandon and hurt at lack of love, he has no monopoly on the complex truths of the situations on which he attempts to impose closure and definitive judgment.

The response of critical readers to these dramatic voices in the text has been interestingly contradictory. For Gaetan Brulotte who categorizes the two voices as respectively negative and positive, it is the second voice of the disordered flux of emotion, of the felt, and of passion that is the "authentic" voice, operating at the level of masks removed. The first voice is heard as unauthentic, as a reflexive consciousness or "super-narrator," who, like the superego, speaks the language of order, of social knowledge, and of convention. Censuring any affective coloring in his speech, and only occasionally identifying with his interlocutor by speaking of "Maman" [Mama] rather than "ta mère" [your mother], this "super-narrator," claims Brulotte, employing a Sarraute metaphor, "is to the narrator what the freeway is to the virgin forest. It follows a path laid out already."[9]

Françoise van Roey-Roux, a critic committed to the notions of self-awareness and truth, and to a traditional frame of voice and expression as presence and mimesis, prefers to identify with the voice that acquires its validity from cognition. She hears it as "attentive, sensitive but firm," therapeutic in its expression and lucid assumption of the truths of the past.[10] For Van Roey-Roux, the "masculine" voice, characterized as the voice of the psychotherapist, is the more authentic.

My quarrel with this interpretation is that it postulates the goal of the work to be just such a clear and therapeutic expression or representation of the truth of childhood family relationships, whereas the possibility of expression, lucidity, and truth seem to me to be precisely what is at stake in the debate between the dialoguing voices. In an open discussion following her public reading of the early scene of the child's slashing of the silken sofa at Wellesley College in Massachusetts in late 1986, I asked Nathalie Sarraute whether she had reached a deeper understanding of her relationships with her family by writing *Enfance*. Her reply (also of course subject to "suspicion") was a categorical "no."

What both Van Roey-Roux and Brulotte have recognized is that figures of authenticity (or unauthenticity) lie at the heart of Sarraute's new autobiography. This topos of authenticity is a central one in modern French writing, from Gide's interrogation of the difficulties of sincerity and self-knowledge to Sartre's preoccupation with self-deceptive "mauvaise foi." In his own autobiography, *Les Mots*, for example, Sartre watches himself from the future and without indulgence playing out the role of the infant prodigy that his grandfather imagines him to be. *Enfance* evokes a similar scene in which the young Natacha is called upon to recite a sentimental child's poem for admiring adult guests. Beyond such self-irony and, indeed, beyond narcissism, it is the inner sense of uneasiness with which Natacha conforms to the role of sweet and clever child that Sarraute strives to capture in words. Natacha's feelings of being misrecognized are further developed in the scene of her fascination with the folk story, *The Prince and the Pauper*, and her identification with both Edward the "true" heir, unrecognized and mocked, and Tom the imposter, surrounded by respectful but watchful courtiers. Tom, unsure of the customs of the land and likely to betray himself by drinking from the finger bowl, feels he is an outsider.

In other scenes, the gap takes the form of the child's sense of guilt for not being a normal child, that is, conforming to the ready-made model of a child: "Je n'étais pas un enfant qui aime sa mère. Pas comme doit être un enfant" (p. 97) [I wasn't a child who loves its mother. Not like a child should be]. It is perhaps the case that feelings of being unnatural, the confession of her apparently anomalous suspicious probing and her critical "ideas" ("Le mal était en moi," p. 97 [The disease was in me]) in the search for recognition whose second contradictory face is indeed a sense of being different and beyond common words, are still as much issues for the writer as for the child she once was.

In *L'Etranger*, founding text of French modernity, the protagonist Meursault is also synonymous with the outsider, with the (impossible) attempt to live beyond the alienation or unauthenticity of learned emotional responses and traditional social ceremonies of life, death, and justice. He has discovered foreignness, even violence, at the heart of that to which he is most attached, the sun, the sea, the life of the senses. Meursault too, I would suggest, like Nathalie Sarraute's narrative voices, discovers ambivalence in the figure of the mother, in the mother's learned wisdom ("on finissait par s'habituer à tout," *L'Etranger*, p. 120 [you got used to anything]), and in the received wisdom in respect to the mother ("on n'a qu'une mère," *L'Etranger*, p. 12 [you've only one mother]).[11] The similarity of the set phrase used by Natacha's mother to impose customary mother-child relationships and obligations, "Tu n'as au monde qu'une seule Maman" (p. 101) [You've only one Mama in the world] is perhaps not entirely fortuitous.

Alain Robbe-Grillet situates "the man who lies" of his 1966 film *L'Homme qui ment*, a true Resistance hero "because his name is inscribed on the war memorial," but also a collaborator and traitor, at the center of contemporary narration. His own autobiographical alter ego, the hero-imposter Lord Corinthe is a shadowy figure of Resistance or Fascism, heroism or treachery, a sea/sex monster devouring little girls and devoured by the feminine and a complex and rich assemblage of the questing figures of the Western imagination. Other contemporary narratives of imposture abound in which the double becomes indistinguishable from, or even replaces, the original. Fassbinder's 1977 film *Despair*, adaptation of Nabokov's novel, follows a hero who suffers frequent bouts of dissociation, murders his double whom he has persuaded to impersonate him, and finally attempts to persuade the police that he is an actor playing the role of a criminal. Daniel Vigne's commercially successful film, *Le Retour de Martin Guerre* (1982), adapted the literary and predominantly intellectual theme of imposture to tell the "true story" of Arnaud de Tilh (Dépardieu) who impersonated Martin Guerre and persuaded the whole village and even "his" wife (Nathalie Baye) to believe in his imposture until the "true" Martin returned to pose the problem of identity and authenticity. The theme of imposture was of sufficient general interest for Hollywood to remake the French film, setting its version, *Philsby*, in which the imposter is again a truer husband and father than the "real" one, in the period of the American Civil War.

Lack of authenticity has characterized all of Sarraute's fictional characters. Even the solid "Martereau" in the novel to which he gives his name finally begins to tremble and fissure, to become not quite what he seems. The question of authenticity is also the subject of Sarraute's critical study of the work of Flaubert. The pompous, glossy, polished, balanced style, the precision, descriptivity, and rhetoricity of Flaubert's classical language, his portrait of a society, and his construction of images, claims Sarraute, carry beneath them a new psychological substance able to pierce the unauthentic ("percer à jour

. . . l'inauthentique").[12] This lack of authenticity serves nonetheless as a locus from which authentic feelings can proceed. In Sarraute's reading of Flaubert, the most worn-out images and texts of Romanticism are at once recreated authentically by Emma's emotion (le bal de la Vaubyessard) and unmasked by Flaubert as clichés in a "subtle" and "complex" work. Sarraute's account of the complex, even contradictory, relation between style and content, between two different paradigms (classical and modern) in Flaubert's novel, in fact, sheds great light on the nature of the struggle with words in her own writing project. Authenticity in her work, too, would seem to arise in the interplay and differences between an existing unauthentic code and a new authentic substance that can be outlined only in the gaps and holes of the old texts that give them form.

The self of the autobiographical writer is constituted from the common words of the other and their effects, and also from the writer's own original work on words. To evoke memories of childhood, both the first and second voices take voices from the "outside" as their point of departure. The relationship with the stepmother can be partially constituted from what emerges in her words and ready-made phrases; in the rejecting "It isn't your home" ("Ce n'est pas ta maison," p. 127), and the Russian phrase "Tiebia podbrossili" (p. 172) ("On t'a abandonnée" [You've been thrown out/unloaded on me]) that is felt to be so much more wounding than its French translation. Her response to Nathalie's question, "Why can't you do that?" ("Pourquoi on ne peut pas faire ça?") by taking refuge in a commonplace: "Because it isn't done" ("Parce-que ça ne se fait pas," p. 177) and to Nathalie's "Tell me, do you hate me?" ("Dis-moi, est-ce que tu me détestes?" p. 252) with "How can anyone hate a child?" ("Comment peut-on détester un enfant?" p. 253), suggests her bad faith as she resorts to the protective clichés that situate her with normal people and implicitly marginalizes the child while denying her fears. To the stepmother's own words, the text adds words used about her that cumulate evidence for the prosecution. And yet, these ready-made categories also cause the child to "retract" and to "refuse" in a conflict of feelings. The early judgment passed on the stepmother by the mother, "Vera is stupid" ("Véra est bête"), "package" that the child takes away to examine at leisure, is developed in the mother's superior and categorical: "That Vera's not altogether normal . . . it seems she's an hysteric" ("Cette Véra n'est pas tout à fait normale . . . il paraît que c'est une hystérique," pp. 237–38). There is some debate on these disparaging labels within the narrative and some nuancing. Discussing the negative phrase used by Vera to describe the articulate intellectual revolutionaries she hosts so stiffly, "Ils ont bonne opinion de soi" (p.193) [They have a good opinion of themselves], the second voice works to give Vera the benefit of the doubt. It is not, concludes this voice, that Vera is "stupid" and giving vent to her own feelings of inadequacy and inferiority; hers is indeed an informed response to the complacency, self-sufficiency, and self-confidence of the group of men.

The commonplaces of the language do seem to attach to common psychological movements and Sarraute's relationship with her mother is the saga of the movement between the child's early adoring loyalty to that parent's injunctions and a fierce resistance to the hidden control exerted by her words. Cliché confronts cliché: the mother's edict "a child who loves its mother thinks that no one is more beautiful than she" ("un enfant qui aime sa mère trouve que personne n'est plus beau qu'elle," p. 93) is resisted by the irrepressible critical "idea" provoked by the aesthetic epiphany of the doll framed in the shop window—"Elle est plus belle que Maman" (p. 92) [She is more beautiful than Mother] and accompanied by other negative judgments. "Maman a la peau d'un singe" (p. 96) [Mama's skin is like a monkey's].

The second voice could be considered to originate in the emotional tremors emanating from the imaginative recall of these words, voices, and images; to be exploring and reworking the repressed hurt, incomprehension, anxieties, desires, and rebellions of the child in the present as these feelings well up and subside in the movement of the writing. It would be closer to Kristeva's preverbal "semiotic" or Lacan's "imaginary" than to the "symbolic" of language and socialization where we might situate the first interrogative voice. Here, a self-aware nondivided subject in the present of adult fairness and objectivity, seeking critical but also, on occasions, charitable, understanding—of Véra's own insecurities and unmet needs, of the mother's charm—can look back over time at the child and her mother(s) as objects separate from (her)self. The second voice evokes/constitutes the child adult's desire to make contact, to cling, to belong, and to be accepted in the world of the maternal, the warm and the soft; the first is closer to the adult child's (contradictory) need for "masculine" separateness, solitude, and critical independence.

This opposition is evoked in the very first scene of childhood in which the child plunges the pointed ends of the sewing scissors into the beautiful soft floral silk of the sofa on which the two are sitting to lay bare a greyish, flabby matter beneath the slit. The young Natacha responds to the German-speaking governess's prohibition, the firm, insistent, inexorable pressure exercised by her words "*Nein, das tust du nicht*" [No, you're not to do that] with her own defiant speech-act, "*Ich werde es zerreissen*" [I'm going to slash it]. The "masculine" voice is alerted, is critical: "En allemand . . . Comment avais-tu pu si bien l'apprendre?" (p. 13) [In German . . . How could you have learnt it so well?]. The first voice concedes that the possibility of an actual and remembered utterance, a "real" reference is slight: "Oui, je me le demande . . . Mais ces paroles, je ne les ai jamais prononcées depuis . . ." [Yes, I wonder . . . But those words, which I have never said since . . .].

Nathalie Sarraute herself confirmed in her public lectures that these words are not "called up" from the past.[13] They are rather words called upon to "evoke" (to call up and bring to the contemplation of the mind), to put voice to "childhood memories" ("souvenirs d'enfance," p. 9). The paradigm of the soft floral silk of the sofa (of the mother's skin) and the sharp steel points of the scissors (the dissecting of the myth of the mother by the writer's pen) is, as Valerie Minogue has so perceptively demonstrated, the basic structuring principle of *Enfance*.[14] The "remembered" phrase is a generator.

By sound, rhythm, repetition, metaphor, in a complex textual work, it creates sensations. "'*Ich werde es zerreissen*' . . . 'Je vais le déchirer.' Le mot 'zerreissen' rend un son sifflant, féroce, dans une seconde quelque chose va se produire . . . je vais déchirer, saccager, détruire . . . ce sera une atteinte . . . un attentat . . . criminel" (p. 13) ["*Ich werde es zerreissen*" . . . "I'm going to slash it." The word *zerreissen* has a hissing, ferocious sound, in one second something is going to happen . . . I'm going to slash, devastate, destroy . . . it will be an outrage . . . a criminal attack].

Fear and anxiety and the exhilaration of independence accompany this tearing of the fabric of sacred relationships, of the smooth surfaces of the good mother and the loving daughter. These feelings are not represented or mirrored by the text but are very consciously created by a work on words, a work characterized structurally by ellipses and break, by the presentation of alternatives (competing paradigms) along a syntagmatic axis, and by different layers of functioning. The revolt against controlling words announced by the first person (child and adult) voice is self-consciously organized in the text by the paradigm ("soft"/"warm") that characterizes the mother.

> Je vous en avertis, je vais franchir le pas, sauter hors de ce monde décent, habité, *tiède* et *doux* je vais m'en arracher, tomber, choir dans l'inhabité, dans le vide. (p. 13, my italics)

> [I'm warning you, I'm going to take the plunge, leap out of this decent, inhabited, *warm*, *gentle* world. I'm going to wrench myself out of it, fall, sink into the uninhabited, into the void.]

As earlier chapters noted, for many postmodern writers and theorists, the void can be a productive principle and a locus of (im)possible self-discovery. Literature is not life nor is it feeling. Memory here is a recreation, triggered in a linguistic and literary interaction with sensation set in movement by a text. The critical impulse ("I'm going to slash it"), common to Natacha and to Nathalie, can be read as the founding impulse of Sarraute's writing.

In a subsequent scene, the first narrative voice remembers that in obedience to the absent mother's instructions, the child, not yet six, on holiday in a Swiss hotel with her father, refuses to swallow her food until it is "aussi liquide qu'une soupe" (p. 16) [as liquid as soup]. Stubborn to all cajolement, pointed out as a bad example to the other children, as a punishment she must eat her meals alone. The first voice, once again, is critical of an evocation that is obviously a present construction in adult language and image. "Des images, des mots qui évidemment ne pouvaient pas se former à cet âge-là dans ta tête" (pp. 17–18) [Images, words, which obviously couldn't have come into your head at that age]. Philippe Lejeune interprets this minidrama as metatextual reflection on an aspect of the writing process in which it is, in fact, language that is worked on patiently and stubbornly, or "liquified."[15] The child's resistance is (re)created by metaphor and the linear (syntagmatic), rhythmic organization of the terms of a conventional paradigm: "Je suis toujours là, à mon poste . . . je résiste . . . je tiens bon sur ce bout de terrain où j'ai hissé ses couleurs, où j'ai planté son drapeau" (p. 17) [I'm still there, at my post . . . I'm resisting . . . I'm holding out on this bit of territory on which I have hoisted her colors, on which I've put up her flag].

Once again, it is the distinctive voice of the writer, Sarraute, that is heard in the movement of the text and in the choice and organization of metaphor. The metaphors, military metaphors in this instance, are, of course, themselves the voice of the tribe or of the forms of our collectivity and carry multiple (and opposing) ideological charges. Is the child's fierce loyalty to the death noble, or is it, rather, unreasoned and misguided? Yet, "trembling" behind this intellectual textual drama, there is the evocation of a self-sufficient, "authentic" feeling that seems to inhere in the absolute, unquestioning devotion of the infant to the mother and the heroic defense of the mother's territory against any outside threat.

The critical second voice does not fail to point out that these military images are obviously not those of the child. The voices in the text and the voice that controls the text are not natural but literary. The vibrations of a particular narrative voice may indeed emanate from an emotional input into the writing, but they take full form only in the writing process. They are not the vibrations of childhood but of the calling up of childhood and the strong emotion and the disquiet this excavation of the intimate and the sacred provokes. The child of the text is not the young Natacha or even the writer understanding the secrets of the young Natacha. She is the product of selections and constructions of the writer and of the dialogue between the two narrative voices created by the writer taking form in interaction with remembered parental "voices" and the voices of European middle-class society in the early years of the century. Indeed a careful reading of *Enfance* reveals the importance of an omniscient narrative voice that takes over from the voices of the various interlocutors, in the discussion of the child's awareness (or lack of awareness) of her Jewish origins, for example. These authorial voices, often close to the first person voice, are apparently present to themselves in consciousness as they perceive, weigh up, and judge the events of the past. At other moments, the psychological detective fiction becomes a critical metafiction and the narrative voice is recognizable as that of Nathalie Sarraute, critic of her own work and of literature.

What is most audible or perceptible in this writing, then, is the continued splitting within the flux, the lack of single definition despite the overriding voice, ellipses that are at once the attempt to describe, and the impossibility of describing with language, an unknown, psychological substance in constant transformation buried under ("enfoui") the smooth, unauthentic linguistic surfaces.

The constitution of the new "I" that replaces the old stable ego of modernism, predator of the other, requires interlocution—subjectivity thus entailing intersubjectivity as Benveniste claims. For the linguist, the "I" only uses "I" in order to address someone who in this address becomes a "you." The "I" who addresses the "you" is itself a "you" for that "I." For Benveniste, it is dialogue that constitutes the "person."[16] In *Enfance*, the pair of the first voice and his interlocutor, perhaps also a figure of the ideal reader in the text, function within a set of other such dialogic interactions—the speaking self and the self spoken in the judgments of others, the subject(s) of the enunciation and the enunciating subject, the child and the adult, the "feminine" and the "masculine" (fusion with the maternal body and the break to the structure of the father's law), the emotional and the analytical.

The first voice is, at moments, explicitly suspicious of the autobiographical enterprise, seeing it as a possible manipulation of the reader by the choice of material and by its organization, (much as Rousseau (re)arranged his "true" "self" to prove his innocence and his victimization to his reader in the *Confessions* and the *Rêveries*). This metatextual suspicion may sensitize the reader to the character and the ordering of the authorial selection and organization of the minidramas played out; scenes, for example, that imply Véra's neglect or dislike. Natacha has head lice, Véra is absent from the sickroom when Natacha is suffering from a serious reaction to an inoculation. The bananas are hidden in the closet to keep them for Véra's daughter, Lili. Natacha makes sure Véra is not present when she shows her excellent grades to her father. The servants' words tend to reveal Natacha's lack of status in the household, the negative judgment implicit in the words of the "perfect" servant Adèle, for example, "Didn't anyone teach you, then, at your mother's place, that that isn't the way to pass scissors?" ("On ne t'a donc pas appris, chez ta mère, comment on doit passer les ciseaux?" p. 153).

The child is pinned down in deprivation by the words of her stepsister's nurse: "What a tragedy, though, to have no mother" ("Quel malheur quand même de ne pas avoir de mère," p. 116). Despite the narrator's assertion that Véra is mellowing, even showing some affection, the reader is led to wonder not only whether the stepmother's organization of a rare Sunday excursion for Natacha that will just happen to coincide with the mother's visit to Paris is really without ulterior motive but also whether the writer's evocation of this uncertainty is itself innocent.

Fragments are selected in which the mother answers her daughter's question about where babies come from with a story about eating dust, deceives the child over a painful operation—Natacha is told that her grandmother is coming to visit and, instead, finds the surgeon waiting to perform a tonsillectomy—and gives dire and misleading cautionary warnings, about the telegraph poles, for example: "If you touch that, you'll die" ("Si tu le touches, tu meurs," p. 29) that show the child's absolute faith in the mother's words to be rationally unfounded. Like the remembering of the mother's words of impatience with the nursing duties imposed by Natacha's convalescence from a childhood illness while on an "ideal" holiday with her cousins at Kamenetz-Podolsk, the metaphor selected that evokes the specter of the expulsion or abandon, the outsider status, that would send the child to live in Paris with the father and the stepmother, "un corps étranger" (p. 73) [a foreign body], deepens the suspicion of the inadequacy of the mother's love. This is confirmed by the father's words when the mother offers to take her daughter back: if he does nothing, he claims, no one will appear to take Natacha to Russia.

The critical attack on the mother by the "masculine" voice is sometimes direct and explicit. "Combien de temps il t'a fallu pour en arriver à te dire qu'elle n'essayait jamais, sinon très distraitement et maladroitement, de se mettre à ta place?" (p. 28) [How long did it take you to realize that she never tried—unless very absent-mindedly and clumsily—to put herself in your place?]. But the second voice attenuates, nuances, and responds that the mother's indifference, curiously, was part of her charm, observing that, in any case, as a child, it did not occur to her to ask questions of this kind. "Et ma mère était toujours pour moi, aussi bien que mon père, au-dessus, au-delà de tout soupçon" (p. 70) [And for me, my mother, just like my father, was always above, beyond suspicion]. As the critical voice probes and pushes the "tu" to label negatively—was mother indeed "miserly" in her apportioning of food and "ungrateful" as the servants' words and their dinner portions suggested—the second voice resists such attempts at generalization. The gaps of memory or meaning are not filled, and the reader, while encouraged to sustain the seeking after truth, is made aware of the difficulty of any definitive nonlocalized (re)solution or completion. The fastidious attempts to establish clear and single meaning by the first voice are constantly nuanced by his "feminine" interlocutor.

Michael Sheringham wonders whether the apparently liberating process of opening up the autobiography to the reader does not, in fact, do the opposite; forestalling the reader's response, shutting us out of the action and protecting the writer from us.[17] Ann Jefferson reads the second voice as a represented reader within the text who is "continuously validating the authenticity of the autobiographical narrative so that the reading role requires little more than passive assent."[18] I would argue that the reader's participation is not limited to one voice and that Sarraute's project is above all to draw the reader into the stream of shifting uncertain tropistic movements in transformation, into open-ended debate. The critical voice never decisively wins its case for the prosecution—against the mother or against Véra—although the author's orderings seem to stack the odds somewhat in its favor. As Valerie Minogue argues against Jefferson's reading: "The questioning dialogue of the two voices, while indicating the effort towards authenticity, never reaches, nor claims to reach, any safe point of rest."[19] Nor indeed is the first voice only negative. Its peremptory tone is very much that of the refusal of self-indulgence and recalls the father's detestation of what he called "vainglory" and his scrupulous moral honesty. This has been an aspect of Sarraute's own public appearances, videotaped interviews, and writings. In *Enfance*, significantly, a similar intellectual austerity and moral exigency characterize the father.

The second voice cannot be limited to the role of a guarantor of an autobiographical "pact" with the reader, in a text reduced to what Stephen Heath has called "a practice of writing." In Jefferson's model, the "real" and the "I" are immanent in the textual conventions. While Nathalie Sarraute herself has admitted that her words are not those of the past, she has also consistently denied that her "real" is uniquely textual. My own sense of the text is that it positions me somewhere between sensation and its exploration in and through writing, beyond the traditional subject-object dichotomy and in a displacement of conventional dialectic, moving with the circulation of the pronouns between a number of different places from which the self can speak. Sarraute's new autobiographical text, linguistic and thus symbolic process, is clearly not a copy, a mimesis of an original "I" or a true or natural experience, but nor is it a pure linguistic construction, a network of intertexts that intersect, or a meeting-place of the theoretical literary experiments of our time.

The changes in conceptual positions that Jardine identifies as characterizing the theoretical texts of "modernité"—changes from time to space, from mastery to nonmastery, from same to other, from paranoia (male) to hysteria (female), and from truth to fiction—do not appear to have been completely effected in *Enfance*. Rather, the text continues to move between the pairs, no longer irreconcilable or dialectical opposites, but simultaneous alternatives, at once asserted and challenged, according to the frame of reference invoked. These pairs, this study has suggested, are "complementary" in the sense of Bohr and Heisenberg's interpretations in the New Physics (that is, mutually exclusive but valid within the appropriate paradigm—traditional Newtonian mechanics or contemporary quantum physics). Liberal and humanist ideology based on naturalized categories (childhood, motherhood, love, reality, and truth), on concepts like Experience, or the Ethical, are the ground from which Sarraute's work proceeds. This "natural" voice we have learned to recognize as that of our everyday experience, a voice that at once makes sense of and masks the world, is put into question, but not completely invalidated, by the venturing of the narrative into new incompatible tropistic spaces. The relationship between the two worlds or the two voices is both "complementary" in the Heisenberg sense and interrogative. We might postulate that the disquiet, the sense of sacrilege, felt by the daughter in her excavations of the relationships with the mother and her childhood is doubled by the writer's ambivalence toward her metatextual deconstruction of a Western logocentric psychology and artistic system (mimesis) that is limited, limiting, but still the secure and stabilizing shared framework of almost all everyday life and traditional art.

Neither voice in Sarraute's writing is a self-present fullness; the traditional essentially single voice of self is put into question by the processes of interlocution and made more complex by the manipulation of both voices by the writer. Neither the interrogative nor the responding voice is uniquely author or authority. Happiness, the text tells us, is not one of "their" words. Yet at the center of the childhood "memories," there is, indeed, a scene on a park bench in the Luxembourg Gardens that evokes an intense feeling of oneness, completeness, and harmony in the world. Significantly, the "joy" ("joie") evoked in this passage results from the loss of self merged with the natural world, from the assimilation of the natural world (the sun, the flowers, the water) to self in a disappearance of boundaries between subject and object. This central existential or metaphysical experience is curiously reminiscent of Rousseau's well-known autobiographical accounts of experiences of intense "being" in fusion with the universe and loss of self in the second and fifth *Rêveries du promeneur solitaire*. In Sarraute's fragment, the presence of the father and the "mother" (Véra) on the bench with the child allows her to experience its completeness.

This scene, which appears to recall a powerful unmediated sensation/experience of being from which the Cartesian cogito is absent, is nonetheless a knowing of that feeling at second hand through narrative process, rhythm, metaphor, language, and fiction. Unlike Plato's myth of the soul and its fall into forgetfulness from true being and truth now situated beyond the heavens, hidden, but still present, Sarraute's exploration does seem to take account of the possibility that the original "signified," that is, unity and presence (Logos, the Word) may be, as Derrida puts it, "never absolutely present outside a system of differences."[20] (These differences, we recall, are those of a language in which, since Saussure's postulation of the arbitrariness of the sign, meaning arises only in the play of differences within phonemic, morphemic, and semantic systems). The Platonic myth comes to serve Derrida's analysis of the fall of Western thought from presence into discourse. In *Enfance*, on the park bench, beside the child Natacha, lies a book of fairy tales.

The fragment, moreover, is itself constructed from the dichotomies of traditional dialectical thinking (father/mother, nature/book, subject/object, presence/absence, present/past). Sarraute's writing process attempts to displace this polarity of opposites based on sexual analogy, a polarity that in organizing our language subsequently directs our thought and our perceptions. Classical oppositions are not assumed in a mediation, but are now both present in a non-contradictory "complementary" way. Meaning, in permanent circulation, arises from "différance" (deferral and difference) between the pairs of these oppositions and between feeling and text.

Or again, as Julia Kristeva expresses this notion, all speaking subjects have a certain bisexuality that is precisely the possibility to explore all the sources of signification. Such a bisexuality is manifest in the two opposing projects in *Enfance*, one a narcissistic self-purging of reminiscence, of subtle sensations and suspended states, the other the constitution of knowledge. One reminisces and the other works on the phonetic texture of language, its syntactical and semantic articulation of the theoretical conflicts of our time. One posits meaning, the other "multiplies," "pulverizes and finally revives it."[21] Such a "bisexuality," which does not attempt to expel the other in a power struggle, would seem to characterize the structure of *Enfance* and its two voices eminently well.

We might also see this nonexclusive dialogic structure in terms of the intrasubjective and intersubjective movements where boundaries become fluid between self and others in the self and between self and outside other. It could also be sited at the intersections of the Oedipus complex and the language of the other, "the subject's never completed break away from the holistic space and rhythm of the maternal body into the time and syntax of patriarchal language,"[22] using the framework of Lacanian psychoanalysis.

The deconstruction of the silken, ready-made language/mother is not only a potentially sacrilegious but a delicate enterprise for, the signifier in free play, however productive, might pass unawares alongside or over the essential, that is, for Sarraute, the unknown hidden by the known. On the other hand, although the expressions used by the mother, stepmother, and father derive from conventional (received) psychology, their reworking may also filter, in intonation or in the reconstruction of tropistic movements of hidden impulse and desire, something not able to be formulated, something authentic. The desire to cling to the mother, to merge with the soft, warm silk in a loss of self and the desire to stand outside alone, to "know" in the domain of the symbolic are complementary. The author who emerges in the interplay behind both voices is controlling *and* controlled by the emotional power of the (m)other's traditional words; mirrored in her own gaze at the mother.

Sarraute (for whom words always have meanings) claims that the text can give voice to microscopic, indefinable, evanescent but intense and self-sufficient inner movements, outside language. These sensations that "slide into words," "melt" with a language from which they become "inseparable," bring to the "outside" (clear consciousness and language?) "something still intact," something which has not already been "taken over by language, something still vague."[23] In this sense, there is, in the work of Sarraute, both a truth of the bio-graphy (a writing of the body) and a work of language on language. Her writing can be seen as an indirect imaging forth of the psyche whose tropistic sensations and emotions are "seized," "captured," "fixed," but indirectly, in and by literary forms. There is every possibility that the child Natacha, seeking confirmation of being loved and wanted, suspicious of possible indifference or dislike in those near to her, developed a hypersensitivity to the hidden implications of the words and gestures of others. But, in *Enfance*, this sensitivity once again comes into play in interaction with writing. "Nein, das tust du nicht" (a speech act of authoritarian prohibition and challenge) is a catalyst for instinctive reactions in the child that can come into clear consciousness for us, and for Sarraute, in a subsequent creative work on language. This imaging forth has a conscious, analytical face that challenges the established taboos and veneration that (already) constitute the "realities" of the mother/daughter relationship.

To this extent, the ivory tower approach and formalist writing with which Simone de Beauvoir reproached Nathalie Sarraute may be unfair criticism. According to the critic Yolande Patterson, Sarraute's formalist approach stems from the lack of a "real" childhood, a loving mother, and "united, fair and calm parents."[24] The critic's words here are indeed those of Nathalie Sarraute's first person voice. "Et aussi elles me semblaient pour la plupart charmantes, ces jeunes Anglaises candides, toutes fraîches écloses de leurs enfances champêtres de filles de pasteurs, d'instituteurs . . . des enfances qui n'avaient pu être que ce que sont les 'vraies' enfances vécues dans l'insouciance, dans la sécurité, sous la ferme et bienveillante direction de parents unis, justes et calmes" (p. 244, my italics) [And also, for the most part, I found them charming, those ingenuous young English girls, fresh blown from their country childhoods as the daughters of parsons, of school-masters . . . childhoods which could only have been what "real" childhoods are, lived in insouciance, in security, under the firm, benevolent guidance of united, fair and calm parents].

In the subsequent lines of this passage that appears, at first sight, to be a self-indulgent or self-pitying recollection, the writer links the nostalgia for a secure "real" childhood to the memory of an outside judgment of her stepmother Véra. One of the young English girls, Miss Philips, who had come to the house as governess for the capricious stepsister, Lilli, characterizes Véra in terms of "nightmare" when Nathalie Sarraute encounters her as a nanny twenty years later in the Bois de Boulogne ("I still see your step-mother in my nightmares," p. 245). Previous categorizations of Véra by hearsay or gossip as stupid, mean, hysterical, jealous, and resentful of the burden of her stepdaughter add their weight to other vignettes that authorize the nostalgia for "real" parents. There is, for example, the image of "les Florimond," the perfect wise and adult couple who appear to personify a united and calm union and correspond to the father's clear-cut values. These "packages" of words and images, however, like the simple words "my daughter" spoken by the father already appear less natural and more complicated to the young Natacha than they seem to appear to others; I would argue that they continue to pose problems for the older Nathalie, some nostalgia notwithstanding.

We note the skeptical inverted commas around "real" childhoods ("vraies" enfances) in the Sarraute text, the past tense and semantic uncertainty of the verb "semblaient," and recall the curious fascination of gossip in all of Nathalie Sarraute's work—words of the group that can serve as a gross repository for the settling out of underlying tropistic feelings, but that may, at the same time, conceal more authentic, complex feelings and reactions behind cliché and established judgments. Whenever Véra begins to harden into a fixed and univocal character, a "wicked" stepmother of folk-tale tradition and psychosocial commonplace, or a metaphorical hissing "viper," wildcat, or "volcano" of repressed resentments and fury, other contradictory or attenuating circum-stances—the father's austerity and the age-gap between the couple, Véra's sepa-ration from her family in Russia—introduce uncertainty and complexity. The beloved Baboutchka, Véra's mother, for example, with her affectionate accounts of her daughter's youth, gaiety, and love of dance, reinforces such doubt about the permanent fit of any definitive characterization. Viviane Forrester com-ments on the demonstration of the inadequacy of a single word or image ("marâtre" [stepmother] or "nightmare") to define Véra or any woman.[25] In the refusal by the child of the mother's paralyzing judgments and of the father's habit of transforming moving people into fixed "characters," both of the voices in *Enfance* reiterate the adult writer's rejection of ready-made, single labels, of "intolerant," "fascist," and "terrorist" words which repress "freedom of ideas."[26]

When Natacha hears the strong and stubborn Véra sobbing in childlike distress in her bedroom and goes to comfort her, the very adjectives—"silken" and "soft" and "warm" ("je caresse sa tête *soyeuse* et *douce*, toute *tiède* . . . et peu à peu elle s'apaise" (p. 191, my italics) [I stroke her *soft*, *silky*, *warm* head and she gradually calms down]—that have become symbolic of the "beloved" aspect of the mother are used to describe the stepmother. Such a consciously organized circulation of words and expressions between individual objects and characters further effaces clear outlines, fixed identities, and even distinct roles. By transferring these epithets to Véra, she becomes the "Véra-Maman" of the child's desire for tenderness and warmth. But, to Véra's written request for permission for Natacha to use the name "Véra-Maman," the mother answers her daughter with the paralyzing and prescriptive injunction: "You only have one Mama in the world" (p. 101). The "warm," the "soft," and the "smooth" that can migrate from the now paralyzing, now radiant and liberating mother to Véra, like all words in Sarraute's work, are suspect. And the "silken," the "golden," the "delicious" (Mother, childhood emotions and needs) do not fail to call forth the dissecting scissors.[27] The adjective "pointu" [pointed], associ-ated with childhood fears, also circulates through the text, appearing in the description of Véra's "pointed" pregnant stomach (an indication of the incipient sibling jealousy) and in the illustration of a childhood storybook that shows a greenish man with a pointed nose brandishing scissors dripping with blood.

Even the most critically competent readings of *Enfance*, that is, readings that take account of the patterning of the whole text and of all the voices that speak (the dialoguing and split adult narrators, the child Natacha, the mother(s), the father, the servants), that consider the discontinuity and incompleteness of the fragments creating the shifting relationship with the mother, the stepmother, and the father, cannot avoid the sense of pain that wells up from behind the objective investigative project. Valerie Minogue, for example, concludes that Nathalie Sarraute's writing quest is, at least in part, a "quest for identity and a home"[28] and concedes that: "The narrative line . . . is a tightrope, for in many ways, this is a classic 'unhappy childhood,' the child torn between mother and father and meeting rejection from mother and stepmother alike."[29] Such "unhappiness" is borne out by the omniscient narrator who informs the reader that the young English governesses who had experienced "real" childhoods with calm, fair, and united parents "se sentaient perdues ici, aux prises avec les passions obscures, les réactions sauvages de Véra" (p. 244) [felt lost here, grappling with Véra's obscure passions and savage reactions].

Yet, as we have noted, there are simplifications effected by these common-sense words and assumptions about the naturalness and universality of "real" childhoods, "loving" mothers, and "united" parents—and, indeed, of a language naturally giving form to the world. It seems apparent that Nathalie Sarraute, as a trained lawyer and upper middle-class French wife and mother of three daughters, shares a social, pragmatic involvement in such common-sense notions, values, and orderings of the world by language. I am also persuaded that the suspicion of the unauthentic character of these ready-made psychological categories (the natural link between mother and child, the absolute and natural goodness of the maternal), and the desire to open up or pull apart this transparent language, are predominant in the play between the narrative voices and in the battle of words against words.

Sarraute's voice(s), as Derrida warns us, may not be real presence. They may indeed be fragmented and heterogeneous. And yet, they are not disembodied as they function somewhere between life and text in ardent and earnest seeking after forms of authentic being through the text. The self of Sarraute may appear to be something of a contradiction in this movement between the unauthentic and the authentic, in the quest for an "I"/"We" that may perhaps reside in the collective "tropism" but can only take form in a new and singular text. Yet there is something distinctive in the text that we can indeed identify if not as Sarraute's, at least as Sarrautean, voice(s).

The narrative voice, then, is at least double in *Enfance*, a product of interlocution and of both conflict and exchange between "masculine" and "feminine" voices. Gender, too, is dialogic and relational, that is, different but not mutually exclusive ("complementary"). The "feminine" is predominantly flux, feeling as it arises, and subjectivity; the "masculine" voice is critical objectivity. As it has been pointed out, this pair is analogous to the "complementary" pair of the analysand and the analyst in psychoanalysis or the I-you of interlocution. Behind the two voices, at the level of the *énonciation*, the voice of the writer, creating, organizing, can also be discerned.

Sarraute has always vehemently resisted being situated as a "woman" writer, in any way different from the great (male) writers of the past. She has consistently situated her work in the tradition of Proust. The refusal of any gendered quality of the voices in *Enfance* may conceal anxieties of influence and self-image. The questions posed by the gender of voices in the new autobiographies and, in particular, in Sarraute's work, also have implications for a significant debate within Anglo-American literary circles.[30] Essentially pragmatic, seeking women's lives in portraits of mother-daughter (father-daughter) relationships and a distinctive place to stand, attempting to discern an excluded or other (feminine) voice that is not identical to the (masculine) voice in power, a mainstream strand of American feminist criticism accepts the existence of a language that would reflect a feminine essence and meanings that are independent of the logical processes that produce them. One way such a critical approach has read *Enfance* is as the story of a child abandoned by "false" (that is, nonloving, noncaring) mother(s) who, through lack of the warmth and security offered by the maternal presence, seeks refuge in the "masculine" space of a cold and formal text.[31] Such a pragmatic, essentialist, or political approach to reading texts can also affirm (and in this contradiction lies a dilemma) that the "nature" of "woman" is an ideological construction by the (masculine) power in place. In Sarraute's textual play, the child who refuses institutional authority, the future writer taking form in opposition to the clichés of others, reveals in and through herself, in and through the textual movement between the soft and silky protection of the known and the manipulation of the steel-tipped scissors, something as yet disorganized but which, for Sarraute, arises not only from ideology but also from life. This life gives birth to her text but necessarily within an interaction with the texts in power.

It could be argued that Sarraute's thematics and her war with words reveal identification with the father (or the "masculine") as much as they suggest the attraction of (and resistance to) the feminine—the self-centered charm, even radiance, of the mother and the hysteria of Véra. In *Enfance*, almost as many scenes are marked by the relationship to the father as are devoted to the mother. His austerity, his love for and unspoken complicity with his daughter concealed behind reserve and a lack of ease ("une gêne") with emotion, contrasts with the mother's extroverted gaiety, absence, and lack of understanding, even though the impressionistic portrait of the father, like the mother's, is a patchwork of both emotional impulse and critical distance. It is, of course, essentially in rebellion against the mother that Natacha asserts her earliest independence. The evocation of this childhood rebellion may involve the adult Nathalie's refusal of the mother's qualities—charm, insouciance, spontaneity—in favor of the father's sense of duty and moral responsibility and reluctance to show his feelings even to his daughter, who must use trickery to get him to say "I love you." Behind the exclusive and protective relationship that the father's use of the term "my daughter" evokes, the child (the adult?) senses the hidden "challenge" to emulate and be worthy of the father's approval. *Enfance* recalls the pain and guilt of being caught stealing as a child less through Véra's virulent indignation than through the father's condemning bedtime words. When his daughter confesses that she stole candy because "she wanted it," the father's bitter outburst at his daughter's selfish lack of moral restraint implicitly links her to the disappointing mother. While the voice of the addressed interlocutor foregrounds the affective power that the charming, independent-minded, and active mother exerts over the abandoned father, the adoring stepfather, and the desiring daughter, the addressing voice focuses on the mother's lack of the father's qualities of responsibility, scrupulousness, and self-denial. These are the qualities that Sarraute seems to have identified with closely in her own life and that would have been necessary to ensure paternal legitimation.

Sarraute appears to be at pains to deny the origins of her own writing career in the profession of her mother, a writer of children's stories. Indeed, *Enfance* stages a scene in which the mother somewhat insensitively shows off her daughter's stories to a friend whose negative critical response (the child needs to learn to spell before she tries to write) is presented as inhibiting her writing career for many years to come. The text evokes an unspoken, intangible bond that develops between Natacha and her father in the unhappiness of life with an unpredictable and resentful Véra and with her stepsister, Lilli. Whereas physical charm is situated implicitly on the mother's side, the father is presented as awkward and cerebral. This may constitute one explanation of the exclusion from Sarraute's work of desire and sexuality.

At the level of these textual thematics, of her public life, and of her own paratextual pronouncements (at Cérisy in 1989, for example), Sarraute refuses to assume a gendered "feminine" position and thereby situates herself closer to the traditional "masculine"—presented as universal. In her texts, however, I would argue, gender is rewritten in the polyphony of voices, in movement toward the authentic out of the sense of imposture, and in the movement between life and text, between the power of words reworked and the prison-house of language. This is a complementary textual/sexual movement creating a mobile complementary masculine/'feminine' identity that is always shifting and incomplete. It is not the fullness of an essence but, rather, what Teresa de Lauretis would call an essential difference (or set of differences).[32] De Lauretis situates this "essential" difference in social situation, in life-experiences, in history, in individual context, and above all, in sex (different for women than for men), that is, in the different impulses and values that, as a consequence of a particular social history, distinguish women from men. There is no assimilation of opposites in Sarraute's shifting voices in *Enfance*, no synthesis or traditional dialectic, but, rather, a "complementary" movement that allows free movement from one virtual gendered position to another. This choice of possible positions permits difference, contradictions, and opposition to coexist without requiring the suppression of one or the other or the maintenance of opposite poles. At the level of the *énonciation*, then, there is, I argue, a reconfiguration of the sex of the text.

The dialoguing shifts between two major dramatic voices do, in most cases, seem to correspond to changes in position. These shifts extend to the pitch, tone, stress, timbre, color, rhythm, or choice of words and syntax that constitute physically, in their different movements, different writing selves and bodies of text. Although the "masculine" voice is interruptive, manipulative, and seeks to impose his version of events, there is no dominant narrative position, no single authorial voice. As we have seen, both voices and frames of probing and understanding remain partial, uncertain, and even contradictory and can be overridden by authorial voices. What is the exact nature of the "scorn" for the mother sensed by the child in the relationship between her mother and her father, or of the "fear" the father may inspire in Véra, for example. Once again, in making sense of these situations, in naming and grasping, the probing (adult) voice(s) may mask, even as they reveal, the complex, moving, psychic realities behind them.

In the dialogic movement, there is perhaps a physical metaphor of the inscription of the "différance" that the writing (symbolic) process introduces into the "real" of unmediated feeling. Yet the first and second voices are not always clearly different or clearly the same in spite of their predominately differential marking for gender, and slippages and empathic communions occur between the "I" and the "You," between the "masculine" and the "feminine," to elide even these boundaries and categories, at their margins. The fixed oppositions imposed by the functioning of language, the division of the emotional flux into discrete categories, and the organization of these categories around oppositions remain operations under suspicion.

Voice in Sarraute's writing is neither "masculine" nor "feminine," neither single and unified, nor double and symmetrically oppositional; nor, however, is it integrally plural and dispersed. It is, in part, an assemblage of other voices and of ready-made literary and clichéd words and metaphors. There is, nonetheless, in the manner of its own assemblages, in the movements in and out of the authentic and the unauthentic, between the conversation and the emotional subconversation, between the "masculine" and the "feminine," and in the physical origins of the text, something clearly recognizable, an *entre-deux* that can nonetheless only be labeled as Sarrautean voice.

seven

THEM AND US

Between Intersubjectivity and Intrasubjectivity in Sarraute's *Tu ne t'aimes pas*

In his now canonical study of the autobiographical genre, Philippe Lejeune argues that the autobiographical "pact" entails identity between the author, the narrator, and the character.[1] His thesis implies the unity of the speaking or writing subject and the "I" as name of the author while recognizing that the autobiographical evoking of the past is simultaneously a self-creation in the present. Sidonie Smith sees such a double function in terms of a split authorial subjectivity; she or he who watches or speaks and she or he who is watched, is spoken for.[2]

The previous chapter described Nathalie Sarraute's *Enfance* (1983) as a dialogic reconstitution of the self as this took fragmented uncertain form through the impact of the living substance captured in the voices of the significant others of childhood (mothers, father, teachers). Sarraute's 1989 *Tu ne t'aimes pas*, a work that draws upon conventions of autobiography, novel, and theater, and that I class, for want of any more suitable category, as an autobiographical fiction, presents the subject as legion, an "immense" and "moving" mass that constitutes an "us." It is only when a member of the "us" seeks to make contact with "them"—those "outside" ("là-bas," "au dehors," p. 12) as one single-faceted delegate that he or she may temporarily assume the role of single subject and use "I." There is no simple identity between Sarraute's characters (or are they rather subcharacters?), this series of delegate "I" addressed by the "we" as a "you" in what is also a subversion of the pronoun set, and the multiple narrators inside ("nous" [we/us]) gendered according to grammatical criteria;[3] no simple identity between inside narrators and the author. The dialogical voices gendered "feminine" and "masculine" (an emotional "feminine" voice and a critical, logical, interruptive "masculine" voice) that characterized the dialogue in *Enfance* as essentially oppositional are carefully avoided in *Tu ne t'aimes pas*. Gender is grammatically determined ("une forte personalité" is a woman). Or it becomes a shifting, potentially multiple complex beyond the "real man" and the "real woman." Gender emerges from the feeling experienced by some of the more introspective interlocutors of being androgynous or a mixture of both man and woman.

The "I" is no longer the name of the author, yet there is an evident community among the ballet of multiple voices of the "we" in *Tu ne t'aimes pas* as these emerge and disappear. I suggest, against the current readings, that *Tu ne t'aimes pas* is not only an exploration of the noncognitive, spontaneous physical events (the shock of tropismic movements) that occur randomly in an anonymous place,[4] but also a choice among them. The complex of interior movements, for me, is intimate and individuated. She who speaks/watches here, however violently she suppresses any "identity" in the preference for the universal, is constituted, at least in part, by her character, experience, and situation as an aging woman. She who creates here is manifest in those she watches and through whom she speaks. Although not all of a piece, and most often oppositional or contradictory, the fragmented delegates and narrators have a clear relationship to Sarraute's own previous texts and images and to that writer's particular preoccupations and aesthetic.

Whereas *Enfance* was an evocation of past memories *and* a present self-becoming in a writing out of "unhappy childhood" and, in the final instance, in an implicit identification with the father, the circulation of voices in *Tu ne t'aimes pas*, each one identifiable as distinctively Sarrautean in their rhythm and movement, operates a kind of self-analysis in the present. This is indeed, once again, an exploration of the emotional impact of the words of the Other. Yet, the phrases selected—"tu ne t'aimes pas" [you lack self-love], "vingt ans de bonheur" [twenty years of married bliss], "c'est pathologique en moi" [it's pathological], for example—constitute a probing, perhaps an exorcism, of a very particular kind of planetarium of thoughts and of emotions.

Identified predominantly with the "we," the writer appears to share their feelings of being a "chaotic" and "contradictory" mixed "world" without clear boundaries. Like the school of fish or flock of birds to which it is compared, the we/you ["nous/vous"] dialogic complex is made up of numerous elements whose source is similar. After a mischievous game in which the break-away "I" causes alarm and rejection by apparently joining the people "over there," using *their* "mass-produced" words, confiding what "belongs to us alone" (p. 126), how good it is for the "nous" to be reunited with the errant "tu," to "be back amongst ourselves again . . . [. . .] to merge, to melt, to be as one" (pp. 126–27).

*Nathalie
Sarraute in later
years. Photo
from Editions
Gallimard,
Paris; courtesy
of Nathalie
Sarraute.*

"Tout se ranime, frémit . . . quelque chose d'impalpable protégé de silence traverse en nous une même substance, remonte à une même source" (p. 127) [Everything is coming back to life, quivering . . . something intangible protected by silence is passing through the same substance in us, returning to the same source]. This is the anonymous universal and living stuff of which tropisms are made, yet in this instance, it is clearly also our "world," our "words," a particular "us."

The intrasubjective "forum" debates competing claims of personality. Being "carefree" and unattached to material objects is juxtaposed with scenes of the anguish aroused by the misplaced or cracked old teapot or coffee-grinder or broken chair springs, to suggest that no single trait is adequate to describe the forum. But as harbingers of Death, these accidents generate a sense of a specific stage in life where death begins, at moments, to be an anxiety-provoking and felt presence, covered over, muses the narrator, rather than revealed by the word that designates it. Even the anti-"portrait" that emerges from the "games" played by an "I" placing itself at a distance from the "you" ("tu") and trying out contradictory outside judgments—"Tu es la bonté même. Qui est plus généreux que toi?" [You're goodness personified. Who is more generous than you?] or "Tu es égoiste. Je ne connais personne de plus mesquin . . . de plus rancunier que toi" (pp. 124–25) [You're selfish. I don't know anyone more petty . . . more spiteful than you]—is organized around specific (self-loving and unselfloving) complexes.

A "we" (self-portrait) emerges piecemeal and indirectly who can be characterized as (hyper)sensitive and refined despite the fact that its element is also the down to earth and the pragmatic. Possessing "departments with products of all kinds," for all needs, in emergencies, it claims to take particular pleasure in the sensations elicited by the touch of the smooth, worn stone rim of the well that speaks to the heart, by the humpbacked parapets of old bridges. It is attracted to the child's sensitive new skin, or to that "source of feeling" where "words circulate, alight, designate" (p. 123). This soft and sensitive "we" seeks to distance itself from the abstract purity of the straight lines, the cubes of concrete, the hard contours that characterize the self-loving, superior leader. The lack of the wholeness and coherence that would be guaranteed by self-knowledge, self-possession, or power, a lack designated by the charge "You don't love yourself," contrasts with the solidity, sense of self, and control of the strong personality evoked by the outside clichés of the Other: "Je suis comme je suis" (p. 153) [I am what I am], "Je me connais" (p. 154) [I know myself], "Qui aime bien châtie bien" (p. 154) [Spare the rod and spoil the child].

Both narrators and outside others are defined by their relation to such a determined "strong personality." They are ready to submit or surrender to his law or whim ("his heavy paw on you"), to be invaded and pushed to abject submission by his implacable occupying power ("as he digs in his claws"), or to be irradiated by the well-being inspired by the strength of his self-love. One spokesperson ("I") is portrayed critically as particularly anxious to live up to the superiority assigned her by the honor of an invitation to share a holiday in the country with another such "strong personality." Desirous of doing everything possible to deserve and please, she is profoundly affected by her host's implicit accusation of mediocrity ("When conversation descends to such a level").

The fascination exerted by such strength and domination, as by humilia-tion, rejection, or criticism, is echoed in the curious scene in which a strong self-loving other discovers the private diary of his old acquaintance hidden in a stove and unmasks unsuspected masochistic impulses in the apparently dig-nified and elegant scholar. In the diary his colleague describes being taken to an extreme limit of humiliation, experiencing blows and slaps that he does not return, a pain not chosen and controlled as by Proust's Baron Charlus but perhaps, he confesses, submitted to out of obscure desire rather than from fear. Images appear, very old images that rise from a common stock and float, suspended ("Des images arrivent, de très vieilles images montent d'un stock commun . . . elles flottent, suspendues," p. 185), slightly different in each of the followers but produced from a single model "locked within us all over a very long time" ("enfermé en nous tous depuis longtemps," p. 185) and pro-voking a nervous, childlike tittering in the audience. Stripped of his clothes, his bare flesh shivering, this little manikin, held up in the air between two fingers and rolled over from one side to the other for inspection by the pure and perfect superior Colossus, reacts only with a tremor, as if of satisfaction at being noticed when he thought he was on the scrap heap, of satisfaction at being brought to life.

Such a portrait of hypersensitivity and masochism at the level of the out-side characters recalls other sadomasochistic struggles in Sarraute's work and reinforces the sense of individuated authorial preoccupations. For the self-as-surance, invulnerability, and monolithic self-love of the leader seem also to tremble and fissure for an instant in the light of the indiscretion, voyeurism or even sadism suggested by his fascinated probing into the other's masochistic intimacy. In this scene, there is an implicit fracturing of the leader's intellec-tual doctrine that seeks the purity of straight lines converging and the eradica-tion of the suspect traces of emotion, the suppression of feelings of guilt or discomfort or nausea. Although the positive self-assurance with which the leader "irradiates" his neophytes is taken to derive from self-evident qualities, these followers, the text suggests, may simply be victims of a persuasion, deceived by the apparent invulnerable transparency of their leader, by his self-love.

The tiny inner movements and miniconflicts concealed in these conversa-tions, that is, the personally selected inner impressions, the movements "on which my attention had been fixed for a long time. In fact, it seems to me, since childhood,"[5] are part of an individuated self-scrutiny. But it is through phrase-gazing that Sarraute's domain takes form, that is, in attention to speech acts that have made an impact on the selves and been internalized, sometimes in latency, in response to outside judgments that touch the authentic roots of feeling. This is a distinctive universe of outside voices evoking evanescent and often violent sensations and an authorial voice that hears and simulates them in her own language rather than, for example, a Proustian rewriting of involuntary memory. The writer's retention of particular words and her invention of new dialogic narrative strategies, gaps, silences, breaks, and metaphors to suggest their emotional resonance in her create a certain individual cohesion. In the final instance, what structures this new autobiographical novel is the fault line between the self-loving others and the unselfloving selves. As Yvette Went-Daoust had described the beginnings of such a process in *Enfance*: "It is as if the writer, taking up a pen to tell her story, had wanted to prove to herself that her story was everybody's and had met only obstacles to these claims to 'normalcy' on her path."[6]

To probe the question of difference, the possible "infirmity" or lack of self-loving and the fascinated refusals of irradiation by self-love that might distinguish him or her from the outside others, one spokesperson puts questions to a fifty-year-old father of Irish origin, selected for his "kindly" and "open" gaze, about his feeling of identity.

> Ecoutez, je voulais vous demander . . . Est-ce qu'en vous-même, enfin dans votre for intérieur, vous avez l'impression . . . mais je dis bien: tout au fond de vous, vous arrivez à vous voir avec une certaine netteté . . . vous avez l'impression de savoir qui vous êtes. (p. 16)

> [Listen, I wanted to ask you . . . Do you, within yourself, in fact in your inmost depths, do you have the impression . . . but I really do mean: in your innermost recesses, that you manage to see yourself with a certain clarity . . . do you have the impression that you know who you are.]

To what extent, asks the spokesperson, does this Irish father feel he is a unified and compact subject, endowed with certain qualities and, of course, with defects but forming a whole, a subject who can look at itself from the outside and see the "I" it loves? The Irishman confesses, on reflection, that when he looks at himself attentively, he sees two contradictory beings, a Dr. Jekyll and a Mr. Hyde. He's sometimes one and sometimes the other: "Je tiens ça de mon grand-père, il disait toujours: 'Il y a en moi un moine et un banquier'" (p. 17) [I get that from my grandfather, he always used to say: "There's a monk and a banker in me"].

Such wisdom passed from father to son is characteristic of the outside, self-loving others—the commonplaces of the monk and the banker, the Dr. Jekyll and Mr. Hyde, the family portraits that include such a splitting as the masculine real brigand and the feminine true saint ("le vrai brigand" and "la vraie sainte"). One of these others, gendered feminine, who cuts her thumb while pruning roses, for example, is taken to task by her self-monitor: "Mais que je me sois fait ça, à moi! [. . .] Ce sont des choses qui ne doivent pas m'arriver" (pp. 134–35) [Just imagine that I did that to myself! {. . .} That sort of thing shouldn't happen to me]. Her watching self clearly considers that "she" has certain qualities possessed only by superior people and has betrayed herself. This woman with the pruning shears has a double or superego at a distance from herself, a "frontier guard," as Sarraute puts it, to protect her beloved body from vulgar attack. Hers is a split and self-protective subjectivity, described also as "a world" but as one that little resembles "ours."

Another self-loving person, this time a man contemplating the hand that he had spread out admiringly in front of us on the table, is characterized by a similar military metaphor. A drumroll assembles soldiers in the court of honor, awaiting his orders. As in the common expression ("il n'y en a que pour lui," p. 24 [he's the only person who counts]), his presence assimilates or obliterates the other: the most apparently trivial details of his morning routine—soup, coffee, and two cigarettes—for his self-satisfaction and the contentment of his intestines become all-important.

The unselfloving "I," on the contrary, is part of a network of sites touched by the circulation of the contradictory feelings of the "we"; feelings of inadequacy, hurt, and imposture, as well as of superiority and uniqueness. He or she is at once the critical site of a self-searching *and* a reaction against the pretension of self-knowledge, of a searching out of the illusions of love and superiority in others, *and* the locus of the desire to please and to be loved by the other (and the others in the self). At another and metatextual level, the "I" emerges clearly as an agent of intellectual deconstruction ("un démolisseur"). It is evident to him or her that simple binary divisions like the "brigand" who abandons wife and family and the "angel" of the family portraits or the Dr. Jekyll and Mr. Hyde syndrome, identified by the father Irishman as a certain complexity within, remain inadequate. The two sides (Jekyll and Hyde) might simply appear to fit together in a preconstituted frame to form an overall whole self that is lovable with faults. But it is recognized that such a splitting within to self and guardian of self, or self and critic of self as in the woman with pruning shears, embodied in another set phrase such as "You've only yourself to blame" ("Tu n'as qu'à t'en prendre à toi-même"), a splitting that characterizes the self-loving, does not constitute an adequate description of the swarming "we."

This chapter explores the directions of flow between the Sarrautean intra-subjective (the "for intérieur" or inner selves and their languages, their constant self-critical questioning and their confessional and emotional impulses) and the intersubjective (the split others and their self-loving words that are not ours). It seeks to tease out some of the implications of the "complementary" relationships in Sarraute's work for a definition of that subject/the author who is the point of origin of both the moral and emotional content (the characters) and of the movements of the articulation (the narrators). Selfhood in Sarraute's latest text, I argue, turns out to be neither (false) transcendence and presence to self, that is, the discovery of an innermost and unique single personal center[7] nor a complete loss of ego boundaries in a free play of desire or of (others') words.

As Louis Sass points out in a study of introspection, schizophrenia, and the fragmentation of self that surprisingly takes Sarraute's texts as a literary model of such phenomena,[8] exigent introspection entails an intentionality that welcomes or rejects. Introspection establishes both identity with, and control over, the stream of social emotions and the episodic states of experience that are revealed to be constituted by tiny and autonomous events at once exterior and interior—memories, phrases, semiconscious urges, sensations, movements of retracting and advancing. But instead of encountering the inner active sanctuary, Sass argues, the analytic impulse and the attention to microscopic details results in a hypertrophy of self-attentive monitoring and self-loss. The absence of ego boundaries or the immobilizing of persons to statues, in this model, derive therefore from self-consciousness itself. They are not the result of any Dionysian or Nietzschean madness of primordial unity and "endemic ecstasies" or from regression to a more authentic state of primitivity or early infantile experience of nonrational fusion as in twentieth-century avant-garde and postmodern literary models or in psychoanalytic psychiatry. Selfhood in *Tu ne t'aimes pas* is paradoxically rendered in the centrifuging stream of outside sense data, words as objects of scrutiny of a self coming apart or dissolving in the objects of a fascination. But words also implode within a subjective consciousness that is distinctively ordered and ordering, have greater or lesser impact and provoke different responses according to the contexts of their reception. A polyphonic subject seeks itself through its recreation in language as it dissolves its own contours through exigent introspection and the desire to know itself. The meticulous, distanced, ironic self-scrutiny that notes the turbulent flow of multiple subjectivities (I, you, us) itself moves between authority and unknowing feeling, between inside and outside voices.

At the very beginning of *Tu ne t'aimes pas*, the words that "flow" from an "I" toward the outside others elicit an image of a humble, fearful, and defenseless personality and give rise to their verdict, "Vous ne vous aimez pas" [You don't love yourself]. The subsequent explorations of the impact of this particular judgment and the adventures in self-detecting that accompany it, will generate most of the drama of the fiction, replacing the traditional sequential narrative of the development of a personality. For what can be known of the inside is the effect on it of outside speech acts. Once back "home" and better protected in the inner sanctuary ("for intérieur," p. 11) or is it stronghold (fort intérieur), the "I" questions his sole responsibility for such an unselfloving condition. Surely the polite "vous" of "vous ne vous aimez pas" does not designate him alone, the buffoon, timid and defenseless, but "all of the rest of you who are me" ("vous tous qui êtes moi," p. 9). "We," after all, are "so numerous" and also include the deserving, the courageous, and the skillful. "We" constitutes a "complex personality" and, indeed, in this respect, is just like those outside, "like all the others" (p. 9). Who then doesn't love whom? The staging of dramas of self-love or lack of self-love, of health and disease that follow set out to investigate these questions of sameness and difference between inside and outside, of degrees of difference tolerable within sameness. In the "for intérieur," the "vous ne vous aimez pas" picked up from the outside is transformed to become the more intimate reproach or question "tu ne t'aimes pas."

The return of the spokesman, the "you" accused of lacking self-love, to the protesting, swarming enclave of the inner self "back to yourself . . . or rather, to us again" ("revenu à toi . . . non, pas à toi, à nous," p. 11) is only temporary. The return to what risks becoming "an enormous shifting mass . . . where you can find anything . . . where so many dissimilar things collide and destroy one another" ("une énorme masse mouvante . . . où il y a de tout . . . où tant de choses dissemblables s'entrechoquent, se détruisent," p. 16) is followed by another excursion into the territory of the outside others required by the debate. The unselfloving spokesman confesses that he or she is in fact not simply double but a universe of infinite possibilities, of internal tugs of war, reproaches, and resentments. Spokespersons who demonstrate a lack of inner trembling or who are even able to make a momentary alliance with the self-loving outside exist. On one occasion, a sudden invasion, convulsive fury, and "involuntary outburst" make the we, unusually, a single solid block, a closed united front with nothing that can be made to waver by the outside others or that is tempted to sally out to subjugate them, indifferent to their presence, radiating that strength, assurance, and perfect liberty that inspires and strengthens them and creates admiration, tenderness, and gratitude. This is indeed what is constantly being given by he/she who is most gifted in self-loving.

Fear of being seen as different, need for self-justification and acceptance, confession, and what has been called "the terrible desire for contact" are, however, much more common movements put into play by the "I" in an anxious soliciting. His or her confidences can cause the outside interlocutor, the Irishman, for example, to retreat in consternation suggesting that such a "loss of sense of self" might call for the counsel, the help, of "someone more qualified." Such indirect outside criticism is internalized toward the end of the autofiction when another delegate or "I" spokesperson again defends himself against the reproaches of the others inside for his confession to the outside ("Ils," "eux"). His exhibitionist self-opening had taken the form of an explosion in the repeated borrowed outside words: "It's pathological with me" ("C'est pathologique en moi," p. 208). In the construction of this scene, the "I" is watched by the cringing "us" or others of the self, first as he makes his exhibitionist confession of malady, then as he subsequently tries to escape from the literal metaphor of the cell where his pathological condition, his self-confessed criminal difference or deviance, has landed him. This time, the embarrassing delegate separates himself completely from the watching others of his group and runs to join the outside others, clamoring that he too is a suitable candidate for their community. The grounds he offers for admission are that he, too, can function as a split subjectivity, see himself, know himself (know his pathology), and apply their rules.

The possible responses of the outside are rehearsed. Will they try to calm him: "It's very common, it isn't anything like what can be called pathological." Will they lay themselves bare like you: "It happens to me too, you know, [. . .] you're like me and there's nothing pathological about it." Or will they give way to their repulsion, get up the courage to stand aside, and listen to you in silence? But in these exchanges, who is the "I" narrator and who the narratee, "you"? This text is surely also readable as a staging of the writer's ironic deconstruction of her own dialogic self-analysis and attempt to arrive at self-knowledge using "their" language and their positions. For, in the final instance, the "other" and self-loving characters are co-opted or invented by the writer as foils for the exploration of difference, the terrible desire for contact, or, to use their term, "pathology." The text puts into play the very split subjectivity of which it speaks—a confessional author performing and watching herself perform at the same time through a multiplicity of spokespersons. The attempt of the "I" (character or writer) to breach the gap between an inside and an outside, between an unselfloving pathology and a self-loving normality, the effort to establish a bridge, a common origin in split subjectivity, is scarcely more successful than in the very first scene of the autofictional drama. In this closing scene of admission of "pathology" as in the opening scene of self-accusation (lack of self-loving), the others in the self distance themselves from the questions the rebel spokesperson puts to others outside, wince at the risks of rebuttal that he takes, and take this shamefaced "I" to task for desertion and collusion with the outside when he returns. Binary divisions of inside and outside are inadequate to account for these movements, just as some of the selves inside are willing, suffering martyrs, others, on the contrary, protect themselves from suffering.

In the final scenes, the word used to qualify the contradictory impulses of the "us" ("nous") ("les tiraillements entre nous," p. 208) reappears to qualify the "them" modified only slightly by an "as if" ("comme tiraillés," p. 210 [as if pulled in different directions]). The vicarious identification with the common language responses of the "them" to the confession of "a pathological" condition concludes with the bringing together of the inside and outside perspectives, of emotional trembling and commonplace analysis, in what the initiated reader will recognize as something of a Sarrautean signature image. Like the selves, claims the text, the outside others must tolerate the discomfort of the "image du clown triste resté seul au milieu de l'estrade, son numéro n'a pas marché, il suit des yeux les spectateurs se hâtant vers la sortie, détournant pudiquement les yeux" (p. 211) [the image of the melancholy clown left alone in the middle of the stage, his act was a failure, he watches the spectators hurrying toward the exit, tactfully averting their eyes]. This image brings together the central theme of the work, the impulse to self-opening despite the risks of humiliation and rebuttal in a masochistic, confessional enterprise; the prefabricated responses of the uncomprehending outside others, in this event, discreetly avoiding the excessive spectacle.

Like many of the sketches or minidramas that make up *Tu ne t'aimes pas*, the scenes of confession of malady or difference began by means of the intrasubjective dialogue between the "vous"/"tu" and the "nous" by evoking the sense of commonality shared by this "we," despite the internal differences. One of the inside voices of the "nous" [we] then ventured to engage with the others outside. In the ensuing drama for three voices—the "I" soliciting, the "we" observing in the embarrassment of the vulnerability of self-opening to the others' judgments, some of the "they" responding with phrases of reassurance and apparent empathy, some standing at a discreet distance—there is again apparent exchange. The delegate (like the writer) may take on the color of the outside group it enters and allow itself "to be cut to the same pattern" ("couper sur le même patron," p. 104), to feel and think only what others think. In any case, the dichotomous slashing between the self-loving and the unself-loving becomes mobile as the polarization demanded by self-love, the demarcated absolute territories, give way to the mobile domain of nonexclusive contradictions, fluid self-boundaries and complexes of sustained tension between self-love and guilt, self-satisfaction and dissatisfaction with self, optimism and anxiety, and sadism and masochism.

However, despite the occasional telescoping of outer and inner (them and us), there is also a sense of the limits and even impossibility of communication. The "we" not only adopts provocative positions in relation to the "they," it also states its preference for transparency, the hat that makes it invisible, that gives it a kind of observer status, and the return to what Sarraute has constantly referred to as her "element." The confessional "unselfloving" first delegate is replaced at one point by another provocatively politically incorrect agent who confesses that he has shaken the hand of a quite unacceptable personality. The "they" may be of analogous stuff, may even be made to tremble for an instant like the "we"; yet their response here is again one of intolerance, the desire to brand, cast out, or execute the terrorist "us." Far from being self-sufficient and independent, the metaphors of the burning of the "doll" or dummy in our image evoke feelings of noncommunication, the misrecognition of the selves by the others for which the selves may be partially responsible. What is cast into the common grave for cowards and traitors is not "us" or our guilt but an effigy we have, in a somewhat perfidious fashion, led them to fabricate from what our delegates have placed before them. Masochism can coexist with a sense of superiority.

The light and warmth generated by the admiration and love of outside others/readers may well also derive from such an illusion or misrecognition, suggests the skeptical writer—from contemplation of figures of the author that are limited and unauthentic—the author discovered as the ironic portraitist of our common tragic condition or the taking of a single, courageous, intransigent, original spokesperson for the author, for example. In any event, such admiration is pernicious, situating the writer in golden cages, palaces, liners, luxury sanatoriums. These images that serve to evoke imprisonment in elitism and aestheticism incorporate both them and us, cliché and its rewriting in their very fabrication. Again, however, there is a "difference," a particularity; the self-critical and unselfloving fear of being captured by the other's reflection of her as the great author.

In the borrowed images of clown and luxury sanatoriums, the writer herself appears to be evoking not only her abjection and pathology but also her isolation; the impossibility of finding words that permit communication of authentic, complex sensations and emotions. Once again, these metaphors and images bring together both fascination with, and resistance to, the prefabricated judgments of the other that are at once a misrecognition and the material from which authentic tropismic physical reactions can be fabricated.

Intersubjective exchange (language/culture and the sets of clichés, judgments this creates) provides the material from which intrasubjective examination and feeling derive. The selves are a function of the responses of the other(s) and the unselfloving self derives in part from its simultaneous implication in, and critical distancing from, the opposite central figure of the strong, self-sufficient great man and his masterpiece. Although the intersubjective interactions between the inside (inner selves or "for intérieur") and the outside others (language) are formative, they are not adequate to explain the authorial position and they conceal as they reveal. The pronouncements of the others, for example, may give more information on these others than on the self they claim to judge. The "strong personality," she "who makes her presence felt," the host who has bestowed the honor on the "I" of an invitation to spend a month's holiday alone with her, and whom the invaded, occupied, hypnotized, submissive, and perfectionist "we" seek to please, to impress, and to entertain, even sending out *agents provocateurs* to work for the oppressor, inciting her to snub brutally, to attack, and to take yet more delight in her strength, later describes her guest to others as sensitive, tolerant, well-balanced, and intelligent despite the earlier aggression of her remark on the lowbrow nature of her guest's conversation. But it would seem that this judgment by an "implacable power," an "occupying force," may simply be making her guest-prisoner confirm her host's own superiority by being worthy of her invitation.

The nature of the outside others, is, however, neither monolithic nor simple. A scene in which the narrator stands up on a terrace at sunset on sudden impassioned impulse and declaims a familiar childhood poem that does not have the prestige of great literature, losing sight of "himself" in what is designated tremblingly as the innocent and moving intactness of the words, provokes surprise in the interlocutors and the suspicion that the narrator may not after all conform to the model of greatness, may not be the genuine thing. Once again, the choice of this particular scene derives as much from Sarraute's distinctive repertoire of images preoccupied with possible unauthenticity and imposture (of the writer) and the crushing tyranny of received opinion as from the ready-made tales and reactions she borrows. The scene of holiday "captivity" turns on a fascination with authority, and her contradictory manipulation of the other to ever greater oppression, a provocation that is ultimately an inverted form of the narrator's own control or superiority. Her relief at being among free people, worthy people, normal people, and innocent words in the train returning home after her holiday is again in contradiction with her sense of separateness from "them" and impulse to push their words around, to pull them apart, to slash them open.

According to the metatextual commentary, the intrasubjective and the intersubjective relation to words and sensations is very different. "They" observe themselves and what is happening within them (in split subjectivity) and apply labels ("je souffrais" [I was suffering], "je pleurais" [I was crying], or "ce que je me serai amusée," p. 133 [I really will have had a great time]), separating, as in this last example, the time of the experience and the frozen time of its remembering, embalming fragile present experience in "a glass casket" or making a future "nest egg" of it. We, on the other hand, are incapable of looking inside ourselves, prodigals, squandering in the present without counting the cost ("de vrais paniers percés," p. 132). In them, it is possible to get hold of words, words for love, "un grand amour" [a great love], for example, or for guilt, to be a lucid righteous judge of self but with indulgence and nostalgia ("Je me connais . . . Alors parfois avant de jeter la pierre . . . Qui est parfait," p. 154 [I know myself . . . Well, sometimes, before casting the first stone . . . No one is perfect]). The words settle into their place, adhere, fit smoothly, solidly, with nothing sticking out or snagging. Words most often slide over "us." What "we" feel is not written anywhere and our "turbulent, ever-changing waves can bear no name" (p. 129).

The "we" is presented as different, as an "exception" in a whole series of contrastive images. Whereas perfect self-love elicits business and military metaphors—the sentinel, the drum roll—transforming what is said and done into treasure for the chests of followers and conferring distinction on them, the "we" is an open place with no safe-box for depositing treasures and no space for hanging medals. In comparison with he who from the earliest age creates an auto-portrait or a statue of himself in the image of the genius, transforming even the negative qualities of laziness, vengefulness, or scorn into aspects of his greatness, our statue is a factitious, constructed, and comic snowman that melts as soon as we return to the solitude that is our element. In he who loves himself ("Chez lui, chez celui qui s'aime," p. 40), one is protected in one's castle, behind fortifications or a code of laws, within the circle of carefully drawn, appropriate boundaries, made for happiness; on the other hand, we are vulnerable, able to be taken captive and forced to please. While they can bring "vingt ans de bonheur" (p. 47) [twenty years of married bliss] out of their jewel case for us to admire, which of "us," even when on duty outside and tempted to show himself off, would ever dare to appear with that? "We" are ill at ease in such a royal palace, in "happiness," not made for such an imposing, sumptuous, and claustrophobic place, situated clearly on the other side of the fault line made apparent by the phrase "Tu ne t'aimes pas" (p. 56). "We" suspect "happiness" of being "a great grey sluggish rubber doll," hiding tedium, locking the "them" into a prefabricated model through their fear of being excluded or of losing the "happiness" they have. Inside their "happiness," we feel like "the wolf dressed up as grandmother," imposters vacillating between a sense of inauthenticity and imposture and fear of being discovered and ejected. Such "happiness" is denounced as a "Castle in Spain," and terrorist action attempts to reduce it to the scraps, stuffing, and sawdust of which it is made.

In spite of our moments of envy and desire to mix, to meld with the outside others, to hide within their "happiness," we are not one of them. Expelled, some of the we—and there are more of us here than we knew—crawl irresistibly toward the suffering that is their "natural element," notice the swollen bellies and the weeping amputated limbs on the exotic golden beaches among the palm trees, feel the earth shake beneath the most solid construction, are conscious of the presence of Death in broken or blemished or lost objects, in what, close to happiness, emanates from stains, fissures, and disorder and has no words to grasp it.

One of the voices of the "we" recognizes the advantages of not being obliged to attach a name ("Happiness") to living and intact sensations. She expresses indignation for the victims of "Happiness," those who are not mothers or fathers and who suffer from believing they are deprived of the one true happiness of families. This does not make it necessary to repudiate her own experience of motherhood. Indeed, counterattacks by the others on the illusions of this "Happiness" paradoxically push the "firemen" in the "we" to leap into the fray, even ignoring truth, in order to protect against counterideology "demolishers."

Both intrasubjective and intersubjective assertions may be subjected to an analytical and critical "démolisseur," but like the author, this deconstructor whose desire is to expose the nature of the power of the leader resembles the "we" more than it represents the "they." This "we" clearly shares characteristics with the writer, Sarraute. Like the majority of the "we," her relation to the outside others selected for investigation is marked predominantly by the fascinated suspicion that works to deflate the inflated dolls of self-love and self-satisfaction, to deconstruct their attraction, to attack their smooth surfaces, and spill their sawdust on the ground, exposing both the intellectual's secret masochism and the great man's sadistic fascination with the flaws of others.

Self-love can be a reflection, seeing oneself in the admiring gaze of others, or being magnified by irradiation from the strength and self-assurance of the supremely self-loving other. The "we," on the other hand, is not able to recognize himself in the other's images; his impulse is often to send out a deconstructor or, more dangerous still, to call down on "our" heads what everyone else wants to protect themselves from. "Why do we arouse threat, provoke anger?" (p. 103). Yet, the guilty or self-punishing impulses in the "we," the "I"'s trembling, also conceals self-aggrandizing impulses and a certain hypersensitivity to any "lack of consideration for our person." Is it not in fact an inverted pride, a more subtle form of self-aggrandizement to present oneself as infinite and incommensurable, as a disconcerting mixture of ages, of genders, unlike the common herd who learn to see themselves as gendered, as little boys, little girls, tomboys, real women and real men, or "the picture of old age" (p. 31)? Reactions to the others' judgments might derive from a different sense of superiority from theirs, from a different kind of self-love.

On the other hand, whether the docile listening "followers" of the self-loving have themselves been endowed by the good fairy with this most natural, faithful, comforting self-love is unclear. Like the we, might they too simply cease to exist in the leader's presence? For even in the most self-loving assured self-portraitist, the loss of love and attachment (his wife has gone off to get away from him) and the horror of the self-annihilation brought about by not being reflected by another's loving gaze evokes the feelings of void of self and abandonment. The line of a well-known poem—"un seul être vous manque et tout est dépeuplé"—suggests inner wounds before these are covered over, replaced by the explanation of his reaction as passing, or as the hunter's instinct to pursue what flees before him. In the leader, the fascination with the vulnerability of the humiliated or lost other, or indeed, self, the quiver that might suggest a possible crack in his facades of authority and self-loving is evanescent, a shifting and rapidly controlled state.

The probing, cerebral writer who attacks the traditional games of portraits and somewhat voyeuristically investigates the nature or possible fissures in those who have a genius (or even a minor talent) for self-loving is also the exhibitionist of another very different kind of portrait. She dares to stage her unself-loving difference from the others that leaves her uncertain and vulnerable, her need to be seen, recognized, and accepted, and her fascination with the elevating, reassuring strength and authority irradiated by the "master" of self-love.

Despite the complex relations between the selves and others and the re-writing of the self as multiple, moving, and variably gendered (or not gendered), between intrasubjectivity and the intersubjective, Sarraute's new autofictional drama does stage a "self" that is not an anonymous signifier but is individu-ated and recognizable. Pattern and even predictability emerge from the disor-der of the disparate contradictory sensations, expressions, and dramas that al-low a new and "chaotic" (order emerging from disorder) game of portraits. Despite all her best efforts at tracking the secret movements of doubt, the fis-sures, behind the other's self-loving words and gestures, despite the occasional unexpected moments of success at self-loving of the narrator's own selves, the gap between the self-conscious, self-loving other and the unselfloving self opened up by the title (the other's words) is never completely bridged. The exploration of the intrasubjective meets competing clichés, a language of the tribe similar to that used by the outside (the intersubjective), but distinctive features and individuated images emerge from the ensuing consultations or confrontations between them and us. Blamed for the wrong we do ourselves and the wrong we do them by our lack of self-love, urged toward self-loving by the outside others infiltrated in the selves, the "we" respond with the feeling that the other face of lack of self-love is the superiority of the nonselfloving.

The distinctive authorial self concludes the autofiction with the question that seems to incorporate the present uncertain wisdom of Sarraute's own life and work in a characteristic Sarrautean dialogic form.

"Comme ce serait bon pour tout le monde . . . comme tout le monde y trouverait son compte si on pouvait, nous aussi, l'éprouver, cet amour de soi . . ."

　"On ne demanderait pas mieux . . ."
　On ne demanderait pas mieux?
　"Pas mieux? Vraiment?"

["How good it would be for everyone . . . how everyone would benefit if we too could experience it, that self-love . . .

　If we could . . ."
　"We would like nothing better . . ."
　We would like nothing better?
　"Nothing better? Really?"]

In *Tu ne t'aimes pas*, Nathalie Sarraute, at 89, is once again pursuing authenticity in an intense commitment to a literary work on the nonstable, successive, and often contradictory states of self and the (im)possibilities of language as of love. This new text emerges from the same swampy land of nonbinary psychological movements that underlies the dialogues and the subconversations in *Enfance* and in Sarraute's earlier fictions. These are the complex, evanescent movements that, once again, cannot be captured by the "coarsely-fashioned" words of mass production "brutally grabbing, encircling, crushing the very thing that escapes them in us, the thing they can't get close to, the thing they dare not touch" ("Des mots de série grossièrement fabriqués, saisissant brutalement, enserrant, écrasant cela justement qui chez nous leur échappe, ce dont ils ne peuvent pas s'approcher, ce qu'ils n'osent pas toucher," p. 126). Within the common stock of words on love ("shared love," a "great love," "love beyond expression," a person with self-esteem ["un amour partagé," "un grand amour," "un amour sans nom," "quelqu'un qui s'aime"]), multiple, contradictory sensations and feelings constitute a much more complex life of that emotion. In this latest and perhaps last work, Sarraute is suggesting that much as the name takes away real presence, the word "la mort" (p. 156), for example, limiting and reducing the feelings aroused by signs of the existence of death, the notions of self-love and of lack of self-love obscure the complex and often intermingled psychological experiences they designate.

The woman writer's confession ("in me, it's pathological") seems to be pleading in her own favor that deception and dangers lurk behind self-love as unique and global dwelling. In the final instance, the lack of self-love, the nonreconciled feeling of guilt for abandoning the outstretched arms of the hungry and the dying in order to live one's own life is preferred to self-love. The self-conscious awareness of the self-loving self's infinite possibilities for egoism and domination may have its own value. More generally, there is a tension between the evocation of feelings of guilt and lack of self-love and the distanced, controlled linguistic analysis of these feelings.

A certain discretion and a self-effacement that are very different from Duras' self-assertive public persona have marked Sarraute's public life. The mixed shame of personal revelation and masochistic pleasure of confessional exhibitionism put into play in her autobiographical fictions may derive from the complexity of Sarraute's personal relation to her writing and to her reader as much as from her dissections of certain linguistic figures of the tribe and the ideologies they carry— "self-love," "self-awareness" ("conscience de soi," p. 71), "happiness," and their opposites ascribed to the writer's own selves, "lack of self-love," "lack of self-knowledge," "not made for happiness." As in Duras' autobiographical works, the boundaries between private and public, inside and outside, become indistinct.

Sarraute's texts draw their material, as has her life, from the clichés, bourgeois brand names, good vintages, reputation, dignity, self-sufficiency, and treasure troves of diplomas and medals enumerated in *Tu ne t'aimes pas* that answer the desire for security and status. They emerge from beneath the literary authority that, as one Sarrautian voice in the text argues, has placed a fine layer of varnish or a smooth layer of plaster over the surfaces of things, over the cracks and the troubling feelings and eliminated objects that speak to the heart. In contrast, certain voices in this Sarrautean text, in which the "je" and the "tu" have been replaced by "nous" and "vous," move toward undignified self-exposure in a search for the roots of feeling, toward confession of "abjection" (preference for the androgynous or the Kristevan domain of the *entre-deux*) and lack of self-love. The complexities of the hypersensitive, defensive, even paranoiac or vengeful, reactions of the self, its ambiguous and complex relations with humiliation, captive of the other in its desire to please, its need for love and approval and fear of abandonment, and its difficulties in sustaining independence are simultaneously disclosures of the impossibility of absolute authorial power or even authority. The nonauthoritarian unselfloving writer(s) may come closer to the missing words that speak to the heart. In any case, the games of the curious children that constitute aspects of the "we," busy taking apart, examining, poking holes in their dolls to reveal their stuffing, eventually cause them to tremble, fissure, or implode, collapsing inward, as self-love is deflated, with a hissing sound.

In her fictions, Sarraute's evocation of love has consistently been discreet and never immediately personal; a subconversation of emotional need associated closely with the fear and fascination of domination and the fear of loss or abandonment. In *Tu ne t'aimes pas*, which can be situated somewhere between a fiction and an autobiography, one fragment organized as a dialogic exploration with an interlocutor takes a line of well-known Romantic verse — "un seul être vous manque et tout est dépeuplé" [A single person is absent and the world is depopulated] — as its generator to investigate some of the multiple, contradictory (but, once again, not mutually exclusive) movements that swarm behind the word "passion." These include the fear of not existing or the fear of being annihilated by the other's abandonment or forgetting, the fear of independence, the impossibility of happiness alone, as well as the hunter's instinct to pursue what flees before him. Whereas a reader familiar with the very few intimate personal details about her life that Sarraute has made available or with the text of *Enfance* might find allusions here to the fear of abandonment by the mothers of her childhood, or to the recent loss of her husband, the movement is, as always in this writer's work, also toward the general, the universal, the tropism. Yet the selection of the tropistic movements, of the commonplaces with which Sarraute works, or of her metaphors, like the rhythms of her rewritings of a ready-made language, are individuated and not anonymous. As for Flaubert's *Madame Bovary* ("Madame Bovary, c'est moi"), the "you" and the "we" (perhaps also the "she," "he," and "they") are, in the final instance, "me"/"us." In this instance, of course, it is a female writer who is (re)searching the undersides of the word "love" and seeking authenticity, not a male writer investigating love as if through a woman's eyes.

In this vision, the (unselfloving) instinct to crawl toward the suffering that waits for those who move outside "happiness" (p. 55), who see the fault, the void, and death, the instinct to succumb to the emptinesss left by a lost object, may have its own authenticity. Perhaps the "happiness" evoked by that word is indeed a ready-made and limiting reality. It also conceals what is beyond words—incandescent points in vast misty spaces that Sarraute claims can have no possible baptism by name ("n'ont pas reçu le baptême," p. 49), moments that remain forever "in limbo" ("ils demeurent toujours dans les limbes," p. 49). And as for Marguerite Duras (or indeed for Rousseau in his *Rêveries*), these ideal moments are less on the side of traditional self-love, on the side of the seduction of the other (the reader, the lover), than on that of self-loss: "Quand on était comme emportés, soulevés, fondus, confondus, dissous . . . On était hors de nous-mêmes" (p. 48) [When we seemed to be carried away, elevated, fused, merged, dissolved . . . We were beside ourselves].

Is Sarraute, already different from her fellow French as an *emigré* from Russia, denounced as a Jew during the Occupation, and coming late to writing, without self-confidence but encouraged by her husband, simply the daughter of a time which inculcated self-effacement in its females along with fascination with the self-love, strength, and domination located in the authoritative (male) other? Or can she, too, be seen as revolutionary in her examination of a topos ("unselfloving") culturally gendered "feminine" but that touches humankind? Is her work a more self-aware, finely wrought approach to the human psyche and to more fluid, mobile ways of rewriting the old words and the arbitrary divisions of the old worlds? In this context, the intrasubjective might be considered that innermost, most personal and intimate domain, normally concealed by the social interactions and formulae with which we save our selves/ our face.

Perhaps, like Duras' carnivalesque inversions of received values, Sarraute's thematics and textual strategies operate a certain recuperation of apparently negative "feminine" qualities while suggesting the narrowness of the prescriptions for a healthy, whole, self-loving self set by the (common) language in power and by its progeny, common knowledge.

It is impossible to translate Sarraute's "masochist" self-explorations or the tropistic movements she attempts to capture without reducing these to the very dolls, the hard, polished linguistic surfaces she attempts to fissure, to squeeze, or slash open, perhaps even somewhat "sadistically." Her metatextual alerting of the reader to the strategies of persuasion that the authoritative text (and she herself, on occasions) employs, and that her scrupulousness pushes her to subvert, or to the traditional autobiographical quest for the reader's love,[9] may discomfort. In this text, sometimes fiercely and sometimes humbly seeking after new kinds of knowledge, we might find, rather, evidence of Sarraute's love for her seeking reader. Perhaps Sarraute's final question mark after "nothing better" (than self-love) should have the final word to these interchanges on "love" and "happiness" between the selves that play the role of authority and censor and a self that is a scapegoat (a scapegoat or sacrificial victim self-designated for an important and subversive cause).

Sarraute's work functions beyond the splitting of the "we" into the "masculine" and the "feminine," the good and the bad, the unconscious self and its self-conscious monitor or keeper, the self-loving and the nonselfloving, or indeed into sadism and masochism, pairs locked in a mutually exclusionary struggle for power or knowledge. The reader of the traditional autobiographical text who is called to love the "I" in spite of his or her split character (strengths and weaknesses) like the "I" himself or herself, in search of self-love, enters a much less unified and more shifting and complex world. This is not only because she or he is caught within the polyphonic, contradictory repeating voices in the closed textual web of postmodern conception, but because, for Sarraute, the textual self is more than the circulation of textual voices. It has a material origin in the complexity of the psychosexual body, of sensations and feelings, of life.

As it rewrites the binary divisions between selves and others, and the play of domination and submission between self and other in the self (ego and superego, ego and id) in multiple, contradictory but coextensive voices, this text, too, draws its meanings in part from its subversive rewriting of traditional language, gender and genre, that is, from its textual politics. The edges of the sameness and the difference that constitute the clear meaning of linguistic signs are blurred as the private and public, the collective and the individuated, the "masculine" and the "feminine," become part of a circulation. Although definitive meaning is deferred and the meanings of the self are constituted only in the present, local play of the text, we are not imprisoned in "the text all alone." As we will argue for Duras' autofictions, in Sarraute's *Tu ne t'aimes pas*, the impulse subversive of ready-made categories and binary distinctions, deriving from inner sensations and hidden infrapsychological movements (a complex circulation including the self-critical *and* the self-loving) creates the power of the writing of the powerless or unselfloving woman.

Marguerite Duras

eight

THROUGH A TEXTUAL GLASS, DARKLY

**The Masochistic in the Feminine Self in
Marguerite Duras' Emily L.**

Autobiography, as Elaine Marks succinctly recapitulates significant origins of
the genre,[1] arises in the narcissistic project of the search for love (self-love,
love for the other, the reader's love). Marks examines three modern autobiographical projects that are not very different from Jean-Jacques Rousseau's classic
search for a transparent mirroring of the self and attempt to persuade his reader
to love the portrait of the good Jean-Jacques. Behind the account of his search
for love in *Si le grain ne meurt*, Gide attempts to win the reader to acceptance
of his ecstatic discovery of pederasty. De Beauvoir hopes to convince the reader
of the value of her self-making experiences in *Mémoires d'une jeune fille rangée*
and Genet to solicit the reader's participation in his celebration of the criminal or deviant act.

In many of the new autobiographies, narcissistic and libidinal mirrors mul-
tiply self-consciously within the texts to serve a number of apparently similar
purposes. In Robbe-Grillet's "returning mirror" (*Le Miroir qui revient*, *Angélique,
ou l'enchantement*, and *Les Derniers Jours de Corinthe*), for example, Corinthe
(or a self-conscious Robbe-Grillet) distances and justifies his own sado-erotic
sexual fantasies, while simultaneously recalling these figures of "feminine"
supplication to text and mind and exposing them to the reader's gaze.

At the very beginning of *L'Amant*, Duras chooses to see herself through the
gaze of a male admirer (the brother of Prévert). Her face, however, no longer
has the transparent beauty of a youthful photograph but is ravaged ("dévasté")
by the irreducible suffering of age and living, by what Julia Kristeva sees in her
crucial article on Duras as "The Pain of Sorrow in the Modern World." This is
the face that he prefers, her interlocutor tells Duras. Product of intersubjectivity,
object of the gaze of the Other, transfigured by collective suffering, the sub-

ject Marguerite Duras also sees/reads herself in the mirror as monstrous and fond object of time's "brutality": "J'ai vu s'opérer ce vieillissement de mon visage avec l'intérêt que j'aurais pris par exemple au déroulement d'une lecture" (p. 10) [I watched this aging of my face unfold with the same sort of interest I might have taken for example in the reading of a book].

These specular and textual images, Durassian inversions of the expected (the preference for the aging face over the beautiful face of youth), and juxtaposition of opposites ("monstrous" and "fond" object of life's ravages) frustrate conventional readings and render any search for love more complex. It is a general feminist tenet that the woman who refuses to be the objectivized "Other" of that dominant "masculine" gaze postulated by Simone de Beauvoir or Laura Mulvey must assert her subjectivity by herself looking at herself, in the mirror, by first loving herself. Yet being seen by the gaze of the outside other/lover or indeed reader ("Regardez-moi") and looking at herself have both always been central to Duras' writing schemes. Spectator and spectacle, reading and being read, writing and being written—Duras is a product of vital constant movements of repeated mirroring and of oscillation, between, for example, active exhibitionism and passive voyeurism, loving and being loved. These movements replace any static photographic dichotomy (seeing/being seen, or self/other) in Duras' work.

In *L'Amant*, which has been portrayed as a work generated from old photographs,[2] the narrator comments that the posed family scenes the mother has taken regularly as a record of her children (being seen) are not a laying bare of a truth but rather a dressing up and a fixing. Likewise, the retouched photo her mother has prepared for her grave in the Vietnamese tradition observes photographic conventions that make everyone look similar and conceal rather than reveal identity. Like existence, identity must take form in response to, or in seeing/reading others, as Marianne Hirsch claims in her interpretation of the mediations of Duras' texts. It therefore has about it much of the indirectness of fiction.

For Hirsch, Duras' earlier novel, *Moderato Cantabile*, is an enacting of such a process of literary reading—an empathetic "imitatio" or imitation. In this novel, Anne Desbaresdes, wife of a factory manager in a French seaside town, and Chauvin, her factory worker interlocutor, meet clandestinely in a bar of the northern port to (re)construct, from the probing of the other's inner life and desires, the story of the *crime passionnel* to which they have both been witness. The setting, the character set, and the central movement of *Emily L.* are very similar to those in this earlier novel. The central movement telescopes the individual and the collective, mirroring the self by reading the other,

and working against excessive textual self-consciousness through this proliferation of doubles. *Emily L.* repeats the oscillation between a sadistic "masculine" position of desire that seeks actively to dominate or hierarchize, to kill
(Chauvin), and a "feminine" position excited by social/sexual degradation
(Anne's desire for the unknown men from the factory passing in the street).
Anne's self-loss in alcohol, willing submission to the desire of the dominating
other, social humiliation and fascination with self-dissolution and death is echoed in *Emily L.* Beyond the thematics of desire, the questions of the writer
as both protagonist and narrator of her story, of writing and the violent doubling (suppression) of life by language, are also already at stake in *Moderato
Cantabile.* As in the later texts of Duras, it is the subordinate and the suppressed that are given place of honor.

    Emily L. (1987) projects a sense of the play of familiar forms duplicated or
multiplied, of ghosts trying out new shapes in the mirror, and of the fierce
returning of subordinate, repressed desire in the ever more present face of death.
The writer as potentially solitary, masterful subject ("Moi, la femme de ce
récit, celle qui est à Quilleubeuf cet après-midi-là," p. 14 [I, the woman in this
story, the woman in Quilleubeuf this afternoon]), selecting and controlling her
characters ("Eux, nous les avions vus au bar de la Marine," p. 16 [We had
taken them in, the couple at the bar]), chooses to oscillate between seeing and
being seen ("cet après-midi-là avec vous, cet homme qui me regarde" [this
afternoon with you, the man looking at me]) and to abdicate power ("Nous
avions dû les regarder sans les voir et puis brusquement les voir. Pour ne plus
jamais ensuite pouvoir faire autrement," p. 16 [We must have looked at them
without seeing them, and then all of a sudden have seen them. And not have
been able to do anything else ever since].

    In *Emily L.*, this process is marked by the splitting of the feminine narrative
positions—the "je"-narrator [I-narrator] (or "we") observing and the "je"/"elle"/
"Emily L."/"la femme du Captain" [I/she/Lady Emily/the Captain's woman]
observed. Such a putting into question of the unified, self-conscious, separate
woman narrator is reinforced by the unreliability of even the authoritative male
narrators (Jacques Hold and Peter Morgan in *Le Ravissement de Lol V. Stein*,
for example, Chauvin in *Moderato Cantabile*, or, in *Emily L.*, the "vous" [you]
or Yann Andréa, the narrator's interlocutor). It is only through the other observed and the observing of the self by the other, in many cases male, lover-
reader ("Regardez-moi" says Marguerite in *L'Amant*, "Regardez-la," says the
Captain of *Emily L.*), that is, through a circulation of desire and intertexts that
I-the writer can speak without being confined to her authority.

    The story of *Emily L.* takes shape in the decision by a narrator, recognizable as Duras, in conversation with an interlocutor, himself identifiable as the younger, homosexual (and thereby perhaps less superordinate) male companion of recent years, Yann Andréa, to write the story of their own relationship indirectly in response to a second couple that they observe two or three times a week, one summer, in the port bar close to where the Seine flows to the sea at Quillebeuf. The story within — or outside — Duras' and Yann Andréa's story, that of the English couple who call regularly into the French port in their yacht, is strangely familiar; *Emily L.* incorporates most of the leitmotiv of Duras' earlier work. The "dying" wife and her husband, "the Captain," waiting, drinking, remembering in self-oblivious dereliction are observed with empathetic fascination by the narrator and her companion. The woman's story is "invented" by this narrator but with the help of her interlocutor much as Anne Debaresdes and Chauvin reinvent the couple of the "crime passionnel" from the words of the crowd, their own adventure, and from Anne's unknown desire in *Moderato* or as the French actress from Nevers responds to the questions of her Japanese lover in *Hiroshima mon amour.*

An absolute passion for her father's caretaker ("gardien") had compelled a young Englishwoman living on the Isle of Wight to break with her wealthy parents. Sacrificing her poetry to her lover's jealousy, she follows him on a yacht traveling the world (recalling Anna, seeking her sailor in *Le Marin de Gibraltar*), returning periodically to the security and prison of her estate (the house, the garden) after the death of her parents, waiting and passing time. Emily L.'s rebellion against parental and societal norms in her uncompromising physical passion, the pain of the impossible loss of a child at birth, ennui, the search for absolute love, the excesses of alcoholism, and the madness that manifest her fascination with self-loss and death are traits of Duras' earlier fictional characters. The lover who holds back or feels betrayed by (or in competition with) her writing belongs to the more recent autobiographical narratives of her own life, *La Pute de la côte normande,* for example. Emily L.'s intense physical attachment to the lover and her defiance of her parents' refusal of her marriage comes to her from her mother and her Durassian women predecessors: "C'étaient des femmes qui ne se séparaient jamais du corps de leurs amants" (p. 74) [They were women who would never separate themselves from the bodies of their lovers].

The aging and convalescing narrator attributes her fascination with Emily L. to the woman's abjection, the "indecency" and the humility, yet lack of shame of her continuing existence so very close to desired death. The narrator's description of the observed couple is a reflection of Duras' own situation with her companion:

Ce qu'on voit, c'est qu'elle est sensiblement plus âgée que lui. [. . .] Que c'est fini pour elle et que pourtant elle est encore là, dans les parages de cet homme, que son corps est encore à la portée du sien, de ses mains partout, la nuit, le jour. Ça se voyait que c'était fini et en même temps, qu'elle était là encore. Ça se voyait de la même façon. Que, s'il était parti d'elle, elle serait morte là même où il l'aurait quittée, ça se voyait aussi. (p. 20)

[But you can see that she's appreciably older than he is. {. . .} It's all over for her and yet she's still with him there, her body within reach of his, of his hands, everywhere, night and day. It was clear it was all over, and at the same time that she was still there. And this was clear too: that if he ever left her, she'd just stay there and die where it happened.]

Little iguana ("petite iguane," p. 106), this fictional double somewhat resembles the description Duras gave in a recent interview with Alan Riding for *The New York Times* of her own diminished state after treatment for alcoholism and life-threatening emphysema. The physically ravaged other, an aging alcoholic isolated on her bar stool alongside her younger husband, no longer able to buy shoes that fit and wearing little children's sandals, no longer willing to enter shops to buy clothes, "a bundle of old clothes, hair with graying roots, dyed and dyed again" ("ramassis de chiffons et de cheveux teints et reteints," p. 106) with broken nails and teeth chipped by falling on the boat at night trying to find the hidden whiskey, laughing and moaning in inarticulate madness, comes to embody the "disturbing strangeness" (the "inquiétante étrangeté" or the *Unheimliche*) of the narrator's own desire.

Desire in *Emily L.*'s narrator is, most immediately, the sudden fierce tenderness of the need to hold the birdlike thinness of the dying Emily L. against herself. But Duras' version of *Love Story* is very different from that popular sentimental film, even if it too requires the suffering and imminent death of the heroine to bring about the spectator's transfiguring identification. It might in fact be argued that the abject specular figures of desire in *Emily L.* have a closer relation to the sadomasochistic images in the Feminist antipornography video *Not a Love Story*. These images of feminine abjection display the social and sexual power imbalance between the sexes but also (and surely inadvertently) the erotic power of this imbalance—the self-conscious staging of abuse does not obliterate libidinal use.

Freud has argued that in a positive Oedipal scenario, the woman will identify narcissistically with the other woman, the mother, her rival for the preferred love-object, the father's phallus, object of desire that the daughter must renounce. In this "normal" Freudian scenario, the "feminine" position is close to a disturbing lack and abjection. Emily L., for her part, as object of Duras' looking and sudden desiring affection, is described as "that bar woman" ("cette femme du bar," p. 26) and "the Captain's woman" ("la femme du Captain," p. 32). This childlike "she"/"her" (L./elle) embodies the self-dispossession of all the fantasmatical recurring figures of loss who traverse Duras' texts and weave together her writing and her life (her desire). She recalls the social destitution of the mad beggar-woman of Calcutta of *India Song*, driven from home pregnant by the shamed mother and the barefoot mother from Savannahkat who abandons her child to Duras' mother in *L'Amant*. "The cheap white girl" or "little prostitute from Sadec" beaten by the shamed mother in *L'Amant* and as if "sold" into prostitution by her mother in *L'Amant de la Chine du nord* is Duras' chosen imaginary image of herself.

In Irigaray's theory of "feminine" speech, there is no unity of the subject or possibility of clear subjectivity or objectivity in this speaking (reading/writing) or indeed looking:

> Pas un sujet qui pose devant lui en objet. Il n'y a pas cette double polarité sujet/objet, énonciation/énoncé. Il y a une sorte de va-et-vient continu, du corps de l'autre à son corps.

> [Not a subject that poses in front of itself as object. There is not that double polarity of subject-object, enunciation-enunciated. There is a kind of continual movement back and forth from the body of the other to one's own].[3]

Self-revelation may come from this self-effacement or displacement, "the mystery of seeing oneself as other"[4] as Sanford Ames describes Lol V. Stein's self-dispossession ("desaisissement") in the rye field as she watches the window of the hotel where Jacques Hold, the narrator who watches her, and Tatiana are making love. Such slippages or oscillations from one position to another, from narcissistic identification (displacement/self-effacement) to libidinal identification or love, from mother to daughter, daughter to father or brother substitute, from feminized minority lover to machistic killer brother, go beyond the fixed masochistic (maternal) or sadistic (paternal) poles that characterize Freudian models.

Discussing the reversal or complementarity of the roles of Alissa, Max Thor, and Stein in *Détruire, dit-elle*, Agnes Beaudry recalls that although it is Max Thor (and the reader with him) who observes Elizabeth with fascination, in a final scene Thor challenges Elizabeth with the statement that it is she who for ten days has been looking at him. Astonishingly, Elizabeth accepts this statement and leaves the hotel followed by her husband. For Beaudry, this puzzling interchangeability reminds us that Elizabeth (who like Emily L. is looked at and does not see) is also a consciousness. In Duras' films too, the camera moves without motivation from assuming the look of a character to an apparent objectivity of the camera eye or narrator. Scenes beginning as the glance of a certain character slip to become a glance at the character.

The anonymity and ambiguity of pronouns that from *Moderato Cantabile* on mark the slippage between selves and others, the self seeing and being seen, recur in *Emily L.* Loving is explicitly equated with seeing the other: "Je ne sais pas si l'amour est un sentiment. Parfois je crois que aimer, c'est voir. C'est vous voir" (p. 139) [I don't know if love's a feeling. Sometimes I think it's a matter of seeing. Seeing you]. This interactive seeing/loving and being seen/loved is both active and passive. *L'Amant*, for example, eddies around the vortex of an "absent" photo in which traces of Duras' own past (being seen) and her present process of remembering and writing from the desiring body (seeing), cohere. This photo is the radically ambiguous and perverse one of the "little prostitute," in "masculine" self-assertive hat and "feminine" seductive silk dress and gold lamé high-heeled sale-price shoes, beside the opulent black limousine of the "inferior" Chinese lover-to-be, on a frail ferry crossing the Mekong river as it sweeps powerfully to the cavities of the sea.

In a study of masochism and male subjectivity, Kaja Silverman argues that the subversion of established hierarchies operated by "perversion" (defined by Francis Bacon as "women governing men, slaves governing freemen"), that is, foreplay displacing heterosexual penetration, or deferral outranking end-pleasure, for example, can operate only within the structuring moment of the Oedipus complex and the premium this places on genital sexuality: "Perversion always contains the trace of Oedipus within it [. . .] always represents some kind of response to what it repudiates, and is always organized to some degree by what it subverts."[5] It can thus be both a capitulation—and Foucault, for example, as Silverman points out, sees perversion as simply extending "the surface upon which power is exercised" (p. 32)—and a revolt against hierarchy, genital sexuality, the symbolic (Father, Truth, Right), disrupting gender, functionality (biological and social), and binarism (pleasure/pain).

I would argue that the oscillations operating in Duras' imagined ideal image, in which transgressive "masculine" affirmation of self through sexual desire takes place against a background of the opposite "feminine" pull toward self-loss in the matrix sea/mother/death (mer/mère/mort), constitute a staging of the possibility of the taking up of both positions, active and sadistic, passive and masochistic, "feminine" and "masculine," subordinate and superordinate, simultaneously. Going beyond a definitive Oedipal choice of subject position, the image acquires subversive potential.

There is, nonetheless, a surprisingly clear favoring of masochism in Duras' work, bias that does not at first sight appear particularly subversive. As Silverman summarizes this, quoting Reik and supported by the work of Krafft-Ebbing, masochism is a requisite element of normal female sexuality. While it may stretch the woman's subjective limits, it does not have the shattering qualities it has for the male who, as a masochist, abandons his "self" and passes over into the "enemy terrain" of femininity. The categories of masochism as out-lined in Freud's essays, "The Economic Problem of Masochism" and "A Child Is Being Beaten," include "erotogenic" masochism, that is, seeking pleasure in bodily pain or being (beaten) in a passive "feminine" sexual relation to the father; "feminine" masochism, that is, being castrated or copulated with, or giving birth to a baby in which the suffering position is almost necessarily male and there is no necessary connection between "woman" and "femininity"; and finally "moral masochism" (that is, pleasure in ego pain where the ego is beaten by the superego). In Duras, all three categories are subtly reoriented and rede-fined by intersubjectivity and the subverting of fixed subject positions. The woman writer's emphasis on masochism and its threat to the stability of the ego is in opposition to Freud's focus on sadism, where sadism's desire to subju-gate and combination of cruelty and sexuality is described as "a serviceable fusion"[6] and sadism seen as simply an exaggerated aggressive component of the normal sexual instinct.

Like Duras' ideal image of the adolescent self, the young woman, Emily L., represents rejection of parental authority and social caste and the affirma-tion, in its place, of desire, the body, and the pleasure principle. But this situ-ates her close to the fascination of the "regressive" impulse to fusion with the Sea/Mother and the death instinct. The text speaks of the drowned slowness of the dissolution of the older Emily L. ("sa lenteur noyée à se défaire"). Emily of the English I(s)-land, Emily L., the Lady, like Anne-Marie Stretter before her in the estranging Colonies, or the migrant mother Emilia [Emily A] of Ivry in the 1990 novel *La Pluie d'été*, strangers in a foreign land and language, are linked to the fantasmatic figures of bliss as death by drowning that have re-curred throughout the work of Duras. The "feminine" figures that conflate love and death in the cavities and hollows of the protective powerful sea can be both male and female, like the young man lost overboard in the immensity of the sea on the liner returning to Europe in *L'Amant* with whom the young girl leaving her love(r) identifies against the background of the Chopin waltz, thrown out over the sea.

After sounding the I(s)-lands ("îles de la Sonde") in the Malaysian Seas or troubled "maternal waters" ("Mers Malaises"/mères malaises) of her youthful wanderings with the Captain, Emily L. spends the space-time of the story in the self-dissolution of drinking in the Bar de la Marine, looking at nothing, and weeping for the ancient loss of a child and the recent disappearance of the yacht's old dog, Brownie. She is the willing scapegoat of pain and death in the world and the ego/victim offering itself to the superego's punishing oversight. This older and diegetically disappointing Emily, in a port bar in France, is not so distant from Anne-Marie, in India, and her impoverished story of abandonment "to the rising tide of the delta and to the oblivion to which it relegates individual lives."[7]

For Marcelle Marini, Duras' work is the recognition by a woman of her "sexual identity" and the inscription of feminine "difference" in the "stifling universe" of the masculine same ("l'inscription de la différence dans l'univers étouffant du même.")[8] Marianne Hirsch, as we noted, identifies in Duras the female sense of connection and receptivity and the self-imagination in which the ego boundaries between self and other/(mother) are exceptionally fluid and undefined that constitute, for this critic, the basis for a distinctive female form of reading. However, if we are indeed in "feminine territories," these spaces are problematically or provocatively marked by masochism. From Duras' "realist" coming of age stories of a woman's life in the 1940s to the predilection for what Marilyn Schuster labels the "interrogations of desire" and the dramas of "criminals of love" in the new novels of the fifties and sixties, and again in the erotic and autobiographical texts of the eighties and nineties, the scene of the powerful erotic attraction of the dominating devouring lover/brother/other is central. One of Duras' early short stories, "Le Boa," presented as perhaps autobiographically inspired ("This happened in a large city in a French colony around 1928"), recounts the excursion of the young boarder with an elderly spinster teacher to the local zoo to observe the cruel but strangely fascinating devouring of a chicken by a sleek and phallic boa constrictor. Taken subsequently to see the teacher's fine silk underwear, the child observes that the aging woman's virginal body has the smell of death. This woman's life is "consumed," states the text, by "the lack of the man who had never come." In the exhibitionist texts of the eighties some three decades later, female pleasure is once again identified with loss and pain, male pleasure with violent phallic activity.

Freud explains the fantasy of being beaten (the fantasy of the incestuous relation with the father repressed to become both punishment and a substitute for the forbidden relation) as appearing only in "unwomanly girls" who identify with the father and in "unmanly boys" who identify with the mother, that is, as resulting from a dangerous negative Oedipal complex. Silverman, on the other hand, analyses the self-display by the male masochist both as the exaggerated acting out of the conditions of cultural subjectivity that are normally disavowed and as the radiation of "a negativity inimical to the social order." The male masochist, continues Silverman, "loudly proclaims that his meaning comes to him from the Other, prostrates himself before the Gaze even as he solicits it, exhibits his castration for all to see, and revels in the sacrificial basis of the social contract. . . . [He] magnifies the losses and divisions upon which cultural identity is based, refusing to be sutured or recompensed."9

Deleuze's recent study *Masochism: An Interpretation of Coldness and Cruelty*, as Silverman points out, goes beyond this explanation of an inversion or subversion of the world to radically reconfigure masochism as a utopian affair between a severe maternal mother and her son. Masochism is presented as a pact to disavow the father's phallus and the mother's lack and write the father out of his dominant position in both culture and in masochism.

Analyzing Freud's explanation of the beating fantasy—boys are being beaten by a male authority figure in the fantasy of the girl who wants to be a boy, while the figure doing the beating is a woman for the "feminine" and "masochist" boy—from the point of view of accounts of masochistic fantasies and performances since Freud, Parveen Adams also concludes that "Something about masochism eludes Freud."10 For Adams, the masochist of either sex might, in fact, occupy any of the three positions, the beaten, the beater, and the observer. "The final form of the fantasy is not fixed, either in the sense that there is one form found in women and another in men, or in the sense that the subject occupies only one position in fantasy or in deed."11 Adams questions whether the terms "passive" and "feminine" are indeed crucial to an account of masochism. She denies that it is the figure of the father who stands behind the figure of the beater and redefines masochism as the participation in a ritual scenario that signifies the abolition of the father in the symbolic and thus also indicates a subversive relation (one of travesty) to the Law.

Masochism in Duras does not appear to suspend belief in the phallus or even to question the production of masculinity and femininity as a construct, as one particular relation to the phallus. It does seem to have some aspects of the "negativity" attributed by Silverman to male masochism or to bear some relation to the "travesty" of Adam's account of (lesbian) masochism. Duras' text has always operated a systematic inversion of traditional sexual morality and a validation of certain negative qualities. Her women characters inhabit a topsy-turvy universe in impudence, rejection of bourgeois roles, in excess, prostitution, and privileging of desire. Yet, as passive other of the male gaze, dependent on a male interlocutor or on male narrative mediation, as bearer of death and as victim of male sexual violence, accepting the inevitability of their solitude in an image of themselves produced by men, they also correspond to what Marilyn Schuster describes as a deeply conservative understanding of what constitutes women's experience.

In Emily's love story, "she" ["elle"/L] is the Captain's loved child and victim. His love is fed by her need of him and her frailty. His violent jealousy of her writing, her world he does not understand, is placated only by her submission and by his destruction of her poem. She is infantilized, rendered speechless, and appropriated by the Captain's words spoken in English — "She's just like a child" (p. 69), "Darling . . . My poor little girl" (p. 98), "Look at her . . . She's my wife . . . Yes . . . [. . .] She's a character . . . Yes . . . Il rit [He laughs] . . . But she doesn't know what she wants" (pp. 102–103). The Captain, claims the narrator, must "speak in her place" ("Il faut bien, chaque soir, un peu, pour elle, à sa place, parler," p. 71).

Writing, on the contrary, would change the relations of power. The Captain knows that his wife's writing excludes him, and burns the poem he sees as a rival, as an unbearable betrayal. Writing would bring about his dependency much as the new generation "caretaker" falls hopelessly in love with the work of Emily, the "unfaithful" poetess. This young muse-lover is not jealous of her strange instinctive knowledge of zones of shadow as is the possesive husband, the "Captain," of an older generation. Emily L., the poetess takes on the fatal attraction of the mysterious Anne-Marie Stretter and the young caretaker inherits the position of hopeless passion of Michael Richardson or indeed of "Jacques Hold ravished by Lol," as Susan Suleiman puts it, even "as he reinvents her ravishment."[12] His now is the waiting, passivity, voyeurism, and self-dissolution in thrall to the beloved. As the narrator (Duras) herself tells Yann Andréa: "Quand j'écris, je ne vous aime plus. [. . .] C'est vous qui m'aimez. Vous ne le savez pas" (pp. 26–27) [When I write, I don't love you anymore. {. . .} It's you who love me. But you don't know it]. Emily's sacrifice of her writing to her lover's jealousy is interpreted by the narrator as a choice, a renunciation of a "flaw deep inside her that she's kept silent about all her life" in order to remain "là où elle voulait se tenir, ces régions pauvres de son amour pour le Captain" (p. 121) [where she wanted to be — in the barren regions of her love for the Captain].

The mirrors of this dialogic autobiographical drama ("I say . . . ," "You say. . . ," The Captain says . . .") of passionate self-abandonment of a woman's talents to the other do not directly represent the story of Duras, the celebrated writer, who is indeed herself writing the tale. Duras does not sit directly facing the woman who renounces her poetry for an ever-receding love. Her looking at Emily L., nonetheless, does model something of the "masculine" and "feminine" desires circulating at the origins of her own life and writing.

Both the framing story in *Emily L.* between the writer and the young man with fair hair and smiling eyes (Yann Andréa), who denies the very existence of their story, and the romance of Emily L. are illuminated by a short autofictional text of twenty or so pages, *La Pute de la côte Normande [The Whore of the Normandy Coast]*, published in 1986. This fragment evokes the terrors of the writing of a book in an apartment overlooking the sea in Normandy. Required to participate in the book's invention, called to see/to love, Yann Andréa, Duras' male interlocutor slips between resistance to this love story, withholding and denial of its interest, and occasional complicity. At one point, ranting against Duras' impossible project, obscurely and obstructively jealous of her excessive work, Yann insults and denigrates the writer: "Vous êtes folle, vous êtes la pute de la côte normande, une connarde, vous embarrassez" (p. 16) [You're mad. You're the whore of the Normandy coast, a cunt, you're an embarrassment]. This humiliating phrase is the one Duras chooses to retain as the title for her text. Yann's anger against the book, his desire to kill "ça" ("that," that is, the Id or writing desire), prevent the writer from continuing, although she says nothing: "Je ne lui disais pas que j'étais empêchée d'écrire à cause de ses cris, et à cause de ce que je croyais être son injustice à mon égard" (p. 14) [I didn't tell him that I was prevented from writing because of his shouting and what I believed was his unfairness toward me]. The completion of the writing project becomes something of a race against the male other. Yann Andréa is hardly a perfect muse. In his defense, it should be said that he nonetheless types the manuscript for the writer and expresses concern lest Duras, fragile after her treatment for alcoholism, should die or abandon her work.

In *Emily L.*, the questions of love for and destruction of the other's projects, of the jealous exclusivity of the Captain's love for the woman poet that makes her writing project impossible, self-forbidden (and yet, at least in part, defiantly or secretly realized), twine through the stories of both couples. The "I" reminds the "you" (Yann Andréa) of his negative role in her current writing project:

Vous ne m'aimiez déjà plus à cette époque-là. [. . .] Et moi j'étais déjà en allée dans ce projet dont je vous avais parlé ce jour-là, d'écrire cette histoire, retenue encore d'y être tout à fait présente à cause de l'amour que je vous portais encore. [. . .] Et vous qui saviez tout de ce projet et de ce sentiment, jamais vous ne m'en parliez. (p. 144)

[By then you no longer loved me. {. . .} And I was already embarked on that project I had told you about that day, of writing that story, but was held back from being entirely caught up in it because of the love I still had for you. {. . .} And you knew all about that project and that feeling, but you never once talked to me about them.]

Emily L. begins, however, not with love but with fear. "Ça avait commencé par la peur" [It began with the fear]. Like the "pain" of Duras' earlier pseudo-diary, *La Douleur*, associated with childbirth as with war, or like the fear in *L'Amant* that woke the heroine in the night at age eighteen and set her face aging in a particular direction, this "fear" becomes invasive and multiform. In *Emily L.*, fear derives from the fearful waking and sleeping nightmares of the recent periods of Duras' treatment for alcoholism and takes the form of the hallucinatory visions that transform the male Asian tanker crew in the bar and the town square into the Other, apparently self-similar and cruel potential "assassins." The indefinite pronoun "ça" speaks, too, of the emergence of the writing and the final line again affirms the writer's growing understanding of the need to write in accordance with what she is experiencing ("laisser tout dans l'état de l'apparition," p. 154 [just leave everything as it is when it appears]), emphasizing, once again, the importance of origins. A journey back into remote primitive regions materially imaged by Emily L.'s voyages to the jagged I(s)-lands, fragmented, thrown up before time in ever threatening volcanic eruptions from profound chasms in the ocean floor, *Emily L.* appears to seek the unconscious origins of Duras' sexual/textual body through its own spontaneous forms.

Madeleine Borgomano suggests that fear as a recurring motif in Duras may be traced to the intense formative early experience of the mother's purchase of a child. The beggar-woman's self-dispossession in the act of abandonment of her child and her own replacement by another "mother," accompanied by the desire for the "velvet annihilation" of death, is, precisely, for Borgomano, the "transparently opaque" generative cell of Duras writing. There are a number of possible readings of such a maternal abandonment that Duras herself has described curiously as "monstrous" and "adorable" ("acte monstrueux et adorable"). In "My Monster/Myself," Barbara Johnson reads Mary Shelley's Frankenstein's monster as a figure for the self-portrait. Jane Gallop argues in "The Monster in the Mirror" that, in alluding to Nancy Friday's *My Mother/ My Self*, Johnson implies that the monster is both self and mother or, rather, the difficulty of separating the two. For her part, Gallop argues that the mother's refusal to mirror the daughter in "good mothering" and her desperate attempt at disentanglement from the ties of motherhood and from the constitutive connections and permeability of self boundaries that for Chodorow and Irigaray exemplify the mother-daughter bond, is a positive assertion of self. Duras can be seen to image both the monstrosity (fear) and the liberating effects of such a separation from the mother.

Other such generative experiential cells can be found in the work of Duras. These might include the daughter's sense of humiliation and defilement at the onset of menstruation and murderous rejection of her mother at the beginning of puberty, evoked in *Les Parleuses*. In a perceptive study that seeks to identify the contours of the unseen monster that roams *Emily L.*, and may not, like Yann Andréa's love, or as in Henry James, the narrator claims, be recognized until after the events are over, Carol Murphy[13] recalls that Duras conflates the twelve-year-old girl's entrance into "ça" (menstruation) as entry both into the feminine and into writing. A further such "primal" scene in *Un Barrage contre le Pacifique* recurs in a somewhat altered form in *L'Amant*, and again in the "sequel," *L'Amant de la Chine du nord*, in which the body of the adolescent is stripped and beaten by her enraged mother, suspicious of her liaison, while the brother listens and encourages from behind the door. The libidinal effects of such scenes are intense if contradictory—revolt, humiliation, a certain pleasure/pain in shame, and pride in the differentiation of herself from the mother through the experience of sexual pleasure. The narrator observes in *L'Amant* that the mother had never known pleasure.

The relation with the mother (or with fear), however, is hardly made clear by these various scenes of "the beast in the jungle." Is this the scenario of the pure mother chastising the impure daughter-whore who asserts her lack of dutifulness and her social rebellion through sexual pleasure? Or is narcissistic identification with the mother in fact the corollary of Oedipal desire for the father-brother-indirect voyeur as primary love object, as Freud would suggest? (We recall that the fantasy "A Child Is Being Beaten" has its unconscious origins in the incestuous desire for the father-phallus). Or, might the mother also represent a cold cruel phallic mother and stand-in, this time, not for the maternal Presymbolic or origin but for the Father's Law? Is she a rival for the love of the professedly "hated" older brother/father substitute or is the relation with the mother primary (archaic or symbolic), and the young girl's jealous fascination with the preferred brother and fascination with the scene of punishment an attempt to be closer to her? Where would we situate the "little" brother with whom Marguerite has a real maternal relationship (presented as incestuous in *L'Amant de la Chine du nord*) and who intervenes to protect his sister and calm the mother? In general terms, I would argue that Duras' texts work against Freudian orthodoxy and oscillate between identification with the mother as love-object and identification with the mother in rivalry for the father—telescoping these contradictions (as between the soft-skinned virile penis of the feminized lover and the powerful beautiful thrust of Hélène Lagonelle's breasts in *L'Amant*).

The fictional daughter's resistance to her rich family in *Emily L.* in her liaison with her father's proletarian caretaker and the autobiographical young girl's defiance and transgressive affirmation of her own sexual desires or pleasure in being desired and in her subversive "shamelessness" in *L'Amant*, are inevitably doubled by these figures of fear and self-chosen degradation. The self-imposed marginalization of the adolescent (the girls at school were forbidden to speak to her), like Emily L.'s stubborn sacrifice of her social position and her poetic gifts to the Captain's exclusive passion and her subsequent self-dissolution in alcoholism seem to have their origin in an affirming of such a "feminine" lack or shame.

Duras writes "organically" close to a collective lost "wild country" of darkness, silence, the unknown, as she claims in an interview with Husserl-Kapit. In this interview, Husserl-Kapit attempts to read Duras' women characters as "mobile, independent, aware, active, and rebellious" and "all your male characters as immobile, dependent, unaware and passive." Duras protests: "I don't see where you find this activeness of women." Duras refuses "authority" or "masculinity" to describe her female characters although she does accept that women have "a power that is almost involuntary . . . it isn't directed."[14] But, sensed intensely in her linguistically artful text is the writer's diffuse, desiring, active, present self marked by the threat of an underlying eruptive violence. This self-affirmation is not so much the Hegelian (or De Beauvoirian) desire to destroy the consciousness that opposes it but an impulse clearly related to both the sexual and to writing, a sadomasochistic desire to enter a fullness of possession/ravishment that takes the intra- and interpersonal form of killing and being killed.

Fear can be located in *Emily L.* both as the fascination of the sadomasochistic relationship between ego and alter at the level of the psyche (between ego and superego, ego and id) and in the relation with the potentially violent other or interlocutor, "C'est de vous que j'ai peur" (p. 50) [It's you that I am afraid of]. The gaze of the male lover that the narrative "I" once followed everywhere "wherever you went," attentive to his needs (forcing herself even now to communicate because she knows her silence makes him anxious), is predominantly violent and annihilating.

When this observer declares that there is "nothing" between them, the female narrator who at moments doubts her own story, can only concur. Death alone, she says, would make their story "fabulous" and "evident." In *Moderato Cantabile*, Anne plays out symbolically with Chauvin the death of the woman beaten, degraded, abject before her lover, willing victim of his "crime passionnel" as the female protagonist of *L'Homme assis dans le couloir* plays out the masochistic role physically in troubling scenarios of solicited physical sexual violence against her body. The self-sacrificial mother in *Un Barrage contre le Pacifique* or *Journées entières dans les arbres*, willing victim of her profligate son, the mater dolorosa of the murdered German soldier in *Hiroshima*, too, would lay down their life for the son. Although the fascination with the fixing and magnifying of the power of love by death is not limited to the female victim—one thinks of the death of the little brother in *L'Amant*, the death of the young man drowned at sea, of Anne-Marie Stretter's young lover as well as the imminent death of Emily L. that so moves the Captain—and, as Kristeva points out, all Duras' work is morbidly necrophilic, it is predominantly the female protagonists who act out scenarios of self-immolation opposite their immolating male lovers. (Claire Lannes, who is not sufficiently intelligent "for the intelligence within her" but who nonetheless cuts up her lover's body and scatters the pieces on trains throughout France in *L'Amante Anglaise*, might be one exception.)

Death, for you, is "nothing" ("Mais pour vous ce n'est rien," p. 61), the interlocutor tells the narrator who is lost in the fear of loss of love. "Je vous aimais d'un amour effrayant" (p. 137) [My love for you was fearsome]. Fear and pain, like the erotic with which they exist in metonymical and metaphorical relation along with death (both violence and self-transcendence) are transformed like this "nothing," inverted, to absorb the fluid multiplicity of the unknown and the unnamed, obscurely, without authority, in innocence, much as Emily L.'s lost poem rushes toward the "unintelligibility of the truth" (p. 89). In the *mise en scène* of "feminine" masochism, a characteristic Durassian inversion of values is operated, perhaps not dissimilar to the writer's surprising use of images of material wealth, the black Morris Léon Bollée, the luxury liner, the private yacht, and the French Embassy ball, to suggest certain human aspirations and oppose them to the limited, the mass produced, or the mean-spirited.

The independent poet's acceptance of her assassination by her lover might of course be seen to represent the writer's fear of the discovery of the fear lodged deeply, darkly, inside, in the solitude of writing:

> Je vous dis encore sur la peur. J'essaie de vous expliquer. Je n'y arrive pas. Je dis: c'est en moi. Sécrété par moi. Ça vit d'une vie paradoxale, géniale et cellulaire à la fois. C'est là. Sans langage pour se dire. Au plus près, c'est une cruauté nue, muette, de moi à moi, logée dans ma tête, dans le cachot mental. (p. 51)

> [I speak to you again about fear. I try to explain it to you. I can't. I say: it's in me. I secrete it. It has a paradoxical kind of origin, in biology but at the same time in imagination. But it does exist though it doesn't have a language to express itself. When you get down to it, it's a kind of dumb and naked cruelty, directed at myself by myself, in my head, in the solitary confinement of my mind.]

Her assuming of the shame for the dog who is dead, however, recalls not only the couple's lost former guard dog "Brownie" but also the dogs tortured on the Kampot plain; the taking upon oneself of the crown of thorns, common-core fear and pain. Emily L.'s unfinished absent poem (paradoxically, in another of Duras' inversions, a "real" poem by the poetess Emily Dickinson) is implicated in the experience of a mystical pain-pleasure, a wounding, that extends to communion with the beggar-woman of Calcutta and the pain and sorrow of the world.

Links between mystical experience and masochistic sexuality are touched on in an interview (a metatext) with a former Carmelite nun that Duras published in the collection of essays *Outside*. Duras asks whether the sisters are aware of the sexual sublimations implicit in the masochistic rituals of penance by group flagellation in the darkened church, rituals described by her interlocutor and which fascinate Duras. In *Emily L.*, as in Bernini's statue of Saint Theresa d'Avila, representations of the martyrdom of Saint Sebastian, or Bataille's work (on which Duras has written), such a wounding is conflated with ecstatic physical love. The rays of the sun through the church windows on Winter Afternoons, described in Emily L.'s lost poem on winter light on the Isle of Wight, "wound" like "celestial swords," "pierce" the heart. Pain, violent self-overthrow, and boundary-crossing, which Reik in fact defines as particularly the domain of male masochism, are similarly equated with intensity in Emily L.'s experience of writing poetry: "cette douleur terrassante . . . cette lumière rougie de sang dans le lieu de laquelle elle entrait seule, dans l'innocence et le mal" (p. 99) [the overwhelming grief . . . the light tinged with blood, into whose realms she entered alone, in innocence and evil].

Such fear is most often interwoven with a sense of exaltation in the assemblage of intertextual material metaphors that create the places of *Emily L.*, in the frail ferries and fragile cross-hatched white guard-rails and the great seagoing tankers against the gulf of the ink-blue river Seine flowing strongly to the sea, in the gulls free-flying in the lyricism of the wind of the summer evening and the chasm of the channel below, and in the smooth surfaces of the Seine and its concealed turbulent flow. The brilliant sunlight pouring out from behind dark storm clouds and the passage from sunlight into the dark sunless spaces that enclose the narrator in the forest near Quillebeuf like the bloody, yellowish mauve light on certain winter afternoons are physical metaphors for the intensity created by this coexistence of opposites.

In *Emily L.* the regression through the metaphorical spaces of Duras' text and mind toward an "ideal image" that for Madeleine Cottenet-Hage marks all of the work of Duras[15] is also both fearful and exhilarated. The originary scene is evoked here in linguistic terms; it is the scar left by "an inner difference at the heart of meaning" ("une différence interne au coeur des significations," p. 114) on the poetess whose heart is pierced by the celestial swords of the rays of sunlight. The phrase is repeated by the Captain in the original English version: "But internal difference where the Meanings are" (p. 114). A similar originary difference or void has appeared throughout the work in other recurring figures of negativity: Anne-Marie Stretter's fatal attraction and her suicide, the beggar-woman's abjection, the absent photo of the self-affirmation of the adolescent through a kind of prostitution, the missing lines of Emily L.'s stolen poem ("Le seul poème véritable est obligatoirement celui qui a disparu," p. 117 [The only real poem is inevitably the one that's lost]), the hole-word in Lol V. Stein.

In a postmodern world where meanings arise in the play of self-similarity and difference and in the circulation of signs, outside the individuated body, in the web of (inter)textual relations and in recursivity, the text can appear at worst self-reflecting and circular, at best a clouded and partial representation or false mirror-mask in which the real presence of self and the world appears to be endlessly deferred. Such a lost, primal "minimal difference" could constitute a form of truth of self in a new autobiographical genre encompassed by the "impossibility of closure and totalization [. . .] of all textual systems made up of tropological substitutions"[16] and that "veils a defacement of the mind of which it is itself the cause."[17] The fearful/fierce compulsion to write and the losing/finding of self in writing that the poet Emily L. experiences, her instinctive attraction to the obscure void at the center of the writing quest as "origin," is the writer's staging of the stakes of her literary life—the minimal difference or absolute text/meaning behind the faces of self that are both goal and absence in her work, reached, she feels obscurely, only through supreme despair and a vision of death.

In Roland Barthes' writing, the "defacement" that for De Man is an aesthetic or intellectual category has bodily and sadomasochistic implications. *Le Plaisir du texte* presents the writer as he who plays with the body of his mother. "Jouissance" or pleasure arises in the "disfiguration" (pp. 60–61) of traditional language/nature, referred to by Barthes as "feminine." This does not prevent the textual "I" that is "defacement," the name that is name of the other, and the writing that Duras herself describes as a forgetting or a replacing and an effacing in *Emily L.* from projecting (and thus ultimately moving toward some knowledge of) the writer's own bodily fear, desire, revolt, and pain. The disintegration of plot, linear time, first and third person narrative, and clear character psychology in favor of moving point of view, anonymous pronouns, dialogic drama, nonsequential verb tenses and the all-importance of rhythm and symbolic repetitions is itself both a defacement and, potentially, a subversive opening up of traditional fiction.

In a study of women's "auto-bio-graphy," which uses the theoretical writings of Irigaray, Leclerc, and Wittig to endorse a feminist thesis that women's writing can be characterized as a self-looking (auto) writing (graphy) of/from the body (bios), Suzanne Wilson argues that while "man" remembers his past through words, "woman" remembers her past through her body. To strengthen her argument that woman's memory and knowledge stem from perception and bodily drives, Wilson cites Duras looking at her own lined face, at the beginning of *L'Amant*. But, however seductive the theory of a woman's writing close to the biological and the lived, the use of the narcissistic mirrors that proliferate in Duras' work (including the figure of Emily L.) to argue for a splitting of writing dialectically into "masculine" words and "feminine" body is questionable. There is always a circulation between body and text. Duras must "read" her face to know it.

The adolescent girl and the poetess are projections of the writer (both of her self-love and her self-dispossession) but at a distance from herself, created by a circulation of pronouns, of words, of intertexts (Emily Dickinson's borrowed poem). The Durassian heroine has been described as floating, abstract, and absent, shrouded in mystery to herself, the very opposite of a body. For

Monique Gosselin, she is a face, a look, a fragile voice of nostalgia, empty waiting.[18] Or like Lol V. Stein, "ravished/enraptured," condemned to live in the desire of a triangulation, outside herself, watching in a total identification the passion and the pain of lost love in the love of others, she is disincarnate, recounted by a "masculine" other. Emily L. is embodied but she is also dialogic and a product of bricolage.

The individuality of Duras' new autobiographical text does not, then, reside in an exclusive "feminine" bodilyness although the inscription of the "feminine" is clearly intensely libidinal. Christiane Makward, for example, has called it hysterical regression ("régression hystérique").[19] It is also a self-conscious attempt to capture, if by indirection, random dialogue, material image, and rhythmic repetition, the unconscious wellsprings of fear and love. Desire is a textual (re)construction in a sadomasochistic relation with the words in power and with received knowledge. It is a war between the ready-made words of the other and words rewritten to become new signifiers. The final passage of *Emily L.* in which Duras wakes her companion, Yann Andréa, in the night to tell him about her new understanding of writing, concludes that formal language must be dispossessed and humiliated, "thrown" on the page, "mistreated" almost ("jeter l'écriture au dehors, la maltraiter presque, oui, la maltraiter," p. 154 [eject what one writes, manhandle it almost, yes treat it roughly]), in order to glimpse the secret country from which it arises, and know what we do not know.

Duras might be rewriting Barthes who in S/Z affirms the need to manhandle ("maltraiter") the unified traditional text and to silence it ("lui couper la parole," p. 15). Yet, as Susan Suleiman points out in her study of the avant-garde, *Subversive Intent,* Barthes reverses the traditional gender coding figuring the classical, "readable text" as replete or pregnant mer/mère, that is, not as "masculine" but as "feminine" and the new decadent, fluid, plural "unreadable" textual fragment as "masculine." The aggressions of the female writer against the traditional text have been considered as aggression against a "masculine" body, her new text as "écriture féminine." Duras does not as clearly gender code the language to be "manhandled" as Barthes. Does she, in fact, stand at opposite poles from what Suleiman sees as Barthes' "homosexual" preference or does she, as I would argue, move into new regions—toward complementarity, for example, or the ambiguity of the *entre-deux*?

What organizes the various levels of functioning of difference within *Emily L.* in its movement around the lost/last minimal difference is the circulating and rewriting of distinctions between the traditional logical opposites of body and text, "feminine" and "masculine," individual identity and indifferentiation.

Differences do indeed exist and are still organized by gender. In the imagining of the differences between Emily L. and the Captain, the narrator hypothesizes that in her drinking and affinity with death, "she" may be hiding from "a belief or fear," "he" from a "murder." Linked to Duras' own childhood memories of cruelty in Indochina—bands of Asian youths taking childlike pleasure in running over undernourished dogs on the Kampot plain—fear lies close to an abstract vision of originary "masculine" violence. The narrator's confession of her idiotic personal fears of the unknown or the unclassified in *Emily L.*, or (in an interview with Alan Riding) simply of leaving the house, are universalized to become fears of holocaust ("les massacres auxquels je m'attendais," p. 14 [the massacres I was expecting]). This death of the world would, the narrator claims, shockingly, be "Japanese," extermination would come from "Korea."

Beyond the political incorrectness of such provocative statements,[20] the experience of fear of difference (the slant-eyed, crew-cut group of "Koreans" "of the night" with "cruel" enigmatic smiles seen as Other and without individuation advancing imperceptibly from the forest), a fear criticized as irrational and ignorant in the dialogue with Yann Andréa, seeks knowledge of itself through representations in the text of its own irrational origins—individuated, tribal, and universal. To a consciousness marked by the war as by colonial occupation, that could not be like that of the French of France after a childhood like hers, says the narrator, causing fear is what constitutes evil. The danger from the Kampot plain is that while they clubbed the dogs to death, the youths went on smiling like children, enjoyed watching the dying contortions of those fleshless skeletons, without awareness of their evil, of causing fear. The narrator is frightened by the "Korean" tanker crew, she explains, because they are unaware that they contain her fear.

The term "Koreans" [*Les Coréens*], suggests Yann, who prompts her toward self-awareness, might be the title of a possible book. This would incorporate a number of disparate experiences—the historical marks left by her birth in the Colonies and her later experience in the war, fear of the unselfknowing other (who has no knowledge of the hidden violence or cruelty within him), confession of the general irrationality of her own fears and prejudices, possibly the sequellae of her alcoholism, fear of being prevented from writing, and intimation of the sadomasochistic relations of ego and alter within the psyche. In spite of the "imbecility" of her fear and of the project itself, this irrational writing of fear may protect from "a certain fear" (p. 55).

Fear is located then in the relationship between the "masculine" and the "feminine," ego and alter, outside and inside, at the level of the psyche and in the relation with the violent other, or interlocutor. The gaze of the male lover that the narrative "I" once followed everywhere, "wherever you went," attentive to his needs (forcing herself even now to communicate, because she knows her silence makes him anxious) is violent and annihilating. The intensity of his gaze indeed prevents him from seeing her, the writer, just as the Captain never really understood the girl from the Isle of Wight he loved. In Duras' work, the death that stamps the pact of passionate love, that seals it in immutability and union, is inevitably "feminine."

The eroticization of the self-deprecation that characterizes the "feminine" writer (Emily Dickinson, Emily L., Duras) by her apparently timeless masochism and her identification with the world in its fear and pain, is problematical. The question is the same as that posed by Sarraute's *Tu ne t'aimes pas.* Will, indeed, she who lays down her life gain it, purified by suffering?

The North American feminist literary critic might also ask, once again (aghast), whether Duras' work, at age seventy-three, on the problem of the sacrifice of Emily L.'s writing to the fierce absorption of her relation with the "Captain" is liberating or even subversive. Is this the final wisdom of the life and career of a women whose writing projects have been considered inspirational or subversive "écriture féminine"? Perhaps Emily L. is simply a passive, masochistic product of the experiences of Colonial Indochina, Asiatic fatalism, and childhood humiliation or of the existence of cruelty, indigence, otherness, aging, and female subordination to the male. Perhaps Duras is a victim of the pain of the war (the conquering older brother) and a daughter of a time which inculcated masochism in its females. Or, taken in hand by her creator, does Emily L. become revolutionary in her courageous assuming and rewriting of a complex that is intimately part of women's lives, in an active seeking of a more self-aware but finely wrought approach to the human psyche that seeks and validates the "feminine" position and more fluid, mobile, ways of mistreating and thus disturbing the old words and old worlds? It is evident from reader-response that poetically the texts of Duras that move beyond the forms of traditional love stories nonetheless remain in very powerful "feminine" territories.

It is equally apparent, once again, that the gap between Anglo-American pragmatic feminist theory concerned with reclaiming for women the strength, visibility, and authority that men have enjoyed and the French writings attempting to deconstruct that gender difference or revalorize "feminine" positions has not narrowed with this "autofiction." As Susan Suleiman points out, Kristeva's semiotic (maternal) theory (in *Des Chinoises*) posits the virtual impossibility for a woman to give up "paternal legitimation" as creative male writers are able to do without falling into madness or suicide. Kristeva argues that while the support of the mother can enable the rebellion against the authority of the father for the male, the only possibilities for the female are acceptance of the father's Law or dangerous regression to the archaic mother. It could be argued that Duras does "create" her own subject position in her invention of, and dialogue with, a double close to madness, suicide, or death (the "mendiante," Lol, Emily L.), or in the oscillatory movement of empathetic regression to and distance from the (archaic or symbolic) maternal, between "feminine" and "masculine," sadistic and masochistic. But as Lacan said of Lol and might have said of Emily L. or indeed of Duras: "Etre comprise ne convient pas à Lol, qu'on ne sauve pas du ravissement"[21] [Being understood is not appropriate for Lol, who can't be saved from ravishing]. As Suleiman says in the context of a critique of the project of psychoanalytic mastery confounded from within by problems of transference, this Achilles heel is a good thing: "Insofar as [. . .] to be vulnerable, to be open to the risk of pain and death is the sign of being human. For a long time and in very specific ways, it has been the additional sign, in our culture, of being a woman."[22]

Translating Duras' intense, intangible, poetic universe of fragmented states ("états successifs sans liens," p. 56) to the prose of everyday practice and politics is difficult and perhaps dangerous. In her excellent 1994 *Marguerite Duras Revisited* for the Twayne World Authors series, Marilyn Schuster expresses grave and thoughtful critical reservations on the reading of a "feminine" paradoxically manifest in the "hole word" or absent images at the heart of Duras' work. While the Lacanian child experiences a sense of wholeness as he acedes to language and recognizable identity, in Duras, she claims, this becomes an experience of the split nature of the self, given power and defined only by the gaze of the male Other, observed and observing her own erasure, consenting in her own victimization. Her look-alike women characters who share a single model of female (hetero)sexuality, deny the cultural and historical specificity that would allow the body to produce as well as demonstrate its cultural significance; Duras fails to contextualize her practices of reading and writing. For Schuster, Duras' identification with the Other, too, the Jew, the immigrant in Paris, the colonized, and her sympathy with injustice, are aspects of the same fatalistic essentialism that ignores differences among others, maintains a privileged viewpoint, and assumes the situation of powerlessness to be immutable.

The attitudes of Duras' female protagonists have also been read as political strength. Germaine Brée contends that whereas Anne-Marie Stretter lets the human misery, the primal disorder, the death of European history that is India (like the cruelty that is Asia in *Emily L.*) flow through her like the river itself, the Vice-Consul's intolerable knowing of the horror leads him to seek a violent double destruction, firing on his own image in the mirror but also on the innocent lepers of Lahore. As in Sarraute's *Tu ne t'aimes pas*, the "weakness" of guilt for the ignored outstretched arms of the poor and suffering in the world, and the recognition of the need of the other's love seem, in the final instance, to be less damaging than the "strength" of self-love.

In the following chapter, I argue that the forms of Duras' explorations take her beyond binary oppositions and integrate logical contradictions into a new system that allows her to write lyrically both of woman's fierce faithfulness to her lover unto death, and of her "unfaithfulness." This is in fact fidelity to waiting, desire, the quest for love—perhaps through many possible lovers of her texts, fidelity to what Brown has described as a "perverse, polymorphous" sexuality. In both faithfulness and unfaithfulness, desire does, however, seem to be inevitably involved with self-abnegation. I would conclude that the auto-fictional (personal and distanced) rewriting of the "feminine" masochistic relations with the "masculine" sadistic Other revealed in a textual glass, and thus necessarily darkly, telescoped with the "seeing" (loving) of the pain of the world, is presented in *Emily L.* as the best hope for the survival of the poetess (Duras) without either her self-accepting assassination or the loss of the origin and well-springs of her passion.

◇

nine

◇

(RE)WRITING POWER IN
DURAS' *L'AMANT DE LA CHINE DU NORD*

In our discussion of Duras' autofictions, as indeed in contemporary critical theory, it has been a concern that "difference" or the "feminine," like the principle of "carnival" or of the disorderly woman, might remain a simple reversal of values, reversal that ultimately serves to reinforce the power structures in place. The transgression of the law—or of narrative—might simply confirm the power of the law or of the language that it transgresses. The central question of whether autofictional writing has the power not only to explore power in place but also to effect change by writing difference and other kinds of power is taken further in this chapter.

It was observed earlier that Nathalie Sarraute's new autobiographies profess to excavate the unknown in the self (the intact or what is untouched by words) through the prodding, the squeezing inside out, and the exposing of the meanings of conventional expressions. An analogous project of entering a "wild country" of "difference" through reversals or transgressions of traditional frames of reference and writing is claimed to lie at the heart of the work of Marguerite Duras. Although these works remain self-consciously aware of the compromised nature of the language that serves as their instrument of investigation, Duras attempts to recover the power of the "wild country" by fashioning a "chaotic" text that models regression to the brutality of primitive states, a text marked by the cry, the gesture, silence, and obsessive repetition of founding scenes of desire. Sarraute is embroiled in a struggle between an unauthentic, unified, polished, surface order of language as it fixes and limits sensations and self and the swarming undersides of these structures, the multiple selves that can be forced for a moment into view, in a war of the words. Both writers have undertaken this "impossible" movement between feeling and saying through the medium of a literary excavation without much certainty of success and with a paradoxical sense of powerlessness/new power.

In the autofictional work of Robbe-Grillet, I argue, "difference" or power "outside power" is a residue; what remains when language is flattened to reveal its ideological basis, when textual play attacks narrative and conventions of genre and deconstructs mythologies and fantasies. This residue of desire or remainder, analogous to Derrida's (anti)concept of "crypt," has the power to transform the ironic, knowing writer-detective into the unknowing, anguished criminal in the prison cell, powerless victim of the beautiful captive; that is, of his own sado-erotic desires. The unsayable, in Robbe-Grillet, is explicitly identified with the ludic display, the pursuit, and the attempt at rewriting of the sado-erotic fantasies by which the writer is pursued.[1]

My study has argued that the "new" power sought in the new autobiographies resides in just this apparent contradiction; the impossible movement, both within and yet somehow reaching beyond that postmodern bind in which self, desires, sensations, fantasies are a construction by language, discursive formations, always-already there. As they transform traditional autobiography, incorporate new scientific models, and expose gender relations, the new autobiographies rewrite the apparently dialectical oppositions (the logic of contradictions) lurking in the very designation of the reversals they effect: a fascination with or preference for the "feminine" in the place of the "masculine," for powerlessness rather than power. These texts write a new "chaotic" character into the circulation between power and resistance to power.

For Michel Foucault,[2] power and the knowledge that is inextricably linked to power are situated within a social dynamic of control characterized by a movement from subversion to containment. Such a movement is essentially a self-canceling equilibrium process; subversion of the system remains within it, within power. Duras' work, I argue, goes further than Foucault's theory allows as power/language/knowledge are abused and used to forge connections with what is not (in) power. This is, as Duras expresses it in Emily L., with the unsayable or unreadable "difference where the meanings are," an avatar of what we have labeled the void of self or what linguistics would see as the "minimal difference" from which the discrimination of meaning proceeds. In Sarraute, the void is the unsayable of the imperceptible, identified with the tiny, affective, tropistic "differences" underlying and deferred in speech yet barely detectable through the speaking voice; in Robbe-Grillet, a sadomasochistic structure of the psyche. Although they participate in the collective circulation of power/resistance to power that constructs both the individual and the truth, a circulation that is, according to Foucault, at once an effect of power and its mode of domination, the "differences" in the new autobiographies also introduce something new (local and approaching agency). It is these local, multiple, and mobile truths that move the ordered Foucault system in equilibrium through minute but recursive changes toward the fluctuating nonequilibrium states and the bifurcation points that may create new forms of knowledge. The forms of the new autobiographies are analogous to the models of the emerging new science, chaos theory, that contests reductive determinism and accounts for the forms of order that, in complex systems, emerge out of unpredictability and disorder. They move beyond the Foucault model to the extent that the circulation of power/knowledge that the earlier Foucault envisaged leaves no place for change or agency.

It has become a commonplace that pre-Oedipal identification is the most obvious route to significations inassimilable to the Patriarchal Law and order in place. This chapter argues that the originality of *L'Amant de la Chine du nord* is that as it experiments with the cinematic and dialogic forms through which some capture of the unconscious or the prelinguistic might be possible in recreation of the selves of the past in a dialogue with the present (the psychoanalytic domain), it simultaneously struggles with the question of whether, as Lacan claims, the unconscious is indeed structured like a language, that is, is of the domain of the semiotic. The character of the "beyond"—beyond the Derridean double bind of the prison-house of language or the Foucauldian "episteme" prefabricated by discourse, beyond conventional notions of power as juridical sovereignty, social contract or right and beyond dialectic and deterministic closed systems—that the new texts model is not simply a regression to the pre-Oedipal. The writing of which Duras speaks in the moment of epiphany at the end of *Emily L.* must participate in the sphere of language as much as in the prelinguistic, be formed by the pen as it moves the pen. Its nature—that of the individual body made word and speaking to the communal body—is contradictory or, rather, "complementary."

The pre-Oedipal identification or the minimal "difference" does not necessarily recover a traditional essence. In her study of Italian feminism,[3] Teresa de Lauretis argues that, despite the mutual exclusion of essentialism and constructionism in current theory, a new form of essentialism, indeed the "essence" of essentialism, based on the individual (different) contexts and individual (different) experiences of women is not incompatible with constructionism, that is, woman conceived of as ideological or linguistic product of her contexts. The problems of constructionism for feminist theory are that it denies women a place of their own to stand and leaves no space for agency. Change, agency, the touching of a beyond might derive, suggests De Lauretis, from the very specificity and uniqueness of female contexts and experiences, from within local interpersonal and intrapersonal differences, hierarchies, and relations of force as much as from the right to the global universal equality theorized by enlightenment humanism. Without attaining the absolute self-determination and freedom of existential humanism in which existence is claimed to precede essence, agency, in this "essentialist" model, could none-theless manifest itself in choices and individual styles.

For Foucault too, in *Power/Knowledge*, the local and the singular have par-ticular significance: "Power is not built up out of 'wills' (individual or collec-tive), nor is it derivable from interests. Power is constructed and functions on the basis of particular powers, myriad issues, myriad effects of power."[4] The individual is not a preexisting entity seized on by the exercise of power but rather "a product of a relation of power exercised over bodies, multiplicities, movements, desires, forces."[5] The traditional relation between the global (as cause and dominance) and the local (as effect and submission/reaction) un-dergoes a radical change. As in the principle of "sensitive dependence on ini-tial conditions" in chaos theory, small local dislocations or effects of power, magnified through the system, can initiate major change in global relations.

Foucault chooses, much as the new autobiographers do, to investigate the network of relations from the bottom, or at the lowest level. But arguing that power is always, already there, that one is always inside power, the philosopher limits his enterprise of knowledge to an intellectual modeling of the ways in which the mechanisms and effects of power have been able to operate. The new autobiographers are writing out of an awareness of such contemporary discourses but they do not seek to elaborate a distancing archaeology of knowl-edge or a history of sexuality as Foucault does. At the limits of their own inti-mate affective experience, they sound the character of intimate power, sexual-ity, personal story in its complementary relation to history, self, and knowledge. Nor can resistance, for Robbe-Grillet, be simply a question of personal opposi-tion to the Law, of cutting off the King's head, or indeed of casting bright light on his own fantasies of the beautiful captive. In Robbe-Grillet's work, Boris, the regicide, is also himself the King/the Law. The "hydra-monster" of theory sprouts new heads as his old head rolls; Stalin replaces the Czar. The marine monster is himself a victim and the confession of his fantasies is also a self-conscious linguistic pirouette. However, in the new interchangeable nondia-lectical, contradictory figures and literary forms they create, in the movement that breaks down the limits between inside and outside, language and life, sadism and masochism, there is, I suggest, a recoding of the relations of power that may alter them.

Foucault claims that the play of power and resistance that generates itself at each moment, at specific points, and in every relation (between male and female, adult and child, etc.) allowing the emergence of "subjugated knowledges," including those of the body, nonetheless remains within power. De Lauretis formulates the hope that struggle against repressive or disciplinary power might take place not in the name of juridical sovereignty or human rights—that is, of the other (resistant) face of global power—but, rather, in the search for a new kind of right.[6]

The limitations of Foucault's poststructuralist formulation of the question of the relation to power (even in resistance, one is inside power) are highlighted by a number of other twentieth-century experiments now entering the general culture that demonstrate similarities with the telescoping ("complementary") structure we have presented as characteristic of the new autobiographies. These experiments appear in the work of Magritte, paintings of landscapes/landscapes painted that are simultaneously inside and outside the room, inside and outside the painting, in *The Human Condition* or *The Beautiful Captive*, for example. They are present also in the scientific discourses that Foucault himself sees as dominant in contemporary society, in the reversibility of the new topological figures of the Moebius strip or Klein worms where inside and outside surfaces meet and are indistinguishable, in Heisenberg's "complementary relations" (matter as both particle and wave), and in the unpredictability *and* pattern in the dynamical systems of chaos theory.

According to the Foucault model, Duras' deconstructionist forms would function within a sexuality constructed by a productive power exercised in both the repression and the stimulation (by advertising, pornography, and so forth) of bodies and desires and in the production of effects at the level of desire and knowledge. Duras' work is characterized precisely by the dramatic rewritings of the effects of such received sex/text. At the same time, her text seeks stubbornly, passionately, outside the mainstream tradition of rationality, to write desire from her own hysterical body in spite of the mixed nature of this desire and the problematic gap between text and life. Foucault, who, as Jana Sawicki puts it, sees the body as the target *and* the vehicle of modern disciplinary practices,[7] calls for a displacement in relation to the sexual centering of the problem of power and argues against the thesis of repression. Duras, on the other hand, seeks to write intense and buried desire, from the individuated body, from sexuality, in a search for new economies of pleasure and forms of community.

Foucault admits he has himself only ever written "fictions" and notes the power of a fiction to go beyond what is in place. "It seems to me that the

possibility exists for fiction to function in truth, for a fictional discourse to in-
duce effects of truth, and for bringing it about that a true discourse engenders
or 'manufactures' something that does not as yet exist, that is, 'fictions' it."[8]
Truth, in this instance, appears to escape its postmodern role of sustaining and
reflecting social systems, its embeddedness in the circulation of power relations. Where truth might engender something that does not yet exist, there is
surely a margin of meanings/origins for those who break with the system, the
writer-agents of the new autofictions, to "gambol" in.

In Duras' work the Law may indeed be constitutive of desire as Marilyn
Schuster would argue. "Difference" as a lost, preverbal, desiring, other side of
the repressive and formative social structures in place is, in any case, perceptible only through the rhythms, semiotic flow, and breaks in the texts in power
that obscure it. But sign-posted in linguistic, thematic, and structural inversions and in the writer's metatextual observations and the fracturing effect of
metalepsis (illicit slippage between levels of the text, between fiction and
metacommentary), desire in Duras is also a complex, nonlinear, nondialectical
product of a pleasure-inducing network of power relations and conflicts and
not simply a dramatization or opposite reaction to repression or disciplinary
normalization of the body. It maintains tensions and interactions at all levels
of functioning of the text, between the pre-Oedipal/prelinguistic (maternal
fusion, oceanic beatitude and self-loss, emotion) and the Oedipal (separation
and individuation, identification with the father's authority, the power of the
phallus, rational control, language).

The engendering by such interactions of something that is not always-already embedded in the circulation of power relations in place in Duras' latest
new autobiography, L'Amant de la Chine du nord (1991), a curious rewriting
of the story of the relationship with the lover, brothers, and mother already
narrated in Un Barrage contre le Pacifique (Gallimard, 1950) and L'Amant
(Minuit, 1984), provides an illustration of what I claim is the new power of a
writing not already wholly contained by the discourses in place and power.

At first sight, an aging writer appears to be at pains to delve yet deeper into
the social and colonial situations she experienced in her childhood in order
to set the record still straighter, in particular into the intimate stories of the
play of power within familial and sexual relations. Although Duras has described L'Amant de la Chine du nord as the most truthful of her autobiographies[9] and begins her text accordingly—"C'est un poste de brousse au sud de
l'Indochine française. C'est en 1930" (p. 18) [This is an outpost in southern
French Indochina. The year is 1930]—this work is also presented as fiction—
("Je suis redevenue un écrivain de romans" (p. 12) [I have become a novelist

all over again] — and as a film scenario envisioned by an "on," a third-person camera eye or spectator, guided by Duras. "L'enfant ouvre le portail. [. . .] Entre dans la maison de fonction. On la perd de vue" (p. 22) [The child opens the gate. {. . .} Goes into the schoolmistress's house. We lose sight of her]. The scenes of the ferry crossing from Sadec, the car ride to Saigon, the adolescent's deflowering in the cubicle at Cholon, scenes from the Lyautey boarding school, like the story of the mother's struggle, are "authenticated" as autobiography because they have appeared earlier. The self-portrait is developed.

> Elle, elle est restée celle du livre, petite, maigre, hardie, difficile à attraper le sens, difficile à dire qui c'est, moins belle qu'il n'en parait, pauvre, fille de pauvres, ancêtres pauvres, fermiers, cordonniers, première en français tout le temps partout et détestant la France, inconsolable du pays natal et d'enfance, crachant la viande rouge des steaks occidentaux, amoureuse des hommes faibles, sexuelle comme pas rencontré encore. Folle de lire, de voir, insolente, libre. (p. 36)

> [She has stayed the way she was in the book, small, skinny, tough, hard to get a sense of, hard to label, less pretty than she looks, poor, the daughter of poor people, poor ancestors, farmers, cobblers, always first in French at all the schools and yet disgusted by France and mourning the country of her birth and youth, spitting out the red meat of Western steaks, with a taste for weak men, and sexy like you've never seen before. Wild about reading, seeing, fresh, free.]

Yet, there is ambiguity here; the "portrait" of her young adolescent self is also presented as text. "Elle, c'est celle qui n'a pas de nom dans le premier livre ni dans celui qui l'avait précédé ni dans celui-ci" (p. 13) [She is the one who has no name in the first book, or the one before it, or in this one]. The ferry is "le bac des livres" (p. 35) [the ferry in the books]. The child is the heroine of the fictional autobiographies and aspects of the portrait of her childhood that Duras chooses to construct in 1991. In answer to the mother's imagined question "What will you write about when you write your books?" ("Tu écriras sur quoi quand tu feras des livres?" p. 25), she is presented as the writer of the book about "Paulo. You. And Pierre too, but just so I can kill him off" ("Sur Paulo. Sur toi. Sur Pierre aussi, mais là ce sera pour le faire mourir," p. 25).

This film scenario, fiction, and autobiography is also a product of a present personal/political struggle for power over the rights to the "truth" of *L'Amant*. Jacques Annaud's erotic cinematic production of that very successful Prix Goncourt novel, a film whose release early in 1992 created a considerable stir in France, was originally to have followed a screenplay written by Duras. The scene was set for a considerable commercial success. *L'Amant* had sold over 800,000 copies in France and was on the best-seller list for more than six months. The English translation, *The Lover*, had also met with market interest. Some critics imputed this to the appeal to women readers of what seemed to them to resemble pulp romantic novels. It is evident that the centrality of forbidden desire and the erotic descriptions attracted interest, as did media attention and a cover feature in the *New York Review of Books*. The film, which also attracted considerable audiences, owed much of its box-office success to its very erotic scenes and its exotic (and generally aesthetically successful) portrait of colonial Indochina. It is, however, equally clear that Duras' lack of respect for traditional narrative, her elliptical, poetic style, her splitting of character, abstractions, and reversals of gender roles take her far from her points of departure in the thematics of mainstream erotic fiction or "women's" fiction. And indeed, Duras fell out with Annaud who, she claims, told a story that she did not recognize.[10] She subsequently published her version in 1991, *L'Amant de la Chine du nord*, thereby preempting (or, at the least, denying the truth or validity of) Annaud's successful cinematic version, produced by Claude Berri and released in 1992.

Rather than simply demonstrating improved recall of real events, or greater sincerity, the rewriting of this "truer" version of *L'Amant* supposedly "without literariness" introduces a number of often small and apparently inconsequential local changes in the stories recounted in the earlier works. These "differences," I suggest, magnify reversibly through the intertextual "system" of Duras' work — not unlike the principle of sensitive dependency on initial conditions in chaos theory — introducing uncertainty and disorder and taking it unpredictably far from its point of departure. The modification of details and the addition of a number of new scenes that alter previous relations of power within familial relations as well as between the former and the present works are surface indications of the power of this writing process to effect change.

One such "new" cinematographic scene takes place in Vinh Long, one evening after a house-washing when the younger brother Paulo has been chased from the house by Pierre. The mother is braiding the child's hair for the night under the mosquito net in the bed shared to prevent the young girl from sneaking in with Paulo. The daughter initiates a dialogue with the mother, accusing her of blind preference for the bullying older brother and neglect of the dominated and slightly retarded younger son. Despite the new diegetic frame, this is, once again, the primal Durassian scene of the family romance — the triangulation or circulation of desire through the mother's unjustified and passionate preference for the violent profligate opium-addicted brother, the daughter's desire to be loved by the mother, fascinated abhorrence for the unselfconscious cruelty of the elder brother, and protective possessive love for the "little" brother. Although the scene is still colored by the young girl's accusing and demanding cries of pain, it is also marked by an attempt on the part of the adult narrator to speak from the mother's position. The narrator recalls the mother's protest that she loves all her children and her admission that Pierre, who takes mysterious pleasure, as she admits in a later conversation, in evil, indeed represents a danger to Paulo's life. In this context, Pierre takes on the form of the negative archaic father of the Oedipus myth, a powerful and tyrannical Laios who would kill any son who threatened to replace him.

The daughter's rage at the mother's attachment to the older "archaic" brother is permeated in this scene by a new understanding of the mother, by the mother's understanding of her daughter's vocation, and an apparent intimacy within the mother-daughter relationship marked by an empathetic affective power. Other such small changes in the writer's still complex and contradictory remembering and rewriting of youthful desire, out of the devastation and desire of age, continue to create a more intense identificatory relation with the mother than existed in *Un Barrage contre le Pacifique* or *L'Amant*. The fluctuations between the child's individuation and separation from the mother and her need for recognition by the mother that marked the account of the mother-daughter relation in *L'Amant* are resolved in this work on the side of a movement toward mutual understanding. Translating this within a psychoanalytic frame, in *L'Amant de la Chine du nord* there seems to be an attempt to resolve the conflict between a pre-Oedipal stage of unity with the mother and a situation of Oedipal conflict in which identification with the mother (as inside, lack of desire, lack of agency and of power) requires renunciation of outside "phallic" desire, excitement, power. Duras is seeking a border territory, margins in which it is possible to renegotiate the apparent opposites of a pre-Oedipal, "feminine" space of freedom from linguistic and patriarchal constraints in "maternal waters" (similar to the space "outside language" posited by object-relations models of analysis) and an Oedipal, ready-made "masculine" language.

Toward the end of the novel, the ambiguities already present in the earlier portraits of the mother in *L'Amant* as punitive and yet, at some level, complicitous with her young daughter's transgressions of the law (her conversation with the director of the Pensionnat Lyautey in which she explains her daughter's need to come and go as she pleases) are also given a new focus by the addition to the story of a meeting between lover and mother. The lover comes to the mother's house as envoy for his wealthy father, who has been solicited by the older brother for compensation for his sister's "dishonor." He is initially indistinguishable from the Chinese creditors waiting for payment of Pierre's opium debts and perhaps represents a similar dishonor for the mother, resembling a client come to pay for the daughter's favors.

The strange dialogue between the mother and the Chinese man could be described as "scattershot," a term that Tom Bishop, talking to Leslie Garis for her article on "The Life and Loves of Duras," uses to characterize his own disconnected exchanges with the writer, whose responses, punctuated by silence or repetition, appear unconcerned with making clear immediate sense. Using rhythm, break, and repetition, and through the shared interest in the young Marguerite and the mother's empathy with the lover's suffering, the exchange succeeds in creating intimacy between the mother and the lover. The subsequent and again new scene between mother and daughter also turns around the daughter's emotional involvement with the Chinese man and her probable future abandonment for a "lawful" young traditional Chinese bride of good family. The mother appears to have an intuitive understanding not only of the desire and empowerment inherent in the daughter's transgressions and socially marginal status but also of the daughter's fierce and tragic desire for the power to bring in money to compensate her mother as defrauded and powerless woman. In such scenes, then, it is together that the mother and the daughter ("Elles") took/got ("ont pris") the money that the too-wealthy Chinese father had to offer in an act of choice that may reverse self-abasement and humiliation to make it self-empowerment. "Avec la mère elles ont fait ça: elles ont pris: l'argent. Doucement, tout bas, elle pleure. D'intelligence. D'indicible tristesse" (p. 173) [That is what she has done together with the mother; they have gotten—the money. Slowly, quietly, she cries. From insight, unspeakable sadness].

Elements of the mother's complicity with the daughter's affair and interest in money were present in many of Duras' previous texts. In *Un Barrage contre le Pacifique*, the mother does not completely reject her very young daughter's well-off suitor, Monsieur Jo, much as the daughter chooses to let this would-be lover see her naked in the shower in return for a diamond ring. Although she does not allow Monsieur Jo to seduce her and maintains her sexual freedom, the daughter, like the mother, is unwilling to let the gift of a diamond slip through "their" fingers. In these scenes, the daughter is tacitly linked to the mother in her awareness of the empowerment brought by money and her "amoral" determination to take advantage of this without shame. Symbol of wealth in *Un Barrage*, the diamond reappears on the ring finger of the Chinese man from Manchuria in *L'Amant* and *L'Amant de la Chine du nord*. Described also as an inheritance or family heirloom given the son by his dead mother, this ring plays a role in the young girl's initial interest in the wealthy Chinese. In *L'Amant de la Chine du nord*, half-laughing, half-serious, the "child" tells her lover her mother had told her never to accept a diamond, just money, and goes on to tell a story about a family unable to sell a diamond for its true value because their poverty makes its origin suspect (another version of the story told in *Un Barrage contre le Pacifique*). Already in *L'Amant*, we are told that it is the lover's "piastres" that pay for the Donnadieu family's return to France. In new scenes in *L'Amant de la Chine du nord*, the lover's father sends money subsequently stolen by Pierre to help pay his opium debts and the lover leaves an envelope with compensation money for the mother in the "garçon-nière" for Thanh to collect. Although Duras' own obsessive relationship with money is well known and her liking for rings much in evidence, money/power is not presented here as simply serving the economic circulation of commodi-ties or as something one acquires or possesses. A metatextual or omniscient commentary claims that the North Chinese lover, too, had understood intu-itively the true and double nature of the desire elicited by the diamond in the pivotal scene of seduction on the ferry crossing the Mekong. "Alors le Chinois avait su qu'elle avait voulu la bague pour la donner à la mère autant qu'elle avait voulu sa main sur son corps" (p. 141) [And so the Chinese knew she had wanted the ring to give to her mother as much as she had wanted his hand on her body].

A second symbol of material wealth and elegance, and power, Monsieur Jo's luxury limousine in *Un Barrage* reappears as the chauffeured black Morris Léon Bollée passing so conspicuously through both versions of the lover's story. In *L'Amant de la Chine du nord*, a new emblem doubles the central symbol of the lover's black limousine on the ferry crossing the Mekong. This black Lancia that the "child" sees on a second ferry crossing the river is the convertible of the wealthy Administrator's wife, Elizabeth Striedter, figure of "feminine" power for whom a young lover was rumored to have killed himself. It is also the ve-hicle of her fictional counterpart, Anne-Marie Stretter, the Lancia of *India Song* and the Embassy ball.

Beyond the pleasure of redressing the mother's humiliation and the Donnadieu family's mixed pleasure in and scorn for the power of money (the black limousine, the diamond ring), it does seem that the political and family power of the wealthy father enhance the child's desire. In the scenes of com-plicity where the mother discusses the daughter's future with the lover in *L'Amant de la Chine du nord*, the mother's implicit understanding of the daughter encompasses a tacit knowledge of such links between sexuality and money as well as an apparent accepting approval of the power and freedom her daughter seeks through her transgressions and her search for pleasure.

> —Je ne t'ai jamais dit . . . mais il faut que tu saches . . . Je n'avais pas ta facilité pour les études . . . Et puis moi, j'étais trop sérieuse, je l'ai été trop longtemps. C'est comme ça que j'ai perdu le goût de mon plaisir.
> La mère dit encore à son enfant:
> —Reste comme tu es. Ne m'écoute plus jamais. (p. 202)

> ["I've never told you, but you should know—I didn't have your gift for school-work. And anyway, I was too serious, I was that way for too long; that's how I lost my taste for pleasure."
> The mother also tells her child:
> "Stay the way you are. Don't ever listen to me again."]

It would not, of course, have been possible for the daughter/the narrator to have been present at a meeting between the lover and the mother. This could only have been imagined or, at best, recounted secondhand. It seems improbable that these additions in Duras' mature years to the novel of childhood have their origin in any single scene lived more than fifty years earlier. They are in apparent contradiction with certain other earlier portraits of the mother's law-enforcing codes and attitudes, and even scenes recalled again in this work in the conversation between the lover and the mother, for example, in which the child, suspected of sexual precociousness, is stripped, humiliated, and beaten by a suspicious, desperate mother egged on voyeuristically by the brutal older brother to "correct" ("dresser") her daughter's sexual promiscuity and save her social reputation. By emphasizing the complicity between mother and lover in the first dialogue, or mother and daughter in the second, Duras may be rewriting one more time, and with a more positive resolution, the complex scars left by this other recursive scene of the mother's anger and despair, the daughter's physical humiliation and the brother's sexual voyeurism.

The truth of the scenes, added in *L'Amant de la Chine du nord*, of the mother's direct complicity in the daughter's affair and "prostitution" and the knowledge that these scenes invoke, derives less from a recovery of factual past event than from its invention in the present, where the body is, in a movement between past desire remembered in the present and desire created through the act of writing. In a number of interviews, Duras has said explicitly that the mother could not have been told of, and could not have accepted, an affair between her adolescent daughter (fifteen and a half in *L'Amant*, fourteen in

L'Amant de la Chine du nord) and a twenty-seven-year-old Chinese. In the final lines of her now well-known interview with Bernard Pivot for the *Apostrophes* program, televised after the appearance of *L'Amant*, Duras reiterates this claim that neither her mother nor her brother ever knew of the lover's existence.

> B. *Pivot:* Est-ce qu'elle, elle avait honte de votre liaison avec le Chinois?
> M. D.: Elle ne la connaissait pas. Ça aurait été pire encore si elle avait appris que sa fille couchait avec un Chinois, pire que le barrage. Elle ne l'a jamais su.

> [*Bernard Pivot:* Was she ashamed of your affair with the Chinese?
> *Marguerite Duras:* She didn't know about it. That would have been even worse if she had learned that her daughter was sleeping with a Chinese, worse than the sea-wall. She never knew.]

There is no reason to doubt the sincerity of this assertion, but it is contradicted in *L'Amant de la Chine du nord.* The truths of Duras' relationships always turn out to be more local, relational, multiple, contradictory, and shifting than any single or global statement can suggest. Perhaps this is because Duras' text has no power to say anything not known directly and locally, that is, through the body in the dialogic act of writing. But at the same time, for Robbe-Grillet, Sarraute, and Duras, as they retell their personal memories in public functions, memory also becomes a public space, mediated by the other—perhaps, it has been suggested to me, even produced by the media. Duras' rewriting of *L'Amant* in *L'Amant de la Chine du nord* as a way of denying the validity of Annaud's film version could be considered as a slightly different case again of a similar production of the personal by the collective.

The scenes of reconciliation between mother, daughter, and lover in *L'Amant de la Chine du nord* do not eliminate the daughter's rage against the injustice of the mother's exclusive love for a "lost" criminal son. The fiction of a complicity on the part of the mother with a lover himself now identified more strongly with the maternally beloved "little" brother does change the relations of power that existed in previous texts. In *L'Amant*, at the dinner he offers the young girl's family in an expensive restaurant, the rich Chinese lover is ignored, exploited, and humiliated. He is presented as weak and ineffectual face-to-face with the older brother in this scene where the young Marguerite joins cruel ranks with her poor, but scornfully racist, white family. The adolescent participates in the mother's fascination with the toughness of her farming brothers and the brute strength of the older brother against the weakness of the lover, although she does resist the brother's absolute tyranny. Jacques Annaud makes this ugly scene a central one in his film, pushing the family's vulgar disdain and the young girl's provocative bravado to burlesque lengths and inventing a subsequent scene of sexual violation in which the lover takes revenge for his public humiliation. In the version of the dinner and its night-club sequel at "La Source" [The Cascade] in *L'Amant de la Chine du nord*, on the contrary, the lover is tacitly accepted by the mother and the little brother. Pretending to be an adept of kung fu, he stands up to and frightens the older brother into less offensive behavior. Indeed, a taller, more confident, less weak and fearful lover is prescribed by Duras to play the lead part of "her" film. Pierre is observed to steal the large tip that the Chinese leaves for the waiter, quite in character, but, in response to the shouts of the unhappy waiter, he is again, surprisingly, "afraid."

In *L'Amant de la Chine du nord*, the power of the "voyou" brother's brute domination is undermined. Although all the elements of potential abuse of power are again put provocatively into play in characteristic Durassian rever-sals in this rewriting—the nymphet, the older man, a diamond, inequality of power—the lover himself moves between positions of power and of weakness that are linked not only to virility or impotence, or to wealth and social situa-tion, but also, and especially, to states of desire. The lover from North China is in the power of his father's law, in the power of the fear of pain, loss, and death and, in the final instance, as much in the desperate power of money ("un désespéré de l'argent") as is Duras' mother, burdened with her son's gam-bling and opium debts and her family's material survival. The lover is also, and most particularly, in the power of his exclusive, excessive passion for the "cruel, unpredictable" underage, white girl much as Jacques Hold becomes the shadow following Lol's desire in *Le Ravissement de Lol V. Stein*. He is also, of course, now completely in the writer's power. In spite of his resistance to the detour that takes them to the quayside and the liner on which the ghostly ball that figures Anne-Marie Stretter's past is unfolding (a ball that had reap-peared most recently in *Emily L.*), the Chinese lover "always winds up going where the child wants to go" ("il finit toujours par aller où veut aller l'enfant," p. 149) even into "the forest of writing still to come" ("la forêt de l'écrit à venir," p. 149).

Voluntarist attitudes in the de Beauvoir style, claims Marcelle Marini, are explicitly refused by Duras ("Je ne veux pas être déclarative"[11] [I don't want to make statements]) or undermined by other involuntary movements of the body. Truth and power for women, according to Duras, derive from desire. "On n'écrit pas au même endroit que les hommes. Et quand les femmes n'écrivent pas dans le lieu du désir, elles n'écrivent pas, elles sont dans le plagiat"[12] [We don't write from the same place as men. And when women don't write from the place of their desire, they don't write, they plagiarize]. Duras, says Marini, takes the figures that De Beauvoir's analysis lays bare—the man who exults in feeling sexually powerful and the woman who is affectively dependent and dispossessed—and explores their underside, their indecency. Her writing removes the taboo on the aggressive violence within us and permits investigation of dereliction, the horror of loss, suicidal crisis, desire to massacre those one loves, or to destroy the sex desired in the body of the other.[13] These undersides reveal unexpected new relations of gender, close to an *entre-deux* or to what Kristeva in *Powers of Horror* calls "abjection," an *entre-deux* that the powerless lover comes to embody and that once again incorporates new relations of power/lack of power.

In many of these reversals, the role of the male changes. He, too, is seen rather than seeing; an object rather than a subject. Even amidst the violent dispossession of the female protagonists in *L'Homme assis dans le couloir*, for example, the male protagonist comes to see himself as Other: "Vous découvrez qu'elle vous regarde" (p. 18) [You discover that she is looking at you]. Marini concludes that the Durassian ethic of pain and joy turns "upside down" the norms of the imagination of thought. The pain of loss and self-baring is experienced at least as intensely by the lover as by the child, and in an unpredictable circulation, is also alternately subject and object of desire.

Fear, desire, and the power of money have the potential to devour or to empower female and male alike. Marini claims:

Loin de confirmer la croyance en un accord fondamental entre l'activité sadique de l'homme et la passivité masochiste de la femme, les oeuvres de MD mettent en scène et en mots un désir bien différent. Celui, par exemple, dans *Le Navire Night*, d'une femme qui mène le jeu, égare l'autre, voit sans être vue, s'éprend d'une poitrine découverte par une chemise, envoie de l'argent—et l'homme suit parce qu'il y gagne quelque chose dont il ne sait rien encore.

[Far from confirming the belief in a fundamental harmony between the sadistic activity of man and the masochistic passivity of woman, the works of MD stage in words a very different desire. For example, in *Le Navire Night*, the desire of a woman who directs the game, misleads the other and sees without being seen, is seduced by the glimpse of a bare chest through an opening in a shirt, gives money—and the man follows because he gains something in this that he is not yet aware of.]

In *L'Homme assis dans le couloir*, Marini points out, the male sex organ is referred to as "elle" [she]. The male, too, can be dispossessed by sex, threatened by mortal fusion, by a devouring, like the chicken and its transubstantiation to a boa in *Le Boa* or the Hollywood kisses described in *L'Eden cinéma* and *Un Barrage contre le Pacifique*. In *Le Ravissement*, man's body is effaced voluptuously by his knowledge of woman's body ("à mesure que le corps de la femme apparaît à cet homme, le sien s'efface, volupté du monde," pp. 49–50 [as the body of the woman appears to this man, his own is effaced, voluptuousness of the world]). Marini cites the reference in *L'Homme assis dans le couloir* to the woman who, "les dents prêtes" [teeth ready], also waits to devour the man's sex (pp. 26, 31). The curious image of the beggar-woman biting off the head of the live fish in *India Song* comes to mind. However, Marini adds the reservation that woman does not kill man. And in *L'Amant de la Chine du nord*, "his" passion is murderous while "the child's" absolute desire carries her not toward murder but toward the fascination of immolation by her lover in the strangeness and desolation of Long Hai.

Madeleine Borgomano's readings of the novels of Duras could be extended to the stories of the power/powerlessness of the mother and of the power/lack of power of money in the autofictions to see the latter as also deriving from the passionate story of the painful and regressive desire for a male body that has disappeared ("le signifiant absent du corps masculin participe de ce vide central du texte durassien" [the absent signifier of the masculine body is part of this central void in the Durassian text]).[14] The dead dog on the beach in the noonday sun, "ce trou de chair" [this hole of flesh] that figures the hollow, the absence, the missing word that contaminate all other words in *Le Ravissement* (p. 48), may be the name or the sex of the father, or his brother/lover substitute. The brother of Françou in *La Vie tranquille* crushed like a dead bird on the rails (a "trou de chair" [hole of flesh]), the dead body of Rodrigo Paestra that resembles a child's body, the young man drowned on the voyage to France in both *L'Amant* and *L'Amant de la Chine du nord*, and Suzanne's single brother in the dangerous primitive forest, initiator into the world turned upside down ("le monde renversé"), are fables of the loss of Duras' own child-lover-little brother. Borgomano quotes the passage in *L'Homme assis dans le couloir* in which the woman takes the man's penis in her mouth and tears come to her eyes. "Je vois que rien n'égale en puissance cette douceur, sinon l'interdit d'y porter atteinte" (pp. 26–27) [I can think of nothing that is equal in power to this softness, unless it is the prohibition of harming it]. We recall the opposite description of Lol, "son corps de fille, sa plaie, sa calamité bienheureuse" (p. 79) [her girl's body, her wound, her happy calamity], or Duras' own account of the indelible stain ("l'ineffaçable salissure") of her first period, so close to the old imprisoning notions of female sexuality as curse. The fables of the loss of Duras' own child-lover-little brother appear, in this reading, to be a traditional Freudian or Lacanian story of loss (of the Phallus).

But, in *L'Amant de la Chine du nord*, the little brother's desired body, like the lover's, is feminized and sexualized. Paulo is also a post-Renaissance Christlike figure, described as a martyr dying of despair and pain. The passionate, protective, and possessive maternal love for Paulo ("C'est comme mon fiancé, Paulo, mon enfant, c'est le plus grand trésor pour moi," p. 29 [He's like my fiancé Paulo, my child, he's my greatest treasure]) is paralleled by a fierce rejection of the kind of cruel and tyrannical power exerted by the older brother Pierre over Paulo and Pierre's exploitation of the mother's love for her imperfect and lost son.

The story of the abuse of the mother was present in the fictional *Journées entières dans les arbres*. It reappeared in *L'Amant* where the brother also defrauds the sister of her inheritance (the mother's forests gambled in a single night) and takes advantage of her hospitality to steal her savings. The mother's blind passionate preference for and deference to her son, the sister's attraction to the sexually free, wild, brother-father-substitutes, the shared hunting of the black panthers at the mouths of the dangerous estuaries and the marvelous initiation into the upside-down world of the forest (the "terre/mer" [earth/sea/mother] where fish swim at the tops of trees in ponds of orchids) were central elements of the early *Un Barrage contre le Pacifique*. In that novel, however, a single brother concentrated aspects of the two brothers to whose "real" existence a plethora of published Durassian family photographs attests. *Un Barrage* writes intimations not only of the sister's jealousy of the mother's preference but also of the ambiguous attraction exerted by the "assassin" in the brother. In *L'Amant*, both the shadow of the hunter and of the assassin (Paulo and Pierre) cross the lover's room. In *L'Amant de la Chine du nord*, there is blood on the hands and body of the lover after he "takes" and hurts the young girl in a deflowering.

Like the figure of the *crime passionnel*, the figure of the assassin, the destroyer of conventions and established repressive orders has been generally celebrated in Duras' work. It seems clear that Duras' rage against and refusal of the older brother's power was less intense or less conscious at the time of the writing of *Un Barrage* than it had become almost forty years later. In *L'Amant de la Chine du nord*, on the other hand, the daughter's fierce love for her victimized brother, first clearly evoked in *L'Amant*, has been pushed to its extreme limits and has become explicitly incestuous. It is only when dancing with Paulo at The Cascade that the white girl's love for the Chinese is over-shadowed.

What was telescoped into a single and passionately admired character in the fictional *Un Barrage* is polarized as good and bad brothers in the autobio-graphical *L'Amant*, and this process is intensified in the sequel. The turbulent extreme states of love and hate, of rage and tears, are very similar. The poles of pain and pleasure, sadism and masochism, power and lack of power, love and hate are contradictory but not mutually exclusive and as troubling in the cir-culation of their distinctive features as the meaning of the accompanying tears that link the lover "taking" the little white girl and those of the little brother "taken" by the sister.

The verb "to take" that also connotes the idea of conquering is transformed by its contexts to signify reciprocity in the incestuous relation with the younger brother. "C'avait été là qu'ils s'étaient pris pour la seule fois de leur vie" (p. 200) [That had been the only time in their lives they took each other] (my translation) and in the triangulation of passion in the desire to give Hélène to the lover: "Je voudrais beaucoup ça, que tu la prennes comme si je te la donnais" (p. 183) [I'd like that a lot, your taking her as if I had given her to you]. The curious self-affirmation that has always been present in consenting triangular relationships in Duras' novels—Maria in *Dix heures et demi du soir en été* and Lol are striking examples of a woman watching her replacement and erasure by the Other woman with vicarious pain/pleasure—is present again in the child's desire to "give" Hélène to her lover. Her fascinated and despairing iden-tification with the Chinese bride is another aspect of this attempt to retain some power over the loved one by sharing his amorous adventures. The para-doxical power of such accepted self-dispossession is played out again in the scandalous "being taken" in the ditches along the roadways, or "being taken for another" by men who do not love her, like the schoolgirl prostitute, Alice, who becomes nothing but the projection of a man's desire. Duras exploits the contexts in which the verb to take ("prendre") recurs to create a network of significations that undermine the traditional semantic distinctive features (+ active + virile) of its active form ("to take") as well as its conventional bi-nary relationship (active/passive) with the passive form "taken." In the repeti-tions of the verb "to take," desire is made to circulate between the passivity and the sexual violence, the voyeurism and the exhibitionism, the control and the renunciation of control that are telescoped in the work of Duras. Again, conventional binary opposition is rewritten in the forms and in the play of the text even if a traditional thematics of female masochism is still troublingly in evidence.

In a similar fashion, the repetition of the verb "to look" is used to effect shifts between seeing and being seen, between being the subject or the object of the gaze. The two are telescoped into a noncontradictory interactive process in which relations of domination have been reconfigured but have not disappeared. On the ferry:

> Il la regarde.
> Ils se regardent . . . [. . .]
> Elle le regarde fort. (p. 36)

> [He looks at her.
> They look at each other . . . {. . .}
> She gives him a straight look.]

In the Morris Léon Bollée, driving toward Saigon, "Lui, il regarde alors les signes de misère" (p. 40) [Then he, he takes in the marks of her poverty]. Later, once again, "Il la regarde très fort" (p. 43) [He gives her a straight look]. The "child" accepts being the object of the gaze and the object of a seduction, but her own looking is also determinedly active. In the bedroom in Cholon, "Elle le regarde. Ce n'est pas lui qui la regarde. C'est elle qui le fait. Elle voit qu'il a peur" (p. 69) [She looks at him. He doesn't look at her. She's the one who does it. She sees that he's afraid]. "C'est elle qui veut savoir" (p. 70) [She's the one who wants to know]. The verbal repetitions may correspond to directions for the camera, but these movements of oscillation and reversal are something more. Significantly, the Chinese fiancée who does not yet have the right to look at the lover plays no active part in the story. What does not permit circulation of power and powerlessness, taking and being taken, looking and being looked at, what is passive only, is rejected. In a footnote that describes the requirements for casting the protagonist of the film, beauty, "some junior Miss France," is excluded because "La beauté ne fait rien. Elle ne regarde pas. Elle est regardée" (p. 70) [Beauty doesn't act. It doesn't look. It is looked at].

At the end of the book in a similar and now characteristic conflating of opposites, this time, of strength and weakness, the lover "avait pleuré. Très fort. Du plus fort de ses forces" (p. 232) [had cried. Very hard. With all the strength that was in him]. The breaking down of another opposition, between the intimate and the public, is continued here in a rewriting of a text from *L'Amant* on the "openness" of the room to the outside, the "exposure" of the lovers in their cubicle separated from the street only by shutters "dans ce passage du dehors dans la chambre" (p. 78) [where the outside came into the room].

The positions of the writer and the young girl she once was are similarly involved in a circulation of opposing elements. Duras' relation with her character, that is, her adolescent self, is sometimes that of a fascinated or admiring mother gazing at "la petite" [the child], sometimes that of empathetic regression to the child's state "je" [I]. Again, past unconscious desire or what Duras has called the inner shadow ("l'ombre interne") surface in the poetic devices of the rhythmic, repetitive writing while, at the same time, there is a narrative stance of present and artful (conscious) control over complex textual relations and intertextual reference.

The extreme masochistic thematics so troublingly present in Duras' earlier works recur in this rewriting in the fascination exerted by Long-Hai and the fantasy of self-loss in the other. The drama of the opening of the body to the other or the outside in the scene of the "little one's" deflowering, the "taking" or breaching of the body, the "bleeding," and the "mind-numbing pain" are presented as a kind of ecstasy and "death." Suffering transforms to pleasure and vice versa in this place where one is "lost" ("naufragé," p. 79) and thought is "defeated" ("terrassée," p. 77), where the ecstasy of the flesh is also despair ("ce désespoir du bonheur de la chair," p. 79). The words that weave the thread of a masochistic mysticism in this scene ("prendre," "naufragé," "terrassée") are repeated at other moments of L'Amant de la Chine du nord and carry over from other Durassian texts. "Elle est emportée par le chauffeur à son amant. Livrée a lui. Cela lui convient. Pendant tout le trajet on reste sur elle qui ce soir regarde le dehors sans le voir" (p. 95) [The chauffeur carries her off to her lover. Delivers her to him. That suits her. The camera remains focused on her the entire ride, as she looks out this evening not seeing a thing].

And again: "Elle devient objet à lui, à lui seul secrètement prostituée. Sans plus de nom. Livrée comme chose, chose par lui seul, volée. Par lui seul prise, utilisée, pénétrée" (p. 96) [She becomes his object, secretly prostituted to him alone. Nameless now. Offered up like a thing, a thing he alone has stolen. Taken, used, penetrated by him alone].

Her identity is reduced to that of "une enfant sans autre identité que celle de lui appartenir à lui, d'être à lui seul son bien, sans mot pour nommer ça, fondue à lui, diluée dans une généralité pareillement naissante, celle depuis le commencement des temps nommée à tort par un autre mot, celui d'indignité" (p. 96) [a girl child without identity except that she belongs to him, is his sole estate—there is no word for that—melded into him, absorbed in a totality that is itself just being born, called since the dawn of time by another, an unjust name: indignity].

In this more recent text, however, the small changes in the rewriting of the passionate relation with the lover and of the gender associations of the pairs of strength and weakness, outside and inside, domination and humiliation go further than *L'Amant* in the modification of the traditional association of "feminine" weakness, inside, and humiliation with the female. The text comments on the inversions it operates. This is where "the story had turned around" ("s'était inversée l'histoire," p. 41). She had taken the hand of the Chinese man, weak, unresisting, and naked, and looked at it: "Ça s'infléchit vers les ongles, un peu comme si c'était cassé, atteint d'adorable infirmité, ça a la grâce de l'aile d'un oiseau mort. [. . .] Elle la regarde. Regarde la main nue . . . La main, docile, laisse faire" (p. 42) [It crooks toward the nails, it might almost be broken, charmingly crippled, it has the grace of a dead bird's wing. {. . .} She looks at it. Looks at the naked hand . . . The hand docilely submits]. In the bedroom, initially, the lover seems to control the scenario ("Avec une sorte de crainte comme si elle était fragile, et aussi avec une brutalité contenue," p. 75 [Almost fearfully as though she were fragile—but with contained violence too]) but he is awed, overwhelmed by his "violation" and, as in *L'Amant*, the child also dominates the lover's abandoned, weak, and unresisting body. "Et c'est alors qu'elle le fait, elle. Les yeux fermés, elle le déshabille" (p. 75) [And then she is the one who does it—she. With her eyes closed, she undresses him].

Again, when the lover returns from the visit to the mother at Sadec before their departure, "Elle le savonne. Elle le douche. Il se laisse faire. Les rôles se sont inversés" (p. 133) [She soaps him. She bathes him. He lets her. Their roles are reversed]. She protects him, maternally; he is her impotent "child" "without strength" who does "what she wants" (p. 133), much as she has been "his blood sister. His child. His love" (p. 81). He is "dead from desire from wanting this child, mad with love. Martyred" (p. 61). As her departure and his marriage approach, his despair and erotic impulse toward death increase "to the point of suicide" (p. 212). On the boat, the young girl closes her eyes to rediscover "his captive eyes" (p. 217) fluttering beneath her kisses.

The thin child is "cruel" (p. 149). But, so, too, in this oscillating movement that is not an equilibrium is the North Chinese lover. Unable to keep the child through fear of his father and weakness before the force of Chinese family law that would have him marry the sixteen-year-old Chinese girl betrothed to him in childhood, he fantasizes the white girl's sacrificial murder at Long-Hai, a place of primitive impulse and madness. In spite of her fear, the young girl shares, but asymmetrically, the fascination of this fantasmatical beach site of loss of power where the mad beggar-women and the dispossessed laugh at the same time as they cry. She, too, becomes fascinated by the fear of martyr-dom, "scared of this stranger of the trip to Long-Hai" (p. 134).

In previous chapters, I interpreted the recurring thematic of "feminine" self-loss and "masculine" violence and domination as the textual imaging of a sadomasochistic (master-slave) structure of the psyche that Jessica Benjamin, for example, sees as characterizing quintessentially the "bonds of love."[15] The remembering of the incestuous nature of the consuming protective love for the little brother that was not present in *L'Amant* might be emblematic of a struggle within the psyche against the superego and its burying ("enfouisse-ment") of powerful impulses. While there is no absolute evidence for a real relation with a Chinese lover, whose name the writer had forgotten—except, paradoxically, the discovery that he died in 1990—or of an incestuous (on one occasion) relation with Paulo, autofiction seeks the recovery of such desires from repression or from the kind of projection that seems to be at work, for example, in the earlier fiction, *Agatha*, in the invention of the meeting be-tween a brother and a sister and their indirect evocation of an earlier incestu-ous love.

Lacan has claimed that Duras' poetic discourses unconsciously repeat his own psychoanalytic constructs ("Elle s'avère savoir sans moi ce que j'enseigne" [It turns out that she knows without me what I teach].[16] Yet, Duras' rewriting of the nondialectical, asymmetric, unpredictable structures of an intrapsychic and interpsychic sadomasochistic desire is surprisingly conscious. It seems to go beyond the fetish of the lost Phallus or indeed, beyond the primal Lacanian "mirror-stage" or scene in which the *jouissance* of (self-)recognition through the other is also (self-)loss as anguished captive of the dislocated image of the other, a splitting and loss accompanied by aggressive tension toward the other. And whereas Lacan takes for granted the primacy of the theoretical discourse, in Duras' text, despite the conscious character of the structuring of the "I" as a fiction and of the systematic deconstruction of traditional meaning, the silences and gaps that clamor the holed or flawed ("lacunaire") character of conscious language, a language that allows the activity of the imagination to penetrate only in a veiled and incomprehensible form, alter traditional power relations between writing from the body and theory. In Duras, these different kinds of discourses themselves become "complementary," are telescoped. The logic of the unconscious, that, for Freud, ignores the dialectic of alternatives much as dream brings together opposites, influences this Barthesian style "mixing of every language."

Duras' explicit, repeated, intratextual paradigms of sexual violence and masochism are troubling. Perhaps, as the narrator in *Emily L.* confesses, the writer has sometimes ventured into dangerous zones that she ought not to have visited. The shifts in the gendering of the active-passive constellation do suggest, however, that "truth" is a construct dependent on one's present position. The conflating of opposites to show their connections in a chaotic and dynamical nondialectical structure directs the reader to make new sense out of the many scenes of excess and contradiction that recall both Lol, who "devait délicieusement ressentir l'éviction souhaitée de sa personne" [who must have experienced the desired eviction of her person with delight] (*Le Ravissement de Lol V. Stein*, p. 124), and the young girl in the pink rose-wood man's hat who actively pursues her desire. There is a case for the defense: Duras' body does indeed show its cultural signification in her texts, as Schuster argues, but her writing is also performative, capable of some remapping of these significations. While I had doubts about the subversiveness of the sexual/textual aggressions against the female body/the body of the text in Robbe-Grillet's texts, which hardly seemed an escape from established relations of sexual power, either, that writer's nondichotomous, or "complementary" and "chaotic," writing practices did appear to have some mitigating potential for change. His *mise en scène* of sadomasochistic thematics foregrounded both the complexity of the power of psychical impulses and energies and the commonplaces of sexuality figured by the "beautiful captive" or the master/slave relation.

My own staging of the sadomasochistic thematics that mark the new autobiographies and, indeed, characterize postmodern texts in general has attempted to reveal the lines of intersection of what Foucault sees as the two dominant views of the domain of sex; at once the place where the "ineluctability of the master" is established and the source of the most radical of all subversions. Power and resistance to power converge at this intersection. Foucault argues that the figure is dialectical, reducing power to a negative law of prohibition that is homogeneous at every level (the family and the state). It enables power never to be considered in other than negative terms and the fundamental operation of power to be thought of erroneously as a speech act (enunciation of law, discourse of prohibition), while its origin is subjectivized and located in the sovereign (p. 140).

For Foucault, the relations of power are also interwoven with other relations—of production, kinship, family, and sexuality. These relations do not take the sole form of prohibition and punishment but are of multiple kinds. In *Power/Knowledge*, he claims:

> Their interconnections delineate general conditions of domination, and this domination is organized into a more-or-less coherent and unitary strategic

form. [. . .] Dispersed, heteromorphous, localized procedures of power are adapted, reinforced and transformed by these global strategies, all this being accompanied by numerous phenomena of inertia, displacement and resistance; hence one should not assume a massive and primal condition of domination, a binary structure with 'dominators' on one side and 'dominated' on the other, but rather a multiform production of relations of domination which are partially susceptible of integration into overall strategies. (p. 142)

Resistances are formed at the point where relations of power are exercised, for, like power, resistance too is multiple.

In the new autobiographical texts, relations of domination are multiform. I have sought evidence for the argument that the multiformity and deviations that create instability in the new autobiographies have their origin in forms of agency, individual history, situation, gender, choice, or style and that they begin to enact a power beyond the Foucault model that has no "margins for those who break with the system to gambol in" (p. 139). In fact, for Foucault too, the local character of criticism is not a "soggy eclecticism" but gives rise to the reemergence of what he calls ordinary knowledge ("le savoir des gens") or "anti-science" (p. 80). The new autobiographers attempt to explore their present relationships with their past through such everyday knowledge or language and through the local and familial. This is why the writer becomes the child of her own past experience and the child the writer in a telescoping of present and past, history and story, ignorance and rhetorical mastery, why outer (the colonial situation, cultural difference) and inner are brought together, as Duras claims to have rediscovered and relived the formative age of her own crossing of the Mekong River during the year she rewrote this new autobiography.

Although the specificity of the historical situation seems generally to be absorbed by or telescoped into the psychic realm in Duras' writing, her transgressive crossings of the spaces of Saigon and wanderings in Cholon that effect the "insertion and reinscription of the Durassian subject in the space of that colonial city," Panivong Norindr argues, open out not only to sexual knowledge but also to some degree of "imaginary understanding of the colonial situation."[17] Referring to herself in the third person, Duras, narrator, also plays critic for her reader in footnotes, analyzing, for example, the unnatural, factitious, but artful, character that paradoxically re-creates naturalness. "L'auteur tient beaucoup à ces conversations 'chaotiques' mais d'un naturel retrouvé. On peut parler ici de 'couches' de conversations juxtaposées" (p. 203) [The author would like to stick with these chaotic conversations, which have a re-found spontaneity. You might call them "layered," parallel conversations] (my translation). She plays with her authorial omniscience by correcting details of scenes from earlier texts—the rattle-trap family car, the B12, from *Un Barrage contre le Pacifique* was perhaps not in such bad condition, after all. Other rewritings are major; the enamored and despised would-be lover of *Un Barrage*, Monsieur Jo, is the son of a dominant white colonial planter.

But writing, as for Peter Morgan in *Le Vice-Consul*, is also always an act of desire and an act of knowledge whose vehicle is empathy with pain and non-knowledge. "Peter Morgan est un jeune homme qui désire prendre la douleur de Calcutta, que ce soit fait, et que son ignorance cesse avec la douleur prise"[18] [Peter Morgan is a young man who desires to take on the pain of Calcutta, who wants this to be done, and his ignorance to cease with the pain assumed]. The verb "prendre" here takes on the meanings of "apprendre," but taking and being taken, knowing and nonknowing, like power and powerlessness, are, once again, telescoped.

The concern with the nature of verisimilitude and truth as ready-made, originating in common knowledge and in texts (as effect of power and mode of domination in Foucault's model or as entry into the Symbolic in Lacanian terms), has characterized both *nouveau roman* and new autobiography from their beginnings. The writer remembers her childhood through her body. "Elle se souvient . . . Elle entend encore le bruit de la mer dans la chambre" (p. 78) [She remembers . . . She still hears the sound of the sea in the room]. Sensation, as in Sarraute or Robbe-Grillet, seems to provide some guarantee of truth. But the memory of the sound of the sea recalls, indistinguishably, her past writing of her childhood. "D'avoir écrit ça, elle se souvient aussi, comme le bruit de la rue chinoise. Elle se souvient même d'avoir écrit que la mer était présente ce jour-là dans la chambre des amants" (p. 78) [And she remembers having written that. As she remembers the Chinese street. She even remembers writing that the sea was present that day in the lovers' room]. There is both an author(ity) controlling and commenting metatextually on these slippages with knowledge, and a staging of the impossibility of knowing. "She," the writer, calls attention in footnotes to the intertextual origin of the "ghostly ball" of the liner that had "already" appeared in *Emily L.*, now watched by the Chinese lover and the little white girl. The "true" origin of this scene is no clearer. Reference is always uncertain, overlapping, or multiple.

In *L'Amant de la Chine du nord*, the fluctuating, local movements toward identification with the mother as intuitive and nonphallic and the imagining of the mother's empathetic understanding of the power of her daughter's transgressive desires effect changes in intimate relations of familial and sexual power.

So, too, does the writing of (or writing out of) the self-assertive power and attraction of the older brother, the settling of accounts with brutal physical power in favor of the interaction with a feminized beloved little brother identified increasingly with the Chinese lover. These shifts in the relations with the mother, brother(s), and lover and with the child she once was, do suggest local and specific agency (the writer seeking present resolution of her own past [selves]). The telescoping movements between past and present, writing and the real, and the gendering of relations of domination and submission both stage and begin to subvert relations of power. Like the "complementary" and "chaotic" forms that carry them, this book has argued, these changes have not always been already there. What is filtered through the repetitions and changes in the text does take Duras further and perhaps not always within power as Foucault would have it. In all of the new autobiographies, these modifications may indeed go beyond the already said to represent not only an analysis or deconstruction of previously existing power (and gender) relations but also a rewriting of the conventions of traditional autobiography and gender that is both the power of this new autobiographical writing and a rewriting of power.

AFTERWORD

This book has argued that the originality of the new autobiographies derives from the fact that although it is preoccupied with the postmodern questions of meaning and origin (as inscribed by an arbitrary linguistic system of "différance" and deferral), this new intergeneric work refuses any hard-line position of "all is language." Autofictions function in the margins between such semiotic theory and the physical practice of writing from the situated gendered body and out of the unconscious. The methodology adopted in my own reading practices consists of what an empathetic critic[1] describes as the "careful tracing and re-tracing of relational and identifiable voices in search of their 'impossible' identity by speaking over and over about their unspeakable past." There is no single unified Truth or Authenticity or Self that emerges from these different voices but a dance of multiple and temporary truths — of so-called inner perceptions, of the affect, of relationships, and of individuated, recursive, desires, fears, and fantasies — as these are framed and carried by selected and combined words.

My thesis is that there is a structural principle of "complementarity" at work in the hybrid texts of autofiction that enables them to make the "impossible" movement between (mutually exclusive) life and text. This afterword, that is, a conclusion without a synthesis or definitive closing, takes up the debate again where the introduction left off by situating the new autobiographies in the wider context of current debates in French intellectual history, in philosophy, and in literary theory. It suggests that this structural principle of "comple-mentarity" may point to paths beyond postmodernism's double-bind, straight intersecting lines, and closed circles; may open up new theoretical perspectives. Duras, for example, as the final chapter sought to demonstrate, writes the imprisoning webs of power and meaning (familial and colonial relations and the Truths of the language in place), while seeing in the repeated rewritings of her own memories and stories a way of making other new altered truths of these determining discursive factors and of unsayable intrasubjective and intersubjective violence. A similar argument, but with greater reservations, was made for Robbe-Grillet's declaredly subversive staging or analytical rewriting of "stock" sado-erotic figures.

Language, the means by which the opacity of the unconscious is expressed is, of course, never itself "adequate to experience. There is no truth that, in passing through awareness, does not lie. But one runs after it all the same."[2] For Christopher Lane, who quotes these statements by Lacan in a study of psychotic (intrasubjective) violence, such a dissociation between subject and signifier "makes all 'rational' explications of behavior, and all consistent predicates of identity, impossible to sustain" (p. 53). Psychosis "foregrounds an anxiety about the stability of the signifier, and a more general crisis at the heart of subjectivity" (p. 53), a crisis of self-reference that manifests acute levels of both internal (psychotic) and external (cultural) violence in our society and suggests a relationship between them.

Yet there are differences at play in these new autobiographies and their investigation of such violence. Robbe-Grillet's autofictions, I claim, are used to stage certain personal sado-erotic fantasies of the writer and a self as enlightened despot in the libertine tradition, while, at the same time, detecting a sadomasochistic structure of the psyche that might cast some light on the prevalence of sexual violence in postmodern writing as in popular representations. In Robbe-Grillet's work, however, Angélique as opposite of the despotic self, sometimes cast as subversive revolutionary figure of revolt or surrealist "convulsive beauty," is most often reduced to the stock figure of seductive siren and (consequently) masochistic consenting victim of punishment. The fictional "masculine" doubles of the writer are situated most commonly at the sadistic or controlling pole. In Duras' work, on the other hand, roles can become interchangeable and notions of inner and outer violence, of "masculine" and "feminine," of the despotism of love become more fluidly gendered. Sarraute, for her part, in another kind of inversion in *Tu ne t'aimes pas*, gives a certain prominence, and even preeminence, to the traditionally negative positioning of the "feminine" at the pole of masochism (lack of self-love, self-doubt, self-punishing hypersensitive guilt, nonviolence, and a flight from despotism).

The postmodern tenet of the nonreferentiality of language—of language as a mirroring system of analogical signs and images that are not the reality they pretend to represent but merely tokens—makes the ghosts of memory and of violence in the autofictional mirror double (and doubly indeterminate) for the (post)modern reader. The only viable option for reader and writer alike might appear to be a cool and distanced theatrical play with signs. Yet language play is clearly not all that I experience in my readings of autofictions.

The differences between the selfconscious "new novel" and the "new autobi-ographies" are evident in this new genre marked by individuation and even intimacy (an emphasis on the inner self without this entailing a return to a traditional conception of full and conscious selfhood). For even within the many rehearsals of the postmodern discovery of the nature of language as nonreferential (signs referring less to things in the world than to other signs) and critical investigation of the traditional representational function of lan-guage, all of these texts demonstrate an understanding of language as some-how itself "complementary," both fiction *and* reality and able to strip away the layers of authorial mask.

The new novel (or metafiction) subverts mimesis as autofiction subverts the conventions of the unity and coherence of the self, and of sincerity and truth-telling of the traditional autobiography. (To "subvert" conventions, in this context, would simply mean to stage, play with, and question the assump-tions of conventions). Yet the autofictions go further again, interrogating many of the assumptions of the metafiction and, in particular, the argument for the all-importance of language as origin. I suggest that they take up the twentieth-century (linguistic) issues of difference between surface and deep or latent structures, introducing new forms of difference into self-conscious texts (meta-fictions). These are the differences between the material bodies that produce (and read) them, between the specific social contexts and world views that shape them, and between the particular intertexts or kinds of texts they choose to put into play. My own sense of the differences between the various auto-fictions include differences in style—the filmic images in Duras, the theatri-cal dialogues of a Sarraute, the pastiche and assemblage of Western narratives in Robbe-Grillet—and in the nature of the gendering of (and gender-struggles in) these bodies of text.

The individuation that marks the autofiction attenuates, then, the postmod-ern notions of the death of the author or the end of (wo)man, lost in the com-mon text. The nature of the sadomasochistic thematics put into play grounds these authors in their time and in their sex because this is determined both by a common structure of the psyche and by the variant forms this takes in indi-viduated social and sexual contexts. Although traditional essentialism is not fully recuperated in this frame, as the importance of particular and individu-ated contexts takes its place alongside linguistic determinism, essentialism is redefined.

Marked by individuation, this new essentialism, and the play of "difference," the new autobiographies cannot be confined within the radical postmodernism that Richard Wolin describes as a celebration of decentered fragmented subjectivity. They stand apart even from what that critic considers to be the "more engaged and less academic texts of antihumanism," the "desiring machines" of Deleuze and Guattari presented as characteristic of late capitalist society or the new technologies of the culture industry, for example.

To read a (postmodern) text is to look critically at sets of relationships with language rather than directly at the real, and this is clearly called for in the reading of the new autobiographies. But it is also to sort out and evaluate differences. Although it may not be possible to decide definitively between lie or truth, real and fiction, the reader of an autofiction is prompted to use a knowledge of other texts to discriminate between the different degrees of the real, to discover the meanings that derive from the difference between pulp or popular texts and their individuated reworking and reorganization in the autofictions. The task of the critical reader (my task), is not only to read empathetically and to analyze the whole texts of the autofictions with sensitivity in order to mediate between author and reader but also to resist certain persuasions and excesses and to detect self-deception and dead end. In this sense, differences call up value judgments.

The authorial presence or self defined by recurrent sado-erotic or sadomasochistic imagery has, in the terms used by Lacan, both symbolic and imaginary reality, that is, derives both from the prelinguistic and from entry into socializing language. "The unconscious voice of the author accompanies the scriptor's machinations of veiling and unveiling" as Ben Stoltzfus puts it,[3] and this includes, I argue, the unveiling of both "the inner violence of the text" and "the pain/pleasure of a personal psychosexual sadistic drive" (*Robbe-Grillet and Modernity*, p. 70). As Stoltzfus observes, noting my "ambivalence about Robbe-Grillet's uses of subversion," "despite metafictions' emphasis on reflexivity and deferred meaning, there is an increasing reader awareness of the turbulence that sexual aggression introduces into the text" producing a "concretization" that transcends the play of signifiers.[4] The motivation behind my analysis of the sadomasochistic thematics that are even more clearly central to the autofictions than to the new novels and films derived precisely from my disquiet at an "invitation" that I had perceived also as an invitation to enter an erotic network, culturally marked as "masculine," in which Robbe-Grillet is avowedly personally enmeshed. My personal response was to resist collaborating in this particular production of meaning even as I attempted to understand its functioning.

Robbe-Grillet's heroine, however, is not only a sexualized female body but also and predominantly language/fiction. His work attempts to harness the explosive potential of the erotic to explore the character (real/fiction) both of the popular discourses (of ideology) and of his own fantasies and to examine the relation between the two. The chapters on the masochistic thematics in Sarraute and Duras conclude similarly that the detecting function is at least as significant as the confessional impulse. The chaotic forms that mark the new autobiographical fictions discussed earlier in this study, like the violence in the psyche and its sadomasochistic structure, suggest the need for new models in literary theory.

The new autobiographies are also a product of the intellectual and political historical contexts in France, particularly since the Second World War, and have implications for French intellectual history in general. In the wake of the Surrealists' early deconstruction of subjectivity and rational consciousness and interest in the unconscious, in reaction to the illusion of intentionality and freedom of Sartrian existential *Pour-Soi* and the Marxist misadventures of the Existentialists, the new novels of these writers emerged in the late fifties against the background of the hegemony of structuralist linguistics. This new linguistic science, in its turn, influenced Levi-Strauss's structural anthropology, Barthes' early semiotics, Lacan's theories of a misrecognized self, and Althusser's political theory and attendant allegiance to Maoist Third World revolution. In the 1960s, "Man" appeared to be being replaced by underlying scientific or linguistic structures. By the seventies and eighties, along with a growing suspicion of all "master" discourses, certain of the claims of scientific structuralism and radicalism were beginning to be deconstructed—some would say "unmasked"—in their turn.

Ferry and Renaut, among others, have critiqued the postmodernism that came out of and after structuralism in the sixties as an "antihumanism." They consider these intellectual movements to have arisen from (or perhaps provoked) a failed 1968 revolution and from sublimation of Maoist and Marxist hostility. According to Ferry and Renaut, the postmodern critique of the modern world that finds ideology or metaphysical illusion in the Western democratic project is incapable of pursuing the promises of modernity. As Richard Wolin sees it, the discrediting of Marxism (Solzhenitsyn's 1974 work, *The Gulag Archipelago*) and Third World revolutionary radicalism, the rise of right-wing revisionist ideology in the form of Le Pen, the trial of Klaus Barbie in 1987, and the drama of the Heidegger debate in France in 1987–88 over that influential philosopher's support of Nazism have increased dissatisfaction with the postmodern ethos. Indeed, the ethos of the French intellectual scene has been changing. The historian Tony Judt has also argued—somewhat sweepingly if one considers the writings of noted moralists such as Gide, Malraux, Sartre, Camus, Mauriac, and de Beauvoir—for an absence of concern for public ethics or political morality among the French intelligentsia of this century. Judt attributes such a lack of ethical values to the French ambivalence toward liberal democracy; some literary theorists, Thomas Pavel, for example, share similar views on the negative implications of postmodern philosophy and literary theory.

In the light of the current uncritical revival of concepts like "man" and "individualism," however, Wolin expresses regret for the loss of certain aspects of this intellectual cultural legacy from the sixties that in the wake of Ferry and Renaut, he, too, labels negatively as "theoretical antihumanism." Wolin notes the emancipatory aspirations of the postmodern critique in its analysis of the traditional ethics of the rational, willing, judging subject, an ethics suspected of concealing the self-justification by an elite of the power it holds. And indeed for many analysts, Baker, for example, the more recent writing practices of Derrida, Levinas, Foucault, and Kristeva, among other postmoderns and their theories of the subject, in fact, demonstrate "an ethical turn." The "new" ethics derives from the analytic goals and artistic writing practices that, while staging social signs in a textual space of pleasure and fantasy, also bring the universe of what Foucault described as intersubjective violence to the surface and to mind. It is evident that the inability to think language outside language, in a system where the sign is both trace of a trace and effacing of a trace, like the discovery of the identity of the self as being grounded in difference and as the reflection of the other, prevent the full recovery of an original subject and indicate certain limits of this "new" (analytical and intersubjective) ethics of deconstruction. Despite its interest in intersubjectivity and the analysis and recognition of the other, the "new ethics" of the self clearly has limitations as well as strengths. Derrida gives his own austere picture of the limitations of this analytical postmodern ethics in a system of intersubjective violence that derives from the fact that words refer primarily to other words. "And if, as I believe, violence remains in fact (almost) ineradicable, its analysis and the most refined, ingenious account of its conditions will be the least violent gestures, perhaps even non-violent, and in any case, those which contribute most to transforming the legal-ethical-political rules." ("Afterword," *Limited Inc.*, p. 112). For Derrida, democracy and human rights cannot escape from the metaphysics of subjectivity, of discourse that he refuses. Although for this master deconstructionist all forms of complicity are not equivalent, they are, he claims, all "irreducible."

For Baker, however, and indeed for Wolin, the philosophy of radical alterity (the difference or exteriority of the other) and the recognition of the positive effects of intersubjectivity, constitute an ethics that might account for desirable real-world effects of the literary theory of deconstruction (postmodernism). The community orientated philosophy of Levinas, for example, presents the self as a relational structure with the Other in which there is neither complete identity nor reversibility of the pairs. Levinas posits "exteriority," defined as the face of the other and the injunction to nonviolence that precedes the establishment of the Law, as exemplary. Derrida's concepts of "remainder," "crypt," and "ashes," too, are indices of the half-hidden presence of such an unspoken Other. A similar Other, instrumental in the constitution of a new decentered subject, figures in various guises at the center of the work of Lacan and Kristeva. Referring to the work of Luce Irigaray, Baker summarizes the new ethics succinctly—"called by the other first, the subject must remain open to this ethical demand, recognizing in the other not merely an alter ego, but an other who is truly other, on whom the subject's freedom depends" (p. 131).

For Wolin, although it is "decentered," this self is not the centerless, fragmented self of postmodernism or Lacanian psychoanalysis. He too refers to the philosophy of intersubjectivity, in this instance to the work of George Herbert Mead, in which conscious subjects do not exist a priori but as a result of social interaction to found his argument that the new self is formed by the internalization of the attitudes and expectations of others. "The 'I,'" wrote Mead, "reacts to the self which arises through the taking of attitudes of others. Through the taking of those attitudes we have introduced the 'me' and we react to it as an 'I'" (p. 104). For Wolin, too, subjective experiences are always an internalization of others' expectations (p. 41) and are intersubjectively mediated.

While a tolerance of other selves and the ability to take the role of the other can be seen as positive—in the current political climate of interethnic conflict in the Balkans and intergroup conflict in Africa, for example—there is also a danger that difference might itself become a new essentialism. Le Pen's use of "differentialist racism" to argue for the return of the Arabs to their homeland (in the interest of "national purity"), on the one hand, and Muslim fundamentalism (in the interest of "religious purity"), on the other, would constitute good examples of an overrating of difference. Wolin notes that the extolling of difference can lead to tribalism or separation from the other on the basis of this difference and concludes that "to celebrate difference at the expense of sameness or unity threatens in no uncertain terms to belittle our common humanity" (p. 30).

It would be an oversimplification of the question of identity and otherness, however, to see exteriority and interiority as positive or negative alternatives (mutually excluding opposites). The risk here is precisely the return of the Cartesian mirror—the Ghost in the Machine theory of dichotomous oppo-

sites (body/mind), one (the public or outer, space-occupying, mechanical entity) defined negatively in relation to the other (private or inner, nonspatial,
self-knowing. Irigaray's theoretical elaboration of a corporeal, nonhierarchical
body, presented as differently sexed, suggests, for example, both that there is
something inassimilable about sexual difference and that this body can feel,
know, and write. Her model breaks down the Cartesian mind/body division
(one is what the other is not) by working on the interactions between them
and postulating both similarities and incommensurate difference.

Earlier chapters presented the interior spaces in Duras and Sarraute, as in
Irigaray, as repositories not only of analogical linguistic representations but
also of spaces of the "feminine" masochism of a self-dissolution and a self-
opening of the body to the "masculine" other. Kristeva's Chora or fusion with
the mother are presented as somehow preceding identity and difference; as
primary. Levinas and Lacan see community-based "exteriority" or the "Real"
and the "Other," respectively, as prelinguistic givens. For Lacan, the ego is the
product of an Imaginary that is itself a product of the "Real" and the "Other"
(a *méconnaissance* or misrecognition). For him, the Imaginary is structured
like a language, and like the layers of the self, as a result of the play of signification, is not only an other, but an other dispossessed. Indeed, the layers of the
Other are also many and perhaps also objects of misrecognition. It may be the
case that the recognition of the other as truly other on whom one's freedom
depends, of which Baker speaks, is a less than self-evident notion. Hegel saw
sexual difference as the founding and meaningful difference but as this was
neutralized and elevated (in an "*Aufhebung*") in sexual union. I have argued
that the new autobiographies move to resolve these contradictions in a complementary movement between (a telescoping of) interiority and exteriority. Here,
the excluded other is both strange to me and at the heart of me; the absent
other impossible to forget (to remember), as in Duras, is the generative void
around which the subject orients its desire.

If there is a turn in postmodernism—and I have argued that such a turn is
manifest in the new autobiographies—this is not a return to the narcissistic
ego delighted by its individuality and elevated to the status of an ethical and
critical paradigm as in the Modernism of a Booth or the texts of Gide. Nor is it
a turn to a language in which there is no alienation of the subject from itself
in the accession to language. It is not a return to a nonalienated language in
which the subject discovers its full and distinctive nature—a "feminine" language, for example.

Politically, these open, playful, inclusive, and polysemous postmodern texts
remain characterized by Foucault's resistance to discourses and to social ar-

rangements in place or to a morality common to all (in the sense that it would be inculcated in everyone) or by Kristeva's similar opposition to normative libertarian politics based on knowledge/power. For Foucault, as the final chapter argued, the interior space of the subject comes into being through power, that is, through technologies of knowledge and forms of discourse as the body is imprinted by the epistemes of history and constituted by both the circulation of this power/knowledge and resistance to such a construction. However, Foucault acknowledges that power can be both repressive and disciplinary and constitutive. His move toward a self-constitution through singular practices of the self in *Le Souci de soi*, it can be argued, does appear to mark an ethical turn in that writer's work. Despite his archaeology of power and his deconstruction of the eternal universal humanist values of freedom and justice, his recent work allows for individual choices to attach preference to just such concepts.

It seems that the new ethics of intersubjectivity, the movement toward "practices of the self" and Durassian-style rewriting may provide some opening, some measure of escape, from a postmodern condition in which Sisyphus would be condemned to endless play and limited to generative textual practices. For the analytical function of deconstruction is never pure. Lucidity and even subversion are not necessarily liberatory. As in the writing or the reading of Robbe-Grillet's work, such a recognition that the staging of linguistic violence is always more or less a complicity with this violence may itself be a starting point for self-knowledge and emancipation.

Eco, as our study argued earlier, suggests that there are indeed motivations behind signifying chains, a language behind language that would permit only a qualified heterogeneity, dissemination, polysemy of signifying practice, Otherness, or openness of interpretative readings. Despite Derrida's concern that if you chose one, you occlude others, there is space in this postmodernism as in the new ethics of intersubjectivity for homogeneity and for heterogeneity, for similarity and for difference, and there are some criteria for preference and critical judgment.

According to the philosopher, Alan Finkielkraut, French thought of the eighties "has been marked by a rationalist, democratic consensus, the most striking feature of which [was] the simultaneous growth of a liberal school of political thought and a rationalist left" (p. 86). The danger perceived here is that the Enlightenment human rights discourse or Renaissance Humanism are themselves both being increasingly colonized by a neoliberal discourse. For Wolin, too, the political participation and civic virtues of self-cultivation of Humanism are being supplanted in this neoliberal culture by individualism, passive citizenship, privatism (family fitness, consumerism, economic accumulation) to the detriment of affective values, libidinal satisfaction, and community solidarity. Perhaps a theoretical discourse that recognizes the identity of the self as being grounded in the recognition and reflection of the other (the ethical turn that Baker finds in postmodernism) might offer a counter to the homogenization that this technoscientific and neoliberal culture threatens to promote. Moreover, the general concern at the apparent devaluation of the discourse of civil liberties and human rights by postmodernism might be alleviated by the recognition increasingly shared by postmodern theorists and evident in the new autobiographies that all discourses are not equal. A distinctive authorial voice emerges from the competing and contradictory voices in Sarraute, for example, without invalidating the latter. It is not the case that anything goes or that there are no criteria for a critical reading. The latter must, precisely, take account of the play between all voices. Notwithstanding the need to take account of the whole text and of all the textual relations, it does still seem possible to read both with and against the grain of the text's persuasions, for a reader to establish her or his own critical distances and practices of the self through particular ways of reading.

The introduction observed that the central question of this study was whether the new autobiographies propose a way out of the postmodern bind without retreating to traditional essentialism or humanism. I conclude that in the French new autobiographies, the "complementary" forms of the remembering of the past, the differences in the gendering of the text, and the rewriting of the self as multiple and intersubjective are just such new models for (re)writing history, story, self, and gender out of/beyond the postmodern.

◇

Notes

◇

I have used the following translations in my text; full publishing information for each may be found in the bibliography. When I have chosen to modify the translation, I have so indicated in these endnotes. All translations in the text from French, other than those listed below, are my own.

For Duras: *L'Amant* (trans. Barbara Bray, 1985). *L'Amant de la Chine du nord* (trans. Leigh Hafrey, 1992). *Un Barrage contre le Pacifique* (trans. Herma Briffault, 1986). *La Douleur* (trans. Barbara Bray, 1989). *Emily L.* (trans. Barbara Bray, 1989).

For Robbe-Grillet: *Le Miroir qui revient* (trans. Jo Levy, 1984).

For Sarraute: *Enfance* (trans. Barbara Wright, 1984). *Tu ne t'aimes pas* (trans. Barbara Wright, 1990).

Introduction

1. For example, in Stephen Heath's *The Nouveau Roman: A Study in the Practice of Writing*.

2. Raylene Ramsay, *Robbe-Grillet and Modernity: Science, Sexuality, and Subversion*.

Chapter 1

1. See Georges May, *L'Autobiographie*, especially "Autobiographie et roman," pp. 169–77.

2. Paul John Eakin, "The Referential Aesthetic of Autobiography," pp. 129–44.

3. Roland Barthes, *Roland Barthes par Roland Barthes*.

4. Eakin, "The Referential Aesthetic of Autobiography," p. 131.

5. To take a single but striking example, the humanist critic and longtime antagonist of the nouveau roman, Jean-Louis Curtis, declared on the literary television program "Apostrophes" (18 January 1985) presenting *Le Miroir qui revient* that he had found Alain Robbe-Grillet's autobiographical scenes "humaines" [human] and even "touchantes" [touching].

6. May, *L'Autobiographie*.

7. Philippe Lejeune, "Paroles d'enfance."

8. Personal interview with Alain Robbe-Grillet in Paris in January 1986 during which we discussed the newly published *Le Miroir qui revient*.

9. Marguerite Duras explicitly identifies the little brother and the lover through the common denominator of their weakness or helplessness during a now commercially available televised interview with Bernard Pivot for "Apostrophes," broadcast in 1984.

10. Interview for "Apostrophes." This "madness" of the mother is reiterated in *L'Amant de la Chine du nord*.

11. It is possible that the following passage in *L'Empire Français* (signed Marguerite Donnadieu et Philippe Rocques) is by Duras although the style is somewhat pedantic and the content ideological. "On a dit de l'Indochine qu'elle était la plus belle des colonies françaises. Elle compte, en tout cas, les plus grandes villes de notre Empire. Son élite indigène est si homogène et si acquise à nos principes qu'on a songé à faire de cette Fédération un dominion. Son outillage des plus modernes s'adapte peu à peu à une vie économique de jour en jour plus parfaite" [It has been said of Indochina that it was the most beautiful of the French colonies. It contains, in any event, the largest cities of our Empire. Its native elite is so homogeneous and so won over to our values that there was some thought of making this Federation a Dominion. Its very modern capital equipment is gradually being adapted to an economic life that is becoming daily more perfect].

12. The Chinese connection is mentioned again. "Jamais mieux que là le colonisateur n'a su concilier une tradition millénaire et respectable, celle de la Chine, avec les nécessités de la vie moderne qui doit assurer à l'Indochine une grande prospérité" (pp. 116–17) [Never better than here has the colonizer been able to reconcile a tradition worthy of respect, going back millenia, the tradition of China, with the requirements of modern living that will guarantee Indochina's great prosperity].

13. See Aliette Armel, *Marguerite Duras et l'autobiographie*, pp. 40–48, and Duras, *Les Yeux verts*, for information and documents on the existence of Elizabeth Stiedter as the origin of her fictional counterpart, Anne-Marie Stretter, and of the fascination the latter exerts.

14. This is my own translation. Jo Levy's translation, "a particular idea of order that might have appeared awe-inspiring" seems to me to make the "real" event suggested by the pluperfect tense ("avait pu") too hypothetical. In the press articles that followed the appearance of *Le Miroir qui revient*, Robbe-Grillet elaborates on this 'confession.' For example, "J'étais le bon fils d'une famille de droite, et comme tel je croyais à l'ordre. Comme dans toutes les familles de droite, le National-Socialisme par rapport au Front Populaire, représentait l'ordre [. . .] Or, je découvre alors [. . .] que le nazisme était un régime de folie pure, et de folie sanglante [. . .] je m'aperçois que sa face cachée, c'est la folie criminelle, l'horreur, le cauchemar [. . .] Voilà la découverte qui me pousse à écrire et mes livres sont faits de ça, la lutte entre l'ordre et le désordre" [I was a good son of a right-wing family, and as such I believed in order. As in all right-wing families, National Socialism represented order in relation to the Popular Front {. . .} Well, then I discover {. . .} that the Nazi regime was one of pure madness, and of bloody madness, {. . .} I realize that its hidden face is criminal madness, horror, nightmare {. . .} This is the discovery that incites me to write and my books are made of this, the struggle between order and disorder]. Entretien, *Libération*, 17 January 1985, 28–29. See also *Art Press*, no. 88 (December 1984): 41 and *Le Magazine Littéraire* (January 1985): 93.

15. Umberto Eco, *Les Limites de l'interprétation.*

16. Dawn Michelle Baude, "Picketing the Zeitgeist: In Search of the Perfect Language," p. 6.

Chapter 2

1. I spoke to Nathalie Sarraute in her Paris apartment in the seizième arrondissement on June 9, 1994, about her recent work. At more than ninety-three years of age, and confined temporarily to bed by a virus, Sarraute still argued clearly and cogently. Discussing my study, she insisted that *Tu ne t'aimes pas* was in no way autobiographical, that just as there was no relationship between Picasso's art and his life, there was no necessary connection between her life and her writing. Accepting that *Enfance* was autobiographical, but claiming that it was a much easier text to write than her other work, Sarraute was particularly preoccupied by the term "new autobiography" and the concern that her work not be claimed by another writer (Robbe-Grillet) as part of his literary movement. Insisting on chronology—the appearance of *Tropismes* in 1939 more than twenty years before Robbe-Grillet or Duras published their first experimental texts—and on the difference between her work and that of the other two writers, this indomitable woman accepted my grounds for situating her work in an experimental tradition but did not want the originality and difficulty of its explorations of hitherto intact regions to be obscured by its appropriation by another.

2. Lejeune, "Paroles d'enfance."

3. Armel (p. 67) discusses Duras' confession in *Les Parleuses* (p. 59) of an erotic experience very similar to Anne's desire to be killed in *Moderato Cantabile.*

4. In *Roland Barthes par Roland Barthes* (p. 109), Barthes reflects on the constructed nature of identity. After describing a typical day during a vacation, he concludes "Tout cela n'a aucun intérêt. Bien plus, non seulement vous marquez votre appartenance de classe, mais encore vous faites de cette marque une confidence littéraire, dont la futilité n'est pas reçue: vous vous constituez fantasmatiquement en "écrivain" ou pire encore: vous vous constituez" (p. 85) [None of this is of any interest. Furthermore, not only do you indicate the class to which you belong, but you make this indication into a literary confidence whose lack of insignificance is not perceived: you construct yourself fantasmatically as a "writer" or, worse still, you construct yourself]. It is of interest that Barthes establishes a scale for the factitious character of identity—degrees of inauthenticity. It is bad enough to construct oneself as a "writer," but worse to construct oneself completely.

5. *Libération,* 17 January 1985, 28.

6. J. Laplanche and J. Pontalis, *Vocabulaire de la Psychanalyse,* "L'Imaginaire," pp. 195–96.

7. Lejeune, *L'Autobiographie en France,* p. 14. In the later *Le Pacte autobiographique* (1975), Lejeune develops the notion of "autobiographical space" to take account of fictional strategies such as the play of multiple identities of writer, narrators, and characters in the constitution of a personality. As opposed to traditional autobiography, "autobiographical fiction" in the case of Gide, for Lejeune, is both personal confession and depersonalization, memory and experimentation, narcissism and self-criticism.

8. André Gide, *Les Faux-Monnayeurs*, p. 987.

9. Michel Leiris. See bibliography for a list of the most significant of Leiris' autobiographies.

10. Serge Doubrovsky, "Autobiographie/Vérité/Psychanalyse," p. 96.

11. Lejeune, in "Friselis: Chronique de lecture," *Romance Studies*, no. 9 (1986) discusses the newly published "novel" by François Nourrissier, *La Fête des pères*, critical of Nourissier's game with the reader as he moves between the stances of literary invention and autobiographical exactitude.

12. The gender of the "voices" in Sarraute is discussed at length in the later chapter on *Enfance*.

13. Ben Stoltzfus, who has written extensively on the new novel and the new autobiographies, read my original manuscript and made a number of perceptive and intellectually generous comments that have influenced my revisions. I am indebted to his knowledge of metafiction and his clear and thoughtful observations.

14. Henri de Corinthe has his literary origins, according to Robbe-Grillet, in Michelet's recounting in *La Sorcière* of an old classical story retold in the Middle Ages and again in the sixteenth century of "La fiancée de Corynthe." Corinthe is discussed at greater length in the chapter on *Le Miroir qui revient*.

15. Insisting on the stereotyped character of the symbol of the white horse, Robbe-Grillet added this example from popular contemporary film to my own list from nineteenth-century painting (personal interview with Robbe-Grillet, Paris, 6 January 1985).

16. Barthes, *Roland Barthes par Roland Barthes*, p. 82.

17. Georges Raillard, "Le Grand Verre d'Alain Robbe-Grillet," p. 6. For Raillard this "fictional" autobiography also poses questions of historical source. "Cet Henri de Corinthe est-il chargé d'assumer des démons droiters, comme le suggère le texte: entre le lieutenant-colonel de la Rocque et le lieutenant-colonel Corinthe, belle anagramme de l'initiale . . . , ou Henri comte de Paris ou Maurice Sachs ou Drieu?" (p. 6) [Is the role of this Henri de Corinthe to take upon himself the right-wing demons, as the text suggests: between the lieutenant-colonel de la Rocque and lieutenant-colonel Corinthe, there is a clever anagram of the initial letter, or is he Henri comte de Paris or Maurice Sachs or Drieu?]

Chapter 3

1. This chapter draws on my article "Autobiographical Fictions: Duras, Sarraute, Simon, Robbe-Grillet Rewriting History, Story, Self," first published in *International Fiction Review* and revised as a chapter in *The Contemporary Novel in France*, edited by William Thompson.

2. The usefulness of certain theories of contemporary physics and of models emerging from chaos theory and the study of dynamical systems for an understanding of configurations of modernity in post-structuralist literary texts is examined at length in Ramsay, *Robbe-Grillet and Modernity*.

3. Quoted in Madeleine Cottenet-Hage and Robert Kolker, "The Cinema of Duras in Search of an Ideal Image," p. 95. The quotation is taken from the catalog for the film, p. 59.

4. Hélène Cixous, "Rethinking difference" in *Homosexualities and French Literature: Cultural Contents*, p. 82.

5. The secrets of this unconscious are perhaps glimpsed in Duras precisely through her discursive effraction of the incest taboo. As Julia Kristeva writes, "Incest prohibition throws a veil over primary narcissism and the almost always ambivalent threats with which it menaces subjective identity. It cuts short the temptation to return, with abjection and jouissance, to that passive status within the symbolic function where the subject, fluctuating between inside and outside, pleasure and pain, word and deed, would find death, along with nirvana" (quoted in Sharon Willis, *Marguerite Duras: Writing on the Body*, p. 20).

6. Joan Brandt, "History and Art in Claude Simon's *Histoire*."

7. Ibid., p. 380. Brandt's translation.

8. Lois Oppenheim, "From Anonymity to Individuation in the Nouveau Roman," Paper read at a special session, "The French Nouveau Roman Thirty Years On," at MLA Convention, New York, 29 December 1988.

9. Michael Sheringham, "French Autobiography: Texts, Contexts, Poetics."

Chapter 4

In this chapter, I have modified Levy's translation of *Le Miroir qui revient* or translated the quotations myself in order to stay closer to the aspects of polysemy and language play in the text.

1. Sheringham, "Ego redux? Strategies in New French Autobiography."

2. R. J. Young, *In Command of France: French Foreign Policy and Military Planning, 1933–40*.

3. Probably a reference to the tragedy of Mers-el-Kébir, a French naval base on the Gulf of Oran (Algeria), which the Royal Navy bombarded on July 3, 1940, killing 1,300 sailors. There is a direct reference to Mers-El-Kébir in *Le Miroir qui revient* (p. 115).

4. *The War: A Memoir*, p. 101.

5. The importance of the fall of the order and efficiency of the Third Reich and the revelation of its second face of Nazi horror, the German "inversion" of signs, is identified by Robbe-Grillet as central in his decision to write in interviews for *Art Press* 88 (December 1984): 44; *Libération*, 17 January 1985, 28–29; *Magazine littéraire* (January 1985): 93; *La Quinzaine Littéraire* 432 (31 January 1985): 6.

6. Julia Kristeva, "The Ethics of Linguistics," in Léon Roudiez, ed., *Desire in Language*.

7. See Barthes, *La Chambre claire: Note sur la photographie*. This aspect of Barthes' work is also discussed in Mary Bittner Wiseman's *The Ecstasies of Roland Barthes*.

8. It was pointed out to me that Michel Tournier's *Le Roi des Aulnes*, a novel partly based on autobiographical events, shows similar preoccupations and also makes constant use of the notion of inversion.

9. Corinthe has been discussed in some detail in a number of essays. Among these are John Michalczyk, "Robbe-Grillet, Michelet, and Barthes: From *La Sorcière* to *Glissements progressifs du plaisir*" and Stoltzfus, "The Language of Autobiography and Fiction: Gide, Barthes, and Robbe-Grillet."

10. Pierre Brunel, "Variations Corinthiennes."

11. Jules Michelet tells the story that according to him was told by Phlégon, Hadrian's freed slave, and is found again in the Middle Ages and the sixteenth century. By giving herself to Corynthe, the fiancée brings about his death. In a 1797 ballad, Goethe makes the fiancée a vampire. Brunel points to other possible sources, Anatole France's *Les Noces corinthiennes* and Charles Nodier's *Smarra*. The latter tells the story of Socrates who goes back to Thessaly and becomes the plaything of the witch Méroé. Lucius finds his friend and believes he witnesses a scene in which Méroé sucks the blood of Socrates, which she makes gush out of the wound in the neck that Socrates had received during the battle of Corinth. The pleasure and danger represented by the female and by sexuality, the fear of a loss of virility or even of life in contact with the female principle is of course also a constant of Western myth and text (Diana and Actaeon, Medusa, Delilah, Salome, Judith, the Lorelei, for example).

12. Sheringham, "Ego redux?" p. 32.

13. Eugen Weber, *Action Française: Royalism and Reaction in Twentieth Century France*; and Henri, Comte de Paris, *Henri Comte de Paris au service de la France: Mémoires d'exil et de combats.*

14. In late 1989 a similarly simplistic "finalist" discourse of the "End of History" reappeared in the proclamation of the ultimate triumph of the superiority of Liberal Democracy over Fascism and Communism: the end of Ideology or competing discourse (preempting new discourses).

15. Nathalie Sarraute and Marc Saporta, "Portrait d'une inconnue: Conversation biographique."

16. Bob Altermeyer, "Marching in Step," in *The Sciences.*

17. Lynn Higgins, "Gender and War Narrative in *La Route des Flandres.*"

18. Ibid., p. 19.

19. Edward Saïd, *Beginnings: Intention and Method.*

20. Stephen Greenblatt, "Towards a Poetics of Culture." Greenblatt discusses Iser's "dynamic oscillation" on page 19.

Chapter 5

1. Ramsay, "The Uses and Abuses of Enchantment," in *Robbe-Grillet and Modernity.*

2. Sheringham, "Ego Redux?" p. 32.

3. Robbe-Grillet, "Entretien." In *Libération,* 17 January 1985, 28.

4. Stoltzfus, "Dead, Desacralized, and Discontent: Robbe-Grillet's New Man."

5. At a Colloquium "Robbe-Grillet at 70/Robbe-Grillet à 70 ans," held at the University of Washington in Saint-Louis, 11–14 October 1992. Robbe-Grillet responded personally to a number of papers.

6. Michel Foucault, *Power/Knowledge: Selected Interviews and Other Writings 1972–1977.*

7. Teresa de Lauretis, *Alice Doesn't: Feminism, Semiotics, Cinema* and "The Essence of the Triangle or Taking the Risk of Essentialism Seriously: Feminist Theory in Italy, the U.S. and Britain."

8. Michel Rybalka, "Alain Robbe-Grillet: At Play with Criticism," in Lois Oppenheim, ed., *Three Decades of the French New Novel*, p. 35.

9. Mireille Calle-Gruber, "Quand le Nouveau Roman prend les risques du romanesque."

10. During a public lecture at a Colloquium in Saint-Louis, "Robbe-Grillet à 70 ans," 12 October 1992 on the occasion of the showing of his film *La Belle Captive* and again at Wellesley College during a public lecture at the Maison Française on 16 November 1992.

11. In an interview at Robbe-Grillet's home ("Portrait de Robbe-Grillet en châtelain"), Michel Contat describes the painting that actually hangs above Robbe-Grillet's desk at Mesnil-au-Grain as a symbolist painting of an insipid young woman on a white horse. The horse has the stance described in *Angélique*, but the young woman is nothing like the Robbe-Grillet version.

12. René Girard, *La Violence et le sacré*.

13. Jessica Benjamin, "Master and Slave: The Fantasy of Erotic Domination."

14. Ibid., p. 282.

15. Ibid., p. 283.

16. Marie Gear and Melvyn Hill, *Working through Narcissism: Treating Its Masochistic Structures*.

Chapter 6

1. Sarraute, in Oppenheim, ed., *Three Decades of the French New Novel*, p. 121.

2. Sarraute's suspicion of the old paradigms of the referential text inherited from the nineteenth century, its conventions of plot, character, psychological analysis, linear chronology/causality, verisimilitude, and the ideological messages these carried was theorized in a series of essays, written between 1947 and 1956 and published in 1956 by Gallimard under the title of *L'Ere du soupçon*. These still constitute her profession of critical faith. See Oppenheim, ed., *Three Decades of the French New Novel*, pp. 119–31.

3. Foucault, *The Order of Things*, p. 304.

4. Jean-François Lyotard, *La Condition postmoderne: Rapport sur le savoir*, p. 7.

5. The question of voice was discussed in depth at a special session at the MLA Convention in New York, 27–29 December 1986. Among the unpublished papers distributed, Paul Kane's "Voice and the Politics of Presence," Peter Elbow's "The Pleasure of Voices in the Text," and Rise Axelrod's "The Problematics of Voice" were the most helpful for this short summary of the history and current theoretical situation of the term.

6. Jacques Derrida in an interview on his *Speech and Phenomena*. Cited by Paul Kane in "Voice and the Politics of Presence," paper presented at the annual meeting of the Modern Language Association, New York, December 1986, p. 8.

7. Derrida, *Writing and Difference*.

8. Sarraute, *L'Ere du Soupçon*, and Oppenheim, ed., *Three Decades of the French New Novel*, pp. 119–31.

9. "D'une part, l'afflux désordonné de l'émotion, du ressenti, de la passion. D'autre part, le langage de l'ordre, de la censure, des lois sociales, des conventions. Le surnarrant

est au narrant ce que l'autoroute est à la forêt vierge: le chemin tracé d'avance (j'emprunte la comparaison à Sarraute elle-même)" [On the one hand, the disordered upsurge of emotion, of feelings, and of passion. On the other, the language of order, of censure, of social laws, of conventions. The super-narrator is to the narrator what the freeway is to the virgin forest: the path traced out in advance (I borrow the comparison from Sarraute herself)] Gaetan Brulotte, "Tropismes et sous-conversation," p. 41.

10. "Elle se montre attentive et délicate, mais ferme, dans l'intention de faire apparaître au grand jour ce qui doit être dit pour que le passé soit pleinement assumé en toute lucidité" [It shows itself to be attentive and sensitive but firm, with the object of bringing what must be said to the light of day in order to come to terms with the past fully and with lucidity] (Françoise van Roey-Roux, "*Enfance* de Nathalie Sarraute ou de la Fiction à autobiographie").

11. Albert Camus, *L'Etranger*, pp. 12, 120.

12. Sarraute, *Paul Valéry et l'enfant d'éléphant—Flaubert le Précurseur*, p. 78.

13. "Nathalie Sarraute," public reading and discussion at Wellesley College, Massachusetts, November 1986.

14. Valerie Minogue, "Fragments of a Childhood: Nathalie Sarraute's *Enfance*." Mother's silky, soft, warm skin can efface all hurt and suspicion. "Je me serre contre elle, je pose mes lèvres sur la peau fine et soyeuse, si douce de son front, de ses joues" (p. 40) [I cuddle up to her, I put my lips on the delicate, silky, soft skin of her forehead, of her cheeks]. "Je la trouvais délicieuse à regarder . . . J'aimais ses traits fins, légers, [. . .] sa peau dorée, rosée, douce et soyeuse au toucher, plus soyeuse que la soie, plus tiède et tendre que les plumes d'un oiselet, que son duvet" (p. 91) [I thought she was often delightful to look at [. . .] I loved her fine, delicate, features, [. . .] her golden, rosy skin, soft and silky to the touch, more silky than silk, warmer and more tender than the feathers of a baby bird, than its down]. Natacha's beloved, well cuddled teddy-bear, Mishka "soyeux, tiède, doux, mou, tout imprégné de familiarité tendre" (p. 49) [silky, warm, soft, cuddly, completely imbued with tender familiarity] shares similar characteristics as an object on which the child projects the same needs and desires. Even the silken tapestry on the wall of the child's bedroom in father's Moscow flat with its "texture lisse" [smooth texture] its "délicate couleur dorée" [delicate golden color], the "éclat soyeux de ses oiseaux, de ses arbrisseaux, de ses fleurs" (p. 52) [the silken sparkle of its birds, its shrubs, its flowers] comforts the child, afraid, in the absence of the mother.

15. Lejeune, "Paroles d'enfance."

16. Emile Benveniste, *Problèmes de linguistique générale*, p. 260. "Je n'emploie je qu'en m'adressant à quelqu'un qui sera dans mon allocution un tu." [I only use I to address someone who, in my address, will be a you].

17. Sheringham, "Ego redux?" pp. 27–35.

18. Ann Jefferson, "Beyond Contract: The Reader of Autobiography and Stendhal's *Vie de Henry Brulard*," p. 53.

19. Minogue, "Fragments of a Childhood," p. 82.

20. Derrida, *Writing and Difference*, p. 280.

21. Kristeva, "Oscillation du pouvoir au refus." Interview by Xavière Gauthier with Julia Kristeva (*Tel Quel*, Summer 1974), reprinted in *New French Feminisms*, pp. 165–67.

22. This is Alice Jardine's formulation of the process that for Lacan and Lacanian theorists brings about the recognition of sexual difference and inner splitting (Spaltung). See Alice Jardine, *Gynesis: Configurations of Woman and Modernity*, p. 107.

23. Nathalie Sarraute was speaking at a colloquium in 1982 at New York University. In Oppenheim, ed., *Three Decades of the French New Novel*, p. 122.

24. Yolande Patterson, "Childhood Memories: Nathalie Sarraute's *Enfance* and Simone de Beauvoir's *Mémoires d'une jeune fille rangée*." Paper given at the MLA Convention, New York, 1986.

25. Viviane Forrester, "Portrait de Nathalie," p. 21.

26. Sarraute and Saporta, "Portrait d'une inconnue: Conversation biographique," p. 22.

27. See Minogue, "Fragments of a Childhood: Nathalie Sarraute's *Enfance*."

28. Ibid., p. 78.

29. Ibid., p. 74.

30. See, for example, Jardine, *Gynesis: Configurations of Women and Modernity* and Toril Moi, *Sexual Textual Politics: Feminist Literary Theory*.

31. See, for example, Patterson's reading in "Childhood Memories: Nathalie Sarraute's *Enfance* and Simone de Beauvoir's *Mémoires d'une jeune fille rangée*."

32. De Lauretis, "The Essence of the Triangle or Taking the Risk of Essentialism Seriously: Feminist Theory in Italy, the U.S. and Britain."

Chapter 7

1. "L'identité de l'auteur, du narrateur et du personnage." Lejeune, *Le Pacte autobiographique*, p. 15.

2. Sidonie Smith, "Self, Subject and Resistance: Marginalities and Twentieth-Century Autobiographical Practice."

3. Valerie Minogue made this observation at the conference on "Nathalie Sarraute et le for intérieur" held at Tucson, Arizona, April, 1994.

4. Mark Lee outlined the nature of the functioning of tropismic movement in Sarraute's aesthetics in a paper given at a conference, "Nathalie Sarraute et le for intérieur," Tucson, Arizona, April, 1994. He examined, in particular, the "aesthenic" response of the hypersensitive narrator, the blank stupor or numbness initially occasioned by the jolt of intersubjective contact and the often embryonic quality of the emotion aroused (the "masse molle" [inert substance]) by the "beauty" of this contact in an anonymous *lieu de rencontre*.

5. Sarraute, *L'Ere du soupçon*, p. 9.

6. "Tout se passe comme si l'écrivain, en prenant la plume pour se raconter, avait voulu se prouver que son histoire était celle de n'importe qui et n'avait rencontré sur sa route que des obstacles aux exigences de la "normalité" (p. 350). Yvette Went-Daoust, "*Enfance* de Nathalie Sarraute."

7. The anthropologist, Clifford Geertz, has described as a fundamental concept of our culture "the Western conception of the person as a bounded, unique, more or less integrated motivational and integrative universe, a dynamic center of awareness, emotion, judgement and action organized into a distinctive whole and set contrastively both against such other wholes and against its social and natural background." *Local Knowledge*, p. 59.

8. Louis A. Sass, "Introspection, Schizophrenia, and the Fragmentation of Self."

9. See, for example, Elaine Marks, "The Dream of Love: A Study of Three Autobiographies."

Chapter 8

1. Marks's article focuses particularly on Gide's *Si le grain ne meurt* (1920), Genet's *Journal du voleur* (1949), and Simone de Beauvoir's *Mémoires d'une jeune fille rangée* (1958).

2. The video presentation of *L'Amant* made by Thames Television for *The South Bank Show*, "Marguerite Duras: Portrait d'une vie," for example, uses old photographs to accompany readings of the text.

3. Luce Irigaray, *Le Corps-à-corps avec la mère*, p. 136.

4. Sanford Ames, "Cinderella's Slipper: Mallarmé's Letters in Duras," p. 249.

5. Kaja Silverman, "Masochism and Male Subjectivity," p. 32.

6. Sigmund Freud, *The Ego and the Id*, p. 31. Quoted in Silverman, "Masochism and Male Subjectivity," p. 34.

7. Germaine Brée, "Contours, Fragments, Gaps: The World of Marguerite Duras." p. 275.

8. Marcelle Marini, *Territoires du féminin avec Marguerite Duras*, p. 269.

9. Silverman, "Masochism and Male Subjectivity," p. 51.

10. Parveen Adams, "Per Os(cillation)," p. 24.

11. Ibid., p. 24.

12. Susan Suleiman, *Subversive Intent: Gender, Politics, and the Avant-Garde*, p. 112.

13. Carol Murphy, "Duras's 'Beast in the Jungle': Writing Fear (or Fear of Writing) in *Emily L.*"

14. Susan Husserl-Kapit, "Interview with Marguerite Duras," p. 426.

15. Cottenet-Hage and Kolker, "The Cinema of Duras in Search of an Ideal Image."

16. Paul De Man, "Autobiography as De-facement," p. 922.

17. Ibid., p. 930.

18. Monique Gosselin, "Voyage au bout de la féminité: Figures féminines dans quelques romans de Marguerite Duras."

19. Christiane Makward, "Structures du silence/du délire: Marguerite Duras/Hélène Cixous."

20. Duras' pronouncements have often involved an unfortunate transposing of admirable personal impulses toward freedom, justice, equality, loyalty (to her friend Mitterrand), and defense of the exploited into very dubious political positions. In the eighties, these ranged from her support of the American bombing of Tripoli, to justification of the French bombing in New Zealand of the Greenpeace ship *Rainbow Warrior* protesting nuclear testing, and to attack on Gorbachev as the embodiment of the tyranny of the Communist Party in Poland on the latter's first visit to France. Her "defense" of Christine Villemin, accused of the murder of her young son, Gregory, a murder that Duras attributed to woman's condition of "ennui" in an article entitled "Sublime, forcément sublime" was also most untimely. (Christine has since been judged not guilty.) Perhaps the best that can be said for Duras' politics is that they do not fear to be "politically incorrect." The inner shadow ("ombre interne") that Duras is pursuing does not necessarily relate to "everyday reality."

21. Jacques Lacan, "Hommage fait à Marguerite Duras, du *Ravissement de Lol V. Stein*," p. 135; quoted in Suleiman, *Subversive Intent*, p. 113.

22. Suleiman, *Subversive Intent*, p. 116.

Chapter 9

1. See Ramsay, *Robbe-Grillet and Modernity: Science, Sexuality, and Subversion.*

2. Foucault, *Power/Knowledge: Selected Interviews and Other Writings 1972–1977.*

3. De Lauretis, "The Essence of the Triangle or Taking the Risk of Essentialism Seriously: Feminist Theory in Italy, the U.S. and Britain."

4. Foucault, *Power/Knowledge*, p. 188.

5. Ibid., p. 56.

6. Ibid., p. 186.

7. On "Foucault and Feminism" in Jana Sawicki, *Disciplining Foucault: Feminism, Power, and the Body.*

8. Foucault, *Power/Knowledge*, p. 193.

9. Leslie Garis, "The Life and Loves of Marguerite Duras."

10. Ibid.

11. See Xavière Gauthier and Marguerite Duras, *Les Parleuses.*.

12. Michelle Porte, *Les Lieux de Marguerite Duras.* Cited by Marini, p. 35.

13. Marini, "L'autre corps," p. 36.

14. Madeleine Borgomano, "Le Corps et le texte," pp. 49–62.

15. Benjamin, *The Bonds of Love.*

16. Lacan, "Hommage fait à Marguerite Duras, du *Ravissement de Lol V. Stein*," quoted in Marini, p. 32.

17. Panivong Norindr, "Errances and Memories in Marguerite Duras's Colonial Cities" (p. 54). Norindr traces a portrait of French Saigon, the capital of French Cochin China, the rigorously organized wide, tree-lined streets and immense café *terrasses* of the upper district and the in-between space of Cholon, the village in the city as a Barthesian "city of Drift." He argues that both the specular self and the power of the "other's" gaze in Duras draw the subject into movement through these cities that are

also spatial journeys across boundaries and "fixed positions of intelligibility" (p. 56). In her dress of masquerade, the young girl can infringe the rules imposed by the policies of French colonial urbanism that separate the European and indigenous districts, French Saigon and Chinese Cholon. Her historicopolitical geographical mapping by a few precise signs or objects of the city of Saigon may not sustain a coherent political position but succeeds, he argues, "in conveying the complex predicament of the postcolonial subject" (p. 73).

18. Duras, *Le Vice-Consul*, p. 9.

Afterword

1. Professor Raymond Gay-Crosier made these comments as a reader of my manuscript for the Humanities Series at the University of Florida. I am indebted to him for his generous reading and thoughtful suggestions.

2. Lacan, *The Four Fundamental Concepts of Psycho-Analysis*, p. vii. Quoted by Christopher Lane in "The Delirium of Interpretation: Writing the Papin Affair," p. 43.

3. Ben Stoltzfus in a review of my *Robbe-Grillet and Modernity* forthcoming in *French Forum*.

4. Ibid.

◇

Selected Bibliography

◇

Altermeyer, Bob. "Marching in Step." *The Sciences* (April 1988): 30–38.

Ames, Sanford. "Cinderella's Slipper: Mallarmé's Letters in Duras." *Visible Language* 12, no. 3 (1978): 245–54.

————. *Remains to be Seen: Essays on Marguerite Duras.* New York: Peter Lang, 1988.

Amouroux, Henri. *Quarante millions de Pétainistes* [Forty Million Supporters of Pétain]. Paris: Laffont, 1988.

Andréa, Yann. *MD.* Paris: Editions de Minuit, 1983.

Armel, Aliette. *Marguerite Duras et l'autobiographie* [Marguerite Duras and Autobiography]. Paris: Le Castor Astral, 1990.

Assouline, Pierre. "La Vraie Vie de Marguerite Duras" [The True Life of Marguerite Duras]. *Magazine Lire* (October 1991): 49–59.

Bajomée, Danielle. *Duras ou la douleur* [Duras or Pain]. Brussels: De Boeck Université, 1989.

Bajomée, Danielle, and Ralph Heyndels, eds. *Ecrire dit-elle: Imaginaires de Marguerite Duras* [Write, She Said: Imaginary Worlds in Marguerite Duras]. Brussels: Editions de l'Université de Bruxelles, 1988.

Barth, John. "Lost in the Funhouse." In *Lost in the Funhouse: Fiction for Print, Tape, Live Voice.* New York: Doubleday, 1988.

Barthes, Roland. *La Chambre claire: Note sur la photographie.* Paris: Seuil, 1980. Trans. Richard Howard as *Camera Lucida: Reflections on Photography.* New York: Hill and Wang, 1981.

————. *Le Plaisir du texte.* Paris: Editions du Seuil, 1973. Trans. Richard Miller as *The Pleasure of the Text.* New York: Hill and Wang, 1975.

————. *Roland Barthes par Roland Barthes.* Paris: Editions du Seuil, 1974. Trans. Richard Howard as *Roland Barthes by Roland Barthes.* New York: Farrar, 1977.

————. *S/Z.* Paris: Editions du Seuil, 1970. Trans. Richard Miller as *S/Z.* New York: Hill and Wang, 1974.

Baude, Dawn Michelle. "Picketing the Zeitgeist: In Search of the Perfect Language." *American Book Review* 15, no. 4 (October–November 1993): 3, 6.

Baude, Michel. "Le Moi futur: L'Image de l'avenir dans l'autobiographie" [The Future I: The Image of the Future in Autobiography]. *Romantisme* (October 1987): 29–36.

Baudry, Agnes. "Détruire, dit-elle: Destruction or Deconstruction?" *International Fiction Review* 8, no. 1 (1981): 41–46.

Beaujour, Michel. *Miroirs d'encre: Rhétorique de l'autoportrait* [Mirrors of Ink: The Rhetoric of the Self-Portrait]. Paris: Editions du Seuil, 1980.

Benjamin, Jessica. *The Bonds of Love.* New York: Pantheon Books, 1988.

———. "Master and Slave: The Fantasy of Erotic Domination." In *Powers of Desire,* ed. Ann Snitow (New York: New Feminist Library, 1983), pp. 280–99.

Benmussa, Simone. *Nathalie Sarraute: Qui êtes-vous?* [Nathalie Sarraute: Who Are You?]. Lyon: La Manufacture, 1987.

Benveniste, Emile. *Problèmes de linguistique générale.* Paris: Gallimard, 1966. Trans. as *Problems in General Linguistics.* Coral Gables: University of Miami Press, 1971.

Berg, Jean de. *L'Image* [The Image]. Paris: Editions de Minuit, 1956.

Berg, Jeanne de. *Cérémonies de femmes* [Women's Ceremonies]. Paris: Editions J'ai Lu, 1986.

Besser, Gretchen. *Nathalie Sarraute.* Boston: Twayne Publishers, 1979.

Bettelheim, Bruno. *The Uses of Enchantment: The Meaning and Importance of Fairy Tales.* New York: Random House, 1976.

Bishop, Michael, ed. *De Duras et Robbe-Grillet à Cixous et Deguy.* [From Duras and Robbe-Grillet to Cixous and Deguy]. *Dalhousie French Studies* 17 (Fall-Winter 1989).

Borgomano, Madeleine. "Le Corps et le texte" [The Body and the Text]. In Bajomée and Heyndels, eds., *Ecrire dit-elle: Imaginaires de Marguerite Duras,* pp. 49–62.

———. *L'Ecriture filmique de Marguerite Duras* [The Film Texts of Marguerite Duras]. Paris: Albatros, 1985.

———. "L'Histoire de la mendiante indienne: Une cellule génératrice de l'oeuvre de Marguerite Duras" [The Story of the Indian Beggar-Woman: A Generative Cell of the Work of Marguerite Duras]. *Poétique* 48 (1981): 479–84.

Brandt, Joan. "History and Art in Claude Simon's *Histoire." Romanic Review* 73, no. 3 (May 1982): 373–84.

Brée, Germaine. "Contours, Fragments, Gaps: The World of Marguerite Duras." *New York Literary Forum,* nos. 8–9 (1981): 267–76.

———. *Narcissus Absconditus: The Problematic Art of Autobiography in Contemporary France.* Oxford: Clarendon Press, 1978.

Brodzki, Bella, and C. Schenck, eds. *Life/Lines: Theorizing Women's Autobiography.* Ithaca, N.Y.: Cornell University Press, 1988.

———. "Mothers, Displacement and Language in the Autobiographies of Nathalie Sarraute and Christa Woolf." In Brodzki and Schenck, eds., *Life/Lines,* pp. 243–59.

Brulotte, Gaetan. "Tropismes et sous-conversation" [Tropisms and Sub-Conversation]. In Saporta and Sarraute, "Portrait d'une inconnue," pp. 39–54.

Brunel, Pierre. "Variations Corinthiennes" [Corinthian Variations]. *Corps écrit* 15 (1982): 117–24.

Bruss, Elizabeth. *Autobiographical Acts: The Changing Situation of a Literary Genre.* Baltimore: Johns Hopkins University Press, 1976.

Butor, Michel. *Frontières* [Frontiers]. Marseilles: Le Temps Parallèle, 1985.

Calle-Gruber, Mireille. "Quand le Nouveau Roman prend les risques du romanesque" [When the New Novel Takes the Risks of Autofiction]. In Calle-Gruber and Rothe, eds., *Autobiographie et biographie: Colloque franco-allemand de Heidelberg*, pp. 185–89.

Calle-Gruber, Mireille, and Arnold Rothe, eds. *Autobiographie et biographie: Colloque franco-allemand de Heidelberg.* Paris: Librairie A.-G. Nizet, 1989.

Camus, Albert. *L'Etranger.* Paris: Gallimard, 1942. Trans. Joseph Laredo as *The Outsider.* London: Hamilton, 1982.

Chodorow, Nancy. *The Reproduction of Mothering: Psychoanalysis and the Sociology of Gender.* Berkeley: University of California Press, 1978.

Cixous, Hélène. "Rethinking Difference." In *Homosexualities and French Literature: Cultural Contents,* ed. G. Stambolian (Ithaca: Cornell University Press, 1979).

———. "Le Rire de la Méduse" [The Laugh of the Medusa]. *L'Arc* 61 (1975): 39–54.

Clavel, André. "Le Nouveau Coup de Robbe-Grillet" [The New Robbe-Grillet Coup]. *L'Evénement du jeudi,* 11–17 February 1988, 104–6.

Clayton, Alan J. "Coucou . . . attrapez-moi . . ." [Coo-ee . . . catch me . . .]. *Revue des Sciences Humaines,* no. 217 (January–March 1990): 9–22.

———. *Nathalie Sarraute ou le tremblement de l'écriture* [Nathalie Sarraute or the Tremors of Writing]. Paris: Archives des Lettres Modernes, 1989.

Conan, Eric, and Henry Rousso. *Vichy, un passé qui ne passe pas* [Vichy, a Past that Does Not Pass]. Paris: Fayard, 1994.

Contat, Michel. "Portrait de Robbe-Grillet en châtelain" [Portrait of Robbe-Grillet as Lord of the Manor]. Interview with Robbe-Grillet in *Le Monde des livres,* 12 February 1988, 15.

Cottenet-Hage, Madeleine, and Robert Kolker. "The Cinema of Duras in Search of an Ideal Image." *French Review* 63, no. 1 (October 1989): 88–98.

Crosman Wimmers, Inge. *Poetics of Reading: Approaches to the Novel.* Princeton, N.J.: Princeton University Press, 1988.

Crosman, Inge K., and Susan R. Suleiman, eds. *The Reader in the Text: Essays on Audience and Interpretation.* Princeton, N.J.: Princeton University Press, 1980.

Crowder, Diane Griffin. *Narrative Structures and the Semiotics of Sex in the Novels of Alain Robbe-Grillet.* Ph. diss., University of Wisconsin, 1977.

De Lauretis, Teresa. *Alice Doesn't: Feminism, Semiotics, Cinema.* Bloomington: Indiana University Press, 1984.

———. "The Essence of the Triangle or Taking the Risk of Essentialism Seriously: Feminist Theory in Italy, the U.S. and Britain." *Differences* 1 (Summer 1989): 3–35.

Deleuze, Gilles. *Masochism: An Interpretation of Coldness and Cruelty.* London: Georges Braziller, 1971.

———. *Présentation de Sacher-Masoch* [Presentation of Sacher-Masoch]. Paris: Union Générale d'Editions, 1967.

Delhez-Sarlat, C., and M. Catani. *Individualisme et autobiographie en Occident* [Individualism and Autobiography in the West]. Brussels: Presses de l'Université Bruxelles, 1983.

De Man, Paul. "Autobiography as De-facement." *MLN* 94 (1979): 919–30.

Derrida, Jacques. *Marges de la philosophie* [Margins of Philosophy]. Paris: Editions de Minuit, 1972.

———. *Writing and Difference.* Trans. A. Bass. Chicago: University of Chicago Press, 1978. Originally published as *L'Ecriture et la différence.* Paris: Editions du Seuil, 1967.

Donnadieu (Duras), Marguerite, and Philippe Rocques. *L'Empire Français* [The French Empire]. Paris: Gallimard, 1940.

Descombes, Vincent. *Modern French Philosophy.* Cambridge: Cambridge University Press, 1980.

Doubrovsky, Serge. "Autobiographie/Vérité/Psychanalyse" ["Autobiography/Truth/Psychoanalysis"]. *L'Esprit Créateur* 20, no. 3 (Fall 1980): 87–97.

———. *Autobiographiques: De Corneille à Sartre* [Autobiographies: From Corneille to Sartre]. Paris: PUF, 1989.

Duras, Marguerite. *L'Amant.* Paris: Editions de Minuit, 1984. Trans. Barbara Bray as *The Lover.* New York: Pantheon Books, 1985.

———. *L'Amant de la Chine du nord.* Paris: Editions Gallimard, 1991. Trans. Leigh Hafrey as *The North China Lover.* New York: New Press, 1992.

———. *Aurélia Steiner* (Vancouver). Film, black and white. 1979.

———. *Un Barrage contre le Pacifique.* Paris: Editions Gallimard, 1950. Trans. Herma Briffault as *The Sea Wall.* New York: Harper and Row, 1986.

———. *Détruire, dit-elle.* Paris: Editions de Minuit, 1969. Trans. Barbara Bray as *Destroy, She Said.* New York: Grove Press, 1986.

———. *Dix heures et demie du soir en été.* Paris: Editions Gallimard, 1960. Trans. Anne Borchardt as *10:30 on a Summer Night,* in *Four Novels by Marguerite Duras.* New York: Grove Press, 1965.

———. *La Douleur.* Paris: P.O.L., 1985. Trans. Barbara Bray as *The War: A Memoir.* New York: Pantheon Books, 1989.

———. *L'Eden Cinéma* [The Eden Cinema]. Paris: Editions Gallimard, 1978.

———. *Emily L.* Paris: Editions de Minuit, 1987. Trans. Barbara Bray as *Emily L.* New York: Pantheon Books, 1989.

———. *L'Eté 80* [The Summer of 1980]. Paris: Editions de Minuit, 1980.

———. *Hiroshima mon amour.* Paris: Editions Gallimard, 1960. Trans. Richard Seaver as *Hiroshima mon amour.* New York: Grove Press, 1961.

———. *L'Homme assis dans le couloir.* Paris: Editions de Minuit, 1980. Trans. Barbara Bray as *The Man Sitting in the Corridor.* New York: North Star Line, 1991.

———. *Des Journées entières dans les arbres.* Paris: Gallimard, 1954. Trans. Anita Barrows as *Whole Days in the Trees.* New York: Riverrun Press, 1983.

———. *Le Marin de Gibraltar.* Paris: Editions Gallimard, 1952. Trans. Barbara Bray as *The Sailor from Gibraltar.* New York: Pantheon Books, 1966.

———. *Moderato Cantabile.* Paris: Editions de Minuit, 1958. Trans. Richard Searer as

Moderato Cantabile, in *Four Novels by Marguerite Duras*. New York: Grove Press, 1965.

———. *Outside: Papiers d'un jour*. Paris: Albin Michel, 1981. Trans. Arthur Goldhammer as *Outside: Selected Writings*. Boston: Beacon Press, 1986.

———. *Les Parleuses*. Conversations with Xavière Gauthier. Paris: Editions de Minuit, 1974. Trans. Katherine A. Jensen as *Woman to Woman*. Lincoln: University of Nebraska Press, 1987.

———. *La Pluie d'été*. Paris: P.O.L., 1990. Trans. Barbara Bray as *Summer Rain*. New York: Charles Scribner's Sons, 1992.

———. *La Pute de la côte normande* [The Whore of the Normandy Coast]. Paris: Editions de Minuit, 1986.

———. *Le Ravissement de Lol V. Stein*. Paris: Editions Gallimard, 1964. Trans. Richard Seaver as *The Ravishing of Lol Stein*. New York: Pantheon Books, 1986.

———. *La Vie matérielle*. Paris: P.O.L., 1987. Trans. Barbara Bray as *Practicalities*. New York: Grove Weidenfeld, 1990.

———. *Le Vice-Consul*. Paris: Editions Gallimard, 1965. Trans. Eileen Ellenbogen as *The Vice-Consul*. New York: Pantheon Books, 1987.

———. *Yann Andréa Steiner*. Paris: P.O.L., 1992.

———. *Les Yeux verts* [Green Eyes]. Paris: Cahiers du Cinéma, 1980.

Duras, Marguerite, and Alan Riding. "Duras and Her Thoughts of Love." Interview. *New York Times*, 26 March 1990, late edition, C11, C16.

Eakin, Paul John. *Fictions in Autobiography: Studies in the Art of Self-Invention*. Princeton, N.J.: Princeton University Press, 1985.

———. "The Referential Aesthetic of Autobiography." *Studies in the Literary Imagination* 23, no. 2 (Fall 1990): 129–44. In Feldstein and Roof, eds., *Feminism and Psychoanalysis*.

———, ed. *Philippe Lejeune: On Autobiography*. Minneapolis: University of Minnesota Press, 1989.

Eco, Umberto. *Les Limites de l'interprétation*. Paris: Grasset, 1990. Trans. as *The Limits of Interpretation*. Bloomington: Indiana University Press, 1990.

———. *Semiotics and the Philosophy of Language*. Bloomington: Indiana University Press, 1986.

Ellison, David R. *Of Words and the World. Referential Anxiety in Contemporary French Fiction*. Princeton, N.J.: Princeton University Press, 1993.

Farges, Joel, ed. *Marguerite Duras*. Paris: Albatros, 1979.

Feldstein, Richard, and Judith Roof, eds. *Feminism and Psychoanalysis*. Ithaca: Cornell University Press, 1989.

Ferry, Luc, and Alain Renaut. *French Philosophy of the Sixties*. Amherst: University of Massachusetts Press, 1990.

Finkielkraut, Alain. *The Defeat of Thought*. New York: Columbia University Press, 1994.

Forrester, Viviane. "Portrait de Nathalie" [Portrait of Nathalie]. *Magazine Littéraire* 196 (June 1983): 18–23.

Foucault, Michel. *Les Mots et les choses: Une archéologie du savoir*. Paris: Gallimard,

1966. Trans. as *The Order of Things: An Archaeology of the Human Sciences*. New York: Vintage Books, 1970.

———. *Power/Knowledge: Selected Interviews and Other Writings, 1972–1977*. Trans. Colin Gordon et al. New York: Pantheon Books, 1980.

———. *La Volonté de savoir; L'Usage des plaisirs*; and *Le Souci de soi*. 3 vols. in *L'Histoire de la sexualité*. Paris: Gallimard, 1976. Trans. Richard Hurley as *The History of Sexuality*. New York: Pantheon Books, 1978.

Freud, Sigmund. "A Child Is Being Beaten." In *Collected Papers of Sigmund Freud*, trans. James and Alice Strachey (London: Hogarth Press, 1924), pp. 172–201.

———. "The Economic Problem of Masochism." *The Standard Edition of the Complete Psychological Works of Sigmund Freud*, 19: 166. Trans. James Strachey. London: Hogarth Press, 1953.

———. *The Ego and the Id*. Trans. Joan Riviere and James Strachney. New York: Norton, 1962.

Friday, Nancy. *My Mother/Myself*. New York: Dell, 1977.

Gallop, Jane. "The Monster in the Mirror: The Feminist Critic's Psychoanalysis." In Feldstein and Roof, eds., *Feminism and Psychoanalysis*, pp. 13–24.

Garis, Leslie. "The Life and Loves of Marguerite Duras." *New York Times Magazine*, 20 October 1991, 44–53, 60–61.

Gauthier, Xavière. *Les Parleuses*. Conversations with Marguerite Duras. Paris: Editions de Minuit, 1974. Trans. Katherine A. Jensen as *Woman to Woman*. Lincoln: University of Nebraska Press, 1987.

Gear, Marie, and Melvyn Hill. *Working through Narcissism: Treating Its Masochistic Structures*. New York: Aronson, 1982.

Geertz, Clifford. *Local Knowledge: Further Essays in Interpretive Anthropology*. New York: Basic Books, 1983.

George, Craig, and Marguerite McGowan. *Moy qui me voye: The Writer and the Self from Montaigne to Leiris*. Oxford: Clarendon Press, 1989.

Gide, André. *Les Faux-Monnayeurs*. Paris: Editions Gallimard, 1925. Trans. Dorothy Bussy as *The Counterfeiters*. New York: Knopf, 1951.

———. *Si le grain ne meurt*. Paris: Gallimard, 1928. Trans. Dorothy Bussy as *If It Die*. New York: Random House, 1957.

Girard, René. *La Violence et le sacré*. Paris: Grasset, 1972. Trans. Patrick Gregory as *Violence and the Sacred*. Baltimore: Johns Hopkins University Press, 1972.

Gleick, James. *Chaos: Making a New Science*. New York: Viking Penguin Press, 1988.

Gosselin, Monique. "Voyage au bout de la fémininité: Figures féminines dans quelques romans de Marguerite Duras." In *Figures féminines et roman*. Paris: Presses Universitaires de France, 1982.

Gratton, J. "*Roland Barthes par Roland Barthes*: Autobiography and the Notion of Expression." *Romance Studies* 8 (1986): 57–65.

Greenblatt, Stephen. "Towards a Poetics of Culture." In *The New Historicism*, ed. H. Veeser (New York: Routledge, 1989).

Gusdorf, Georges. *Lignes de vie: 1, Les écritures du moi; 2, Auto-bio-graphie* [Life Lines:

vol. 1, Writings of the Self; vol. 2, Auto-bio-graphy]. Paris: Editions Odile Jacob, 1991.

Hayles, N. Katherine. *The Cosmic Web: Scientific Field Models and Literary Strategies in the Twentieth Century*. Ithaca: Cornell University Press, 1984.

Hawking, Stephen. *A Brief History of Time: From the Big Bang to Black Holes*. New York: Bantam Books, 1988.

Heath, Stephen. *The Nouveau Roman: A Study in the Practice of Writing*. London: Elek, 1972.

Henri, Comte de Paris. *Henri Comte de Paris au service de la France: Mémoires d'exil et de combats* [Henri Count of Paris in the Service of France: Memoirs of Exile and Combat]. Paris: Atelier Marcel Jullian, 1979.

Hewitt, Leah D. *Autobiographical Tightropes: Simone de Beauvoir, Nathalie Sarraute, Marguerite Duras, Monique Wittig and Maryse Condé*. Lincoln: University of Nebraska Press, 1990.

Higgins, Lynn. "Gender and War Narrative in *La Route des Flandres*." *L'Esprit créateur* 27, no. 4 (Winter 1987): 17–25.

Hofstadter, Douglas. *Godel, Escher, Bach: An Eternal Golden Braid*. New York: Basic Books, 1979.

Holland, Michael. "Sea-Change: Figure in Robbe-Grillet's Autobiography." *Paragraph* 13, no. 1 (March 1990): 65–88.

Houppermans, Sjeff. *Alain Robbe-Grillet: Autobiographe* [Alain Robbe-Grillet: Autobiographer]. Amsterdam: Rodopi, 1993.

———. "Un Miroir enchanté" [An Enchanted Mirror]. *Dalhousie French Studies* 17 (Fall-Winter 1989): 37–45.

Husserl-Kapit, Susan. Interview with Marguerite Duras. *Signs* (Winter 1975).

Hutcheon, Linda. *Narcissistic Narrative: The Metafictional Paradox*. New York: Methuen, 1984.

Irigaray, Luce. *Ce sexe qui n'en est pas un*. Paris: Editions de Minuit, 1977. Trans. Catherine Porter with Carolyn Burke as *This Sex That Is Not One*. Ithaca: Cornell University Press, 1985.

———. *Le Corps-à-corps avec la mère* [The Corps-à-corps with the Mother]. Montreal: Pleine Lune, 1981.

———. *Passions élémentaires*. Paris: Editions de Minuit, 1982. Trans. Joanna Collie and Judith Still as *Elemental Passions*. New York: Routledge, 1992.

Jardine, Alice. *Gynesis: Configurations of Woman and Modernity*. Ithaca: Cornell University Press, 1985.

Jefferson, Ann. "Beyond Contract: The Reader of Autobiography and Stendhal's *Vie de Henry Brulard*." *Romance Studies* 9 (1986): 53–69.

———. *The Nouveau Roman and the Poetics of Fiction*. Cambridge: Cambridge University Press, 1980.

Jelinek, Estelle. "Introduction: Women's Autobiography and the Male Tradition." In *Women's Autobiography: Essays in Criticism* (Bloomington: Indiana University Press, 1980).

Johnson, Barbara. "My Monster/Myself." *Diacritics* 12, no. 2 (1982): 2–10.

Judt, Tony. *Past Imperfect: French Intellectuals, 1944–1956*. Berkeley: University of California Press, 1993.

Krafft-Ebing, Richard. *Psychopathia Sexualis: A Medico-Forensic Study*. Trans. Harry E. Wedeck. New York: Putnam's Sons, 1965.

Kristeva, Julia. *Des Chinoises*. Paris: Editions des Femmes, 1974. Trans. as *About Chinese Women*. New York: Urizen Books, 1977.

———. *Etrangers à nous-mêmes*. Paris: Fayard, 1988. Trans. Leon Roudiez as *Strangers to Ourselves*. New York: Columbia University Press, 1991.

———. "The Pain of Sorrow in the Modern World: The Works of Marguerite Duras." Trans. Katherine Jensen. *PMLA* 102, no. 2 (March 1987): 138–52. Originally published in *Soleil Noir: Dépression et Mélancolie*. Paris: Gallimard, 1987.

———. *Pouvoirs de l'horreur: essai sur l'abjection*. Paris: Editions du Seuil, 1980. Trans. Leon Roudiez as *Powers of Horror: An Essay on Abjection*. New York: Columbia University Press, 1982.

———. *Séméiotiké: Recherches pour une sémanalyse*. Paris: Editions du Seuil, 1969. Trans. as "The Ethics of Linguistics." In *Desire in Language*, ed. Leon Roudiez (New York: Columbia University Press, 1980).

Kuhn, Thomas. *The Structure of Scientific Revolutions*. Chicago: University of Chicago Press, 1962.

Lacan, Jacques. *Ecrits*. Paris: Editions du Seuil, 1966. Trans. Alan Sheridan as *Ecrits: A Selection*. New York: Norton, 1977.

———. *The Four Fundamental Concepts of Psycho-Analysis*. Trans. Alan Sheridan. Ed. Jacques-Alain Miller. New York: Norton, 1978.

———. "Hommage fait à Marguerite Duras, du *Ravissement de Lol V. Stein*" [Homage to Marguerite Duras, on *The Ravishing of Lol Stein*]. Paris: Editions Gallimard, 1964.

———. "The Mirror Stage as Formative of the I." In *Ecrits: A Selection*. New York: Norton, 1977.

Lamy, Suzanne, and André Roy, eds. *Marguerite Duras à Montréal* [Marguerite Duras in Montreal]. Montreal: Editions Spirale, 1981.

Lane, Christopher. "The Delirium of Interpretation: Writing the Papin Affair." *Differences* (Summer 1993): 24–61.

Laplanche, J., and J. Pontalis. *Vocabulaire de la Psychanalyse* [The Vocabulary of Psychoanalysis]. Paris: PUF, 1968.

Leiris, Michel. *L'Age d'homme*. Paris: Gallimard, 1946, 1992. Trans. Richard Howard as *Manhood: A Journey from Childhood into the Fierce Order of Virility*. Chicago: University of Chicago Press, 1992.

———. *La Règle du jeu*. Paris: Gallimard, 1948, 1991. Trans. Lydia Davis as *Rules of the Game*. New York: Paragon House, 1991.

Lejeune, Philippe. "L'Atelier autobiographique de Sartre." *French Literature Series* 12 (1985): 129–64.

———. *L'Autobiographie en France* [Autobiography in France]. Paris: Armand Colin, 1971.

————. *Exercices d'ambiguïté: Lectures de Si le grain ne meurt* [Exercises in Ambiguity: Readings of "Si le grain ne meurt"]. Paris: Lettres Modernes Minard, 1974.

————. "Gide et l'autobiographie." *Revue des Lettres Modernes* 9 (1973): 31–69.

————. *Moi aussi* [Me Too]. Paris: Editions du Seuil, 1986.

————. *Le Pacte autobiographique* [The Autobiographical Pact]. Paris: Editions du Seuil, 1975.

————. "Paroles d'enfance" [Childhood Words]. *Revue des Sciences Humaines* 217 (January-March 1990): 23–38.

Lyotard, Jean-François. *La Condition postmoderne: Rapport sur le savoir*. Paris: Editions de Minuit, 1979. Trans. Geoff Bennington and Brian Massumi as *The Postmodern Condition: A Report on Knowledge*. Minneapolis: University of Minnesota Press, 1984.

Makward, Christiane. "Structures du silence/du délire: Marguerite Duras/Hélène Cixous" [Structures of Silence/of Delirium: Marguerite Duras/Hélène Cixous]. *Poétique* 35 (1978): 314–24.

Marini, Marcelle. "L'Autre Corps" [The Other Body]. In Bajomé and Heyndels, eds., *Ecrire dit-elle: Imaginaires de Marguerite Duras*.

————. *Territoires du féminin avec Marguerite Duras* [Territories of the Feminine with Marguerite Duras]. Paris: Editions de Minuit, 1977.

Marks, Elaine. "The Dream of Love: A Study of Three Autobiographies." In *Twentieth Century French Fiction* (New Brunswick, N.J.: Rutgers University Press, 1980), pp. 72–88.

Marks, Elaine, and Isabelle de Courtivron, eds. *New French Feminisms*. Amherst: University of Massachusetts Press, 1980.

May, Georges. *L'Autobiographie* [Autobiography]. Paris: Presses Universitaires de France, 1979.

Mead, George Herbert. *Mind, Self, and Society*. Chicago: University of Chicago Press, 1934.

Michalczyk, John. "Robbe-Grillet, Michelet, and Barthes: From *La Sorcière* to *Glissements progressifs du plaisir*." *French Review* 51, no. 2 (December 1977): 233–44.

Michelet, Jules. *La Sorcière*. Paris: Garnier-Flammarion, 1867, 1966. Trans. A. R. Allinson as *Satanism and Witchcraft*. New York: Citadel Press, 1993.

Minogue, Valerie. "Le Cheval de Troie: A propos de *Tu ne t'aimes pas*" [The Trojan Horse: On *Tu ne t'aimes pas*]. *Revue des Sciences Humaines*, no. 217 (January-March 1990): 151–61.

————. "Fragments of a Childhood: Nathalie Sarraute's *Enfance*." *Romance Studies*, no. 9 (1986): 71–83.

————. *Nathalie Sarraute and the War of the Words: A Study of Five Novels*. Edinburgh: Edinburgh University Press, 1981.

————. "Sarraute, Auden, and the Great Tall Tailor." *Modern Language Review* 84 (1989): 331–44.

Mitchell, Juliet. "Psycho-analysis, Narrative, and Femininity." In *Woman, the Longest Revolution* (London: Virago, 1984).

Moi, Toril. *Sexual Textual Politics: Feminist Literary Theory.* New York: Methuen, 1985.

Montrelay, Michèle. *L'Ombre et son nom: Sur la fémininité* [The Shadow and Its Name: On Femininity]. Paris: Éditions de Minuit, 1977.

Morgan, Janice. "Fiction and Autobiography / Language and Silence: *L'Amant* by Duras." *French Review* 63, no. 2 (December 1989): 271–79.

Murphy, Carol. *Alienation and Absence in the Novels of Marguerite Duras.* Lexington, Ky.: French Forum, 1982.

———. "Duras' 'Beast in the Jungle': Writing Fear (or Fear of Writing) in *Emily L.*" *Neophilologus* 75 (1991): 539–47.

Nettelbeck, Colin. "Robbe-Grillet and Friends in Nuremberg: Exorcizing the *Service du Travail Obligatoire.*" *French Cultural Studies* 3 (1992): 235–51.

Nicholson, Linda, ed. *Feminism/Postmodernism.* New York: Routledge, 1990.

Norindr, Panivong. "Errances and Memories in Marguerite Duras's Colonial Cities." *Differences* 5, no. 3 (Fall 1993): 52–79.

Nourrissier, François. *La Fête des pères* [Father's Day]. Paris: Grasset, 1985.

O'Callaghan, Raylene. "An Identikit Portrait" and "Text, Sex, and Criminal Project." Interviews with Alain Robbe-Grillet. *Landfall* (June 1986): 180–87. Reprinted in Ramsay, *Robbe-Grillet and Modernity: Science, Sexuality, and Subversion.*

Ollier, Claude. *Déconnection.* Paris: Flammarion, 1988. Trans. Dominic di Bernardi as *Disconnection.* Elmwood Park, Ill.: Dalkey Archive Press, 1989.

Olney, James, ed. *Autobiography: Essays Theoretical and Critical.* Princeton, N.J.: Princeton University Press, 1980.

———, ed. *Studies in Autobiography.* Oxford: Oxford University Press, 1988.

Oppenheim, Lois. "From Anonymity to Individuation in the Nouveau Roman." Paper presented at the annual meeting of the Modern Language Association, New York, 29 December 1988.

———. *Three Decades of the French New Novel.* Urbana: University of Illinois, 1986.

Paris, Comte de, Henri. See Henri, Comte de Paris.

Patterson, Yolande. "Childhood Memories: Nathalie Sarraute's *Enfance* and Simone de Beauvoir's *Mémoires d'une jeune fille rangée.*" Paper presented at the annual meeting of the Modern Language Association, New York, December 1986.

Pavel, Thomas. *The Feud of Language: A History of Structuralist Thought.* New York: Blackwell, 1989.

Perec, Georges. *Je me souviens* [I Remember]. Paris: Hachette, 1978.

———. *W, ou le souvenir d'enfance.* Paris: Denoel, 1975. Trans. David Bellos as *W, or the Memory of Childhood.* Boston: Godine, 1988.

Pierrot, Jean. *Marguerite Duras.* Paris: Librairie José Corti, 1986.

Pivot, Bernard. "Apostrophes." Television program, Paris, 28 September 1984.

Poirot-Delpech, Bernard. "*Angélique ou l'enchantement:* Robbe et Grillet" [*Angélique or Enchantment:* Robbe and Grillet]. Review in *Le Monde,* 5 February 1988, 11, 15.

Porte, Michelle. *Les Lieux de Marguerite Duras* [The Places of Marguerite Duras]. Paris: Éditions de Minuit, 1977.

Praeger, Michèle. "Une Autobiographie qui s'invente elle-même" [A Self-Inventing Autobiography]. *French Review* 62, no. 3 (February 1989): 476–82.

Prigogine, Ilya. *Order Out of Chaos*. New York: Bantam Books, 1984. Trans. from *La Nouvelle alliance: Métamorphoses de la Nature*. Paris: Gallimard, 1982.

Prince, Gerald. *Narratology: The Form and Functioning of Narratives*. New York: Mouton, 1982.

Raillard, Georges. "Le Grande Verre d'Alain Robbe-Grillet" [The Grand Verre of Alain Robbe-Grillet]. *La Quinzaine Littéraire* 432 (16–31 January l985): 6.

Ramsay, Raylene. *Robbe-Grillet and Modernity: Science, Sexuality, and Subversion*. Gainesville, Fla.: University Press of Florida, 1992.

———. "The Sado-Masochism of Representation in French Texts of Modernity." *Literature and Psychology* 37, no. 3 (Fall 1991): 18–28.

Rapp, Bernard. "Caractères" [Characters]. Television program, Paris, 5 July 1991.

Réage, Pauline. *Histoire d'O*. Paris: J.-J. Pauvert, 1954. Trans. Sabine d'Estrée as *The Story of O*. New York: Grove Press, 1965.

Reik, Theodor. *Masochism in Sex and Society*. Trans. Margaret H. Beigel and Gertrud M. Kurth. New York: Grove Press, 1962.

Ricardou, Jean. *Une Maladie chronique* [A Chronic Illness]. Paris: Impressions Nouvelles, 1989.

Ricouart, Janine. *Ecriture féminine et violence: Une étude sur Marguerite Duras* [Feminine Writing and Violence: A Study of Marguerite Duras]. Birmingham, Ala.: Summa Publications, 1991.

Riding, Alan. "Duras and Her Thoughts of Love." Interview. *New York Times*, 26 March 1990, late edition, C11, C16.

Riffaterre, Michael. *Fictional Truth*. Baltimore: Johns Hopkins University Press, 1990.

Robbe-Grillet, Alain. "L'Ange gardien" [The Guardian Angel]. Reprinted in *Obliques*, no. 16–17 (1978): 93.

———. *Angélique ou l'enchantement* [Angelica or Enchantment]. Paris: Editions de Minuit, 1987.

———. *Dans le labyrinthe*. Paris: Editions de Minuit, 1959. Trans. Richard Howard as *In the Labyrinth*, in *Two Novels*. New York: Grove Press, 1965.

———. *Les Derniers Jours de Corinthe* [The Last Days of Corinthe]. Paris: Editions de Minuit, 1994.

———. *Djinn: un trou rouge entre les pavés disjoints*. Paris: Editions de Minuit, 1981. Trans. Yvonne Lenard and Walter Wells as *Djinn*, in *Djinn and La Maison de rendez-vous*. New York: Grove Press, 1982.

———. *Les Gommes*. Paris: Editions de Minuit, 1953. Trans. Richard Howard as *The Erasers*. London: Calder, 1966.

———. Interview. *Art Press*, no. 88 (December 1984): 41; *Le Magazine Littéraire* (January 1985): 93.

———. Interview. *Libération*, 17 January 1985, 28.

———. *La Jalousie*. Paris: Editions de Minuit, 1957. Trans. Richard Howard as *Jealousy*, in *Two Novels*. New York: Grove Press, 1965.

———. *La Maison de rendez-vous*. Paris: Editions de Minuit, 1965. Trans. Richard Howard as *La Maison de rendez-vous*, in *Djinn and La Maison de rendez-vous*. New York: Grove Press, 1982.

———. *Le Miroir qui revient*. Paris: Editions de Minuit, 1984. Trans. Jo Levy as *Ghosts in the Mirror*. New York: Grove Weidenfeld, 1991.

———. Preface to *La Nouvelle Justine* [The New Justine], by Donatien Alphonse François de Sade. Nyons: Editions Borderie, 1979.

———. *Projet pour une révolution à New York*. Paris: Editions de Minuit, 1970. Trans. Richard Howard as *Project for a Revolution in New York*. New York: Grove Press, 1976.

———. *Un Régicide* [A Regicide]. Paris: Editions de Minuit, 1949, 1978.

———. *Souvenirs du triangle d'or*. Paris: Editions de Minuit, 1978. Trans. J. A. Underwood as *Recollections of the Golden Triangle*. New York: Grove Press, 1986.

———. *Topologie d'une cité fantôme*. Paris: Editions de Minuit, 1976. Trans. J. A. Underwood as *Topology of a Phantom City*. New York: Grove Press, 1977.

———. *Le Voyeur*. Paris: Editions de Minuit, 1955. Trans. Richard Howard as *The Voyeur*. New York: Grove Press, 1989.

Roudiez, Léon, ed. *Desire in Language*. New York: Columbia University Press, 1980.

Roudinesco, Elizabeth. *Jacques Lacan and Co.: A History of Psychoanalysis in France, 1925–1985*. Chicago: University of Chicago Press, 1990.

Rybalka, Michel. "Alain Robbe-Grillet: At Play with Criticism." In Oppenheim, ed., *Three Decades of the French New Novel*.

Saïd, Edward. *Beginnings: Intention and Method*. New York: Basic Books, 1975.

Sankey, Margaret. "Time and Autobiography in *L'Amant* by Marguerite Duras." *Australian Journal of French Studies* 25, no. 1 (1988): 58–70.

Saporta, Marc, and Nathalie Sarraute. "Portrait d'une inconnue: Conversation biographique" [Portrait of an Unknown Woman: Biographical Conversation]. *L'Arc* 95 (1984): 5–23.

Sarraute, Nathalie. *Enfance*. Paris: Gallimard, 1983. Trans. Barbara Wright as *Childhood*. New York: G. Braziller, 1984.

———. *Disent les imbéciles*. Paris: Gallimard, 1976. Trans. Maria Jolas as *Fools Say*. New York: G. Braziller, 1977.

———. *L'Ere du soupçon*. 1964. Paris: Gallimard, 1983. Trans. Maria Jolas as *The Age of Suspicion: Essays on the Novel*. New York: G. Braziller, 1990.

———. *Paul Valéry et l'enfant d'éléphant—Flaubert le Précurseur* [Paul Valéry and the Elephant's Child—Flaubert the Precursor]. Paris: Gallimard, 1986.

———. *Tropismes*. Paris: Denoel, 1939. Trans. Maria Jolas as *Tropisms*. New York: G. Braziller, 1967.

———. *Tu ne t'aimes pas*. Paris: Gallimard, 1989. Trans. Barbara Wright as *You Don't Love Yourself*. New York: G. Braziller, 1990.

———. *L'Usage de la parole*. Paris: Gallimard, 1980. Trans. Barbara Wright as *The Use of Speech*. New York: G. Braziller, 1983.

Sarraute, Nathalie, and Marc Saporta. See Saporta, Marc, and Nathalie Sarraute.

Sartre, Jean-Paul. *Les Mots*. Paris: Gallimard, 1964. Trans. Bernard Frechtman as *The Words*. New York: Vintage Books, 1981.

Sass, Louis A. "Introspection, Schizophrenia, and the Fragmentation of Self." *Representations* 19 (Summer 1987): 1–34.

Sawicki, Jana. *Disciplining Foucault: Feminism, Power, and the Body.* Routledge, 1991.

Schuster, Marilyn. *Marguerite Duras Revisited.* World Author Series. New York: Twayne Publishers, 1993.

Sheringham, Michael. "Ego redux? Strategies in New French Autobiography." *Dalhousie French Studies* 17 (Fall-Winter 1989): 27–35.

———. "French Autobiography: Texts, Contexts, Poetics." *Journal of European Studies* 16 (1986): 59–71.

Silverman, Kaja. "Histoire d'O." In *Pleasure and Danger: Exploring Female Sexuality* ed. Carole Vance (Boston: Routledge and Kegan Paul, 1985).

———. "Masochism and Male Subjectivity." *Camera Obscura* (1988): 31–65.

Simon, Claude. *L'Acacia.* Paris: Editions de Minuit, 1989. Trans. Richard Howard as *The Acacia.* New York: Pantheon Books, 1991.

———. *La Route des Flandres.* Paris: Editions de Minuit, 1960. Trans. Richard Howard as *The Flanders Road.* New York: Riverrun Press, 1985.

———. *Histoire.* Paris: Editions de Minuit, 1967. Trans. Richard Howard as *Histoire.* London: Cape, 1969.

———. *Les Géorgiques.* Paris: Editions de Minuit, 1981. Trans. Beryl and John Fletcher as *The Georgics.* New York: Riverrun Press, 1989.

———. *L'Invitation.* Paris: Editions de Minuit, 1989. Trans. Jim Goss as *The Invitation.* Elmwood Park, Ill.: Dalkey Archive Press, 1991.

Smith, André. "Sartre: *Les Mots* sous l'éclairage des *Lettres au Castor*" [*Les Mots* in the Light of *Lettres au Castor*]. *Etudes Litteraires* 17, no. 2 (Fall 1984): 333–56.

Smith, Keren. "Voyeurism and the Void of Self: The Problem of Human Identity in Robbe-Grillet's *Le Voyeur* and Dostoevsky's *Crime and Punishment.*" *New Zealand Journal of French Studies* 9, no. 2 (1988): 34–41.

Smith, Sidonie. "Self, Subject and Resistance: Marginalities and Twentieth-Century Autobiographical Practice." *Tulsa Studies in Women's Literature* 6, no. 1 (1990): 11–24.

Sontag, Susan. "The Pornographic Imagination." In *Styles of Radical Will* (New York: Delta, 1981), pp. 35–73.

Stambolian, George, ed. *Homosexualities and French Literature: Cultural Contents.* Ithaca: Cornell University Press, 1979.

Stanton, Donna, ed. *The Female Autograph.* New York: New York Literary Forum, 1986.

Stoltzfus, Ben. *Alain Robbe-Grillet: Life, Work and Criticism.* Fredericton, New Brunswick: York Press, 1987.

———. "The Body of Robbe-Grillet's Text: Sex, Myth, and Politics in the Nouveau Nouveau Roman." *Neophilologus* 68, no. 2 (April 1984): 192–205.

———. "Dead, Desacralized, and Discontent: Robbe-Grillet's New Man." *Modern Fiction Studies* 27, no. 4 (Winter 1981–1982): 543–53.

———. "The Language of Autobiography and Fiction: Gide, Barthes, and Robbe-Grillet." *International Fiction Review* 15, no. 1 (1988): 3–8.

———. "Robbe-Grillet's Mythical Biography: Reflections of *La Belle captive* in *Le Miroir qui revient.*" *Stanford French Review* 12 (1988): 387–404.

Suleiman, Susan Rubin. *Subversive Intent: Gender, Politics, and the Avant-Garde.* Cambridge: Harvard University Press, 1990.

———. "Reading Robbe-Grillet: Sadism and Text in *Projet pour une Révolution à New York.*" *Romanic Review* 68, no. 1 (1977): 43–62. Reprinted in *Subversive Intent* (Cambridge: Harvard University Press, 1990), pp. 51–71.

———, ed. *The Female Body in Western Culture.* Cambridge: Harvard University Press, 1986.

Suleiman, Susan R., and Inge K. Crosman, eds. *The Reader in the Text: Essays on Audience and Interpretation.* Princeton, N.J.: Princeton University Press, 1980.

Tannenbaum, E. *The Action Française: Die-hard Reactionaries in Twentieth Century France.* New York: John Wiley and Sons, 1962.

Thompson, William. *The Contemporary Novel in France.* Gainesville: University Press of Florida, 1995.

Thiher, Alan. *Words in Reflection.* Chicago: University of Chicago Press, 1984.

Todorov, Tzvetan. *On Human Diversity: Nationalism, Racism, and Exoticism in French Thought.* Cambridge: Harvard University Press, 1993.

Tournier, Michel. *Le Roi des Aulnes.* Paris: Editions Gallimard, 1970. Trans. Barbara Bray as *The Ogre.* New York: Pantheon Books, 1984.

Twitchell, James. *Preposterous Violence: Studies of Fables of Aggression in Modern Culture.* New York: Oxford University Press, 1989.

Van Roey-Roux, Françoise. "*Enfance* de Nathalie Sarraute ou de la fiction à autobiographie" [*Enfance* by Nathalie Sarraute, or From Fiction to Autobiography]. *Etudes Littéraires* 17, no. 2 (1984): 273–82.

Vareille, Jean-Claude. *Alain Robbe-Grillet: L'Etrange* [Alain Robbe-Grillet: The Strange]. Paris: Nizet, 1981.

Veeser, Aram, ed. *The New Historicism.* New York: Routledge, 1989.

Vercier, Bruno. "(Nouveau) Roman et Autobiographie: *Enfance* de Nathalie Sarraute" [(New) Novel and Autobiography: *Childhood* by Nathalie Sarraute]. *French Literature Series* 12 (1985): 162–70.

Vircondelet, Alain. *Duras: Biographie* [Duras: A Biography]. Paris: François Bourin, 1991.

Weber, Eugen. *L'Action Française.* Paris: Fayard, 1985. Trans. as *Action Française: Royalism and Reaction in Twentieth Century France.* Stanford: Stanford University Press, 1962.

Went-Daoust, Yvette. "*Enfance* de Nathalie Sarraute." *Les Lettres romanes* 41, no. 4 (1987): 337–50.

Whiteside, Anna. "Autobiographie ou anti-autobiographie? le cas Barthes" [Autobiography or Anti-Autobiography? The Case of Barthes]. *Neophilologus* 65 (1981): 173–84.

Willis, Sharon. *Marguerite Duras: Writing on the Body.* Urbana: University of Illinois Press, 1987.

Wilson, Suzanne. "Auto-bio-graphie: vers une théorie de l'écriture féminine" [Auto-bio-graphy: Toward a Theory of Feminine Writing]. *French Review* 63, no. 4 (March 1990): 617–22.

Winnicott, D. W. *Playing and Reality*. New York: Basic Books, 1971.

Wiseman, Mary Bittner. *The Ecstasies of Roland Barthes*. London and New York: Routledge, 1989.

Young, R. J. *In Command of France: French Foreign Policy and Military Planning, 1933–40*. Cambridge: Harvard University Press, 1978.

Index

Simon, Claude: on discontinuity of
experience and of history, 59; order and
disorder in, 59; and the war, 63; and
exploration of hidden origin of stories, 63.
See also autofiction; Second World War
skepticism: and critical examination of War
and Holocaust, 3. *See also* postmodernism
Smith, Keren: on void, 60–61
Smith, Sidonie: on autobiographical splitting,
141
snowflakes. *See* chaos
songbird. *See* Angélique
splitting of self as monster and hunter of
monsters. *See* monster
stepmother: Véra as "wicked" stepmother in
Enfance, 128–29, 135–36
Stoltzfus, Ben: on scriptor's machinations
accompanied by unconscious voice of
author, 218
strange attractor. *See* chaos
strategies. *See* narrative
Stretter, Anne-Marie: as figure of fatal
attraction, 22; historical referent for, 226n.
13.
strong personality. *See* self-love
subversion: as sexual transgression in Duras,
32; of traditional narrative use of tenses, 40;
of ready-made expressions and binary
organization in Sarraute, 162
Suleiman, Susan: and Barthes' reversl of
gender coding of texts, 184; on women's
need for "paternal legitimation," 187
super narrator. *See* metafiction
suspicion: the age of, 15; of the autobiographical enterprise, 128; deflates dolls of self-
satisfaction, 156; Sarraute's essays on (*L'Ere
du soupçon*), 231n. 2

telescoping of opposites: self-loss in other and
separation from other, 6; as transformative
of self in new autobiographies, 49; and
masculine and feminine voices in Sarraute,
57; significance of new autobiographies in,
64; in past and present in Duras, 208, 214;
writer and child, 212; detective function
and confessional impulse, 219. *See also*
complementarity
time: blurred by use of present tense, 27; and
tense, 41; and predominance of present
tense, 41; in Sarraute as tropistic movement, 51; in Duras as return to Chora, 52;
in Simon as insignificant detail, 52; in

Robbe-Grillet as monster, 52; and close
relationship to History, 52
Thames Television: documentary on Duras,
15
traditional autobiography: as denial of the
void, 50; new autobiographies seen as
return to tradition of, 11; dialectical forms
in dislocated, 89
tropisms: universal, in Sarraute, 7; and
interpersonal realm, 7, 145; as desire to
master and instinct to flee, 90; as
individuated, 137; and Sarraute's choices
among tropistic movements, 142; analysis of
functioning of, 233n. 4. *See also* self-love
truth: of past as a function of present, 27; of
Barthesian photograph, 50; of bodily
reaction in Sarraute, as pleasure and pain
in Robbe-Grillet, 50; and autobiographical
contradictions, 201; derives from desire,
202; as construct dependent on present, 211;
as verisimilitude and ready-made, 213;
dance of multiple and temporary truths, 215
turbulence: in chaos theory and in new
autobiographies, 51; introduced by sexual
aggression into text, 218. *See also* chaos

uncertainty relations. *See* indeterminacy

vampire: *Fiancée de Corynthe* as, 85. *See also*
Angélique; Corinthe, Henri de
verbs: "to look" [regarder], "to take" [prendre]
transformed by repetition in new contexts,
206; as effect shifts between seeing and
being seen, taking and being taken, 206–7
vertigo. *See* holes; void
victim: Angélique as sacrificial, 105; of incest,
106; Robbe-Grillet as, 107; of words
("happiness") in *Tu ne t'aimes pas*, 155
violence: ritualized, as catharsis, 108; as
revenge on mother, 109; originary
"masculine," 185; analysis of conditions of,
as the least violent gesture, 220. *See also*
Derrida, Jacques; sado-eroticism
voice: dialogic, in Sarraute's *Enfance*, 29, 118;
overlapping of voices of narrator and
character, 34; "grain" of Sarraute's, 117; as
implied author, 118; definitions of literary,
119–20; as presence contested by Derrida,
120; masculine and feminine voices in
Sarraute, 120, 137–40; differences between
voices, 139–40; assemblage of other voices/
individuated voice, 140

void: as absent center in new autobiographies, 59; of self as absence of transcendence, 60; as site of authenticity, 60; meaning of, in *Le Voyeur*, 61–62; as red hole of violent fantasies and of self-loss, 62; as original language for Eco, 64; golden ring metaphor of, 78; in Simon, 92; in Sarraute, 126; that generates desire, absent other as, 222. *See also* holes; self-loss; silence; Smith, Keren

walls of the city: and Robbe-Grillet's fantasies as ready-mades, 7; and material on the walls as pre-text, 82
wild country: as buried desire in Duras, 6; as "ravishing," 6, 179
Willis, Sharon: writing from the body in

Duras, 54. *See also* body; writing
Wilson, Suzanne: and women's auto-bio-graphy, 183. *See also* autobiography
Wolin, Richard: and critique of postmodern ethos and negative antihumanism, 219
words: in best clothes, 37; of the mother in Sarraute, 125
World War II. *See* Second World War
writer: all powerful, 213
writing: cursive, in Duras, 29; role of, in evoking emotion, 29; from body, 50; for Barthes, 50; both bios and graphy, 50; history as rewriting, 74; the lover's jealousy of the woman poet's, 168; changes relations of power in *Emily L.*, 175–76; need to mistreat traditional, 184; as act of desire and of knowledge, 213. *See also* rewriting